D0988711

SPACE AND POWER

For Jamie

SPACE AND POWER

Politics, War and Architecture

PAUL HIRST

Polity

Copyright © Paul Hirst 2005

The right of Paul Hirst to be identified as Author of this Work has been asserted in accordance with the UK Copyright, Designs and Patents Act 1988.

First published in 2005 by Polity Press

Polity Press
65 Bridge Street
Cambridge CB2 1UR, UK.

Polity Press
350 Main Street
Malden, MA 02148, USA

All rights reserved. Except for the quotation of short passages for the purpose of criticism and review, no part of this publication may be reproduced, stored in a retrieval system, or transmitted, in any form or by any means, electronic, mechanical, photocopying, recording or otherwise, without the prior permission of the publisher.

ISBN: 0-7456-3455-9
ISBN: 0-7456-3456-7 (pb)

A catalogue record for this book is available from the British Library.

Typeset in 10.5 on 12 pt Sabon
by Servis Filmsetting Ltd, Manchester
Printed and bound in Great Britain by TJ International, Padstow, Cornwall

Every effort has been made to trace all copyright holders. However, if any have been inadvertently overlooked, the publishers will be pleased to make the necessary arrangements at the first opportunity.

For further information on Polity, visit our website: www.polity.co.uk

Contents

Illustrations

Preface

British politics and culture remain smothered by the past, suffocated by it almost. They have singularly failed to think about the future in an imaginative and compelling way over much of the post-Second World War period. They seemingly remain forever wistfully tethered to reproducing the past, nostalgically and unconsciously longing for its return. As Paul Hirst was so intent on reminding us on every suitable occasion, this is something that typifies the left as much as it does the right.

So, it is extremely difficult to think imaginatively about the future, but it is also urgently necessary to do so. This is something Paul did with great effect in the latter part of his life, and which was exemplified by the books on *Associative Democracy* (Polity, 1994), *War and Power in the 21st Century* (Polity, 2001), to some extent in *Globalization in Question* (Polity, 1999) which I wrote with him, but also in the chapters of this book. By 'imaginative thinking about the future' I do not mean speculative futurology. Paul's thinking about the future was always grounded in an absolutely relevant and realistic account of the possibilities for change and democratic reform.

In his lucid account of several themes organized around space and power in this book, Paul Hirst demonstrates his characteristic knack of finding a level of analysis that builds on both past and current theory, but also transcends its inhibiting grip on thinking, particularly in respect of what we can expect from the future. Thus, here, Paul manages to render problematic the vitally necessary task of thinking imaginatively about the future at the same time as he resolutely provides an utterly realistic contribution to its advancement. If called upon to characterize the methodological protocols that enabled Paul to pull off this move, I would term them a commitment to a 'principled pragmatic scepticism' on his part.

Paul Hirst was a sceptic by nature and he added to this a contrarian twist which always meant he disagreed more often than he agreed with something or with what someone had said. And this attitude was as often applied to himself as much as to others. Thus I suspect Paul would have been among the first to disagree with how I have just summed up his methodological position. He would have been sceptical about the charge of a principled pragmatic scepticism just as he is sceptical in the chapters of this book in respect of the contemporary theories of space that – as chapter 1 demonstrates — he was so determined not to interrogate at any length. But a contrarian turn of mind was a key feature of his scepticism that I am trying to outline and that I would argue pervaded Paul's latter years, because it precisely forces one to *think* imaginatively. Reliance on an abstract and general theory easily endangers thinking because it provides an 'already known' account to which the detail of this or that example or illustration can always turn for comfort. Paul, to the contrary, liked to discomfort his audiences. But he did this at the same time as he provided them with a fascinating account of what the alternatives might be and how they might come about or be operationalized.

As many have noted, as well as being a principled sceptic, Paul was almost an instinctive democrat. His book on *Associative Democracy* was the culmination of a decade's work of thinking and writing about a democratic agenda for the reinvigoration of the political regime in advanced countries, particularly Britain. Paul was pleased with the way he was able to integrate a reform programme for the welfare state into the associative schema outlined in this book. He felt that imaginative thinking about the future of the welfare state was a neglected area, largely because it was not a particularly glamorous or fashionable one. But he thought this a most fitting empirical illustration of the general arguments for the advantages of associationalism. And of course he was additionally pleased by the fact that his conception of associational democracy was something that could in principle appeal to, and be adopted by, a range of political positions, not just those on the left.

Of course, Paul and I cooperated closely on the book *Globalization in Question* and we were actively planning a third revised edition when he died. In this book we were like-minded and pragmatic on the issue of globalization, arguing that its significance had been seriously exaggerated and that there was no reason to think that international trade interdependency and investment integration would necessarily continue to grow in the future. One of the things we were going to develop much more in the new edition involved the future of globalization. We thought there were good reasons why the recent period of the global expansion of economic, political and cultural activity may have peaked, and could even go into decline. Always expect the unexpected in the international system and do not think that what has been going on for several decades will necessarily continue into the future. This was very much our working slogan, and this basic attitude is nicely illustrated in the chapters of this book. Path dependencies are there to be broken, seemingly deep structures there to be reconfigured. Thus, to a great extent, the chapters in the present book illustrate well many of the themes we were going to develop in our third edition.

I think the book *War and Power in the 21st Century* marked a real departure in the public and academic perception of Paul's work. Here was the beginning of a publishing programme on his part that was rich in historical reflection, and which built on his long and sustained interest in matters of warfare and on military architecture, strategy and technologies. He continued this approach in the book of essays included here, where he again shows what it means to rethink the future, in his usual uncompromising style. Paul taught architectural theory and practice at the Architectural Association in London and at the University of Western Australia in Perth. In this book his concerns with architecture and fortifications, with new weapons technologies, and with the nature of space, combine to produce a fitting testimony to his highly fertile mind.

The question is, then, how did Paul think so imaginatively about the future regarding these concerns? There were several features of his intellectual life that contributed to his thinking.

First was his heavy suspicion of the growing *over*-theorization of academic debates. Not for the mature Paul Hirst the fads and fancies of postmodernism and its ilk. As pointed out above, Paul was not against theory, but he was against it if it seemed that it was done very much for its own sake, when it was just too clever for its own good and when it actively got in the way of him understanding the concrete detail of practical life. Was it helpful or not in making sense of detailed examples and empirical illustrations? That was his overriding question. So for him theory often got in the way of thinking creatively about the future. Theory is not an unambiguously good thing, despite its cherished status in academic circles.

Second, Paul also became very suspicious of a continued 'structural' analytical style. Perhaps it was his long engagement and final break with structural Marxism in the 1970s that produced this scepticism, but for Paul 'structural analysis' increasingly came to mean that thinking was confined only to the existing state of affairs. It reproduced the present and was of little help in imagining the future. This was particularly so in the case of all 'depth model' approaches to analytical life: that somehow there is a deeper unseen set of structural relationships that give rise to the phenomenal forms we see around us. With this theoretical approach the task is to penetrate through the hazards and complexity of everyday life to find the deeper and simpler underlying structures that are thought to produce them. But Paul's approach, I think, was the reverse. For him – again as amply demonstrated by the chapters in this book – the hidden and underlying remain complex and chaotic, while the surface is where the orders and the rationalities of space and power adhere, and it is these which give meaning and sense to their respective empirical configurations.

Third, this was all combined with his inherent 'decisionism' in matters of political analysis and policy-making – based upon an admiration for Carl Schmitt's theoretical position (but not an admiration for Schmitt himself, whom he despised). Forget 'structures' and 'structural constraints' so beloved of the social sciences, and instead concentrate on the 'balance of forces' at the conjunctural moment of any decision.

These features may not readily appeal to all the readers of this book, but, locked together with Paul Hirst's formidable intellect, they gave him an uncanny ability to 'imaginatively think the future' that, I would argue, was such a telling feature of his mature writings, and that is so admirably illustrated by the following chapters of this book.

Grahame Thompson
27 July 2004

Acknowledgements

Paul, I know, would want to acknowledge the countless students at the Architectural Association who provided a stimulating audience over many years, and Geoff London and Bill Taylor, who gave him the opportunity to lecture in their department at the University of Western Australia.

I would like to thank Grahame Thompson, David Held and Terry Mayer, without whom the manuscript would not have been published, and Bill Taylor and Lars Bo Kaspersen, who always responded to my many queries, however trivial.

Penny Woolley
December 2004

Part I

1

Space and Power: Architecture, Politics and War

This book is concerned with the various ways in which space is configured by power and in which space becomes a resource for power. It examines how, at different scales and under different social and technological conditions, spaces interact with and are constructed by forms of political power, armed conflict and social control. Space is a resource for power, and the spaces of power are complex and qualitatively distinctive. Hence in this context it makes little sense to theorize about the properties of 'space' in general, but rather to investigate definite space–power systems.

However, space is more than a malleable set of coordinates in the service of power. Spaces have characteristics that affect the conditions in which power can be exercised, conflicts pursued and social control attempted. At the most fundamental level, basic geographical distinctions like land and sea or steppe and sown do have effects on institutions and social practices, even if those effects are mediated by and specific to certain types of social organization and levels of technology. Moreover, even when spaces are deliberately constructed by forms of power, the very properties of those spaces have consequences, and these spatial effects cannot just be read off from the forms of power themselves.

This study operates at three spatial scales: that of the state in relations of cooperation and patterns of conflict with other states, that of the city as both an autonomous political entity and as a self-governing but subsidiary part of territorial states, and that of the building as an instrument of power. It also explores three main themes. First, the tendency for forms of exclusive territorial governance to re-emerge and to persist: thus today we are not witnessing 'de-territorialization', but the reverse. Second, the key role of frontiers of different kinds in different political systems. The chief frontier forms considered here are those between pre-modern empires and their barbarian neighbours, the shifting lines of conquest and settlement between opposed societies of different culture and ethnicity, and the surveyed, mapped and fortified lines demarcating modern sovereign territorial states. Third, the existence of severe spatial and material constraints on communication and social action in the past and their persistence in different forms even today. Thus information supplements, rather than displaces, physical communication: the virtual is not supplanting the real.

The analysis is guided by two main bodies of theory. First, at the macro level of space and power, the approach of close description of qualitatively distinct spaces by the early twentieth-century French historical geographers, Pierre Vidal de la Blache and Lucien Febvre. This has proved far more useful than most modern geographical, philosophical and sociological theorizing about space. It has provided a model of how to think about and how to present the specific spaces shaped by power that in turn condition it. Febvre's account of 'possibilism' provides a way of thinking about space as having effects while at the same time avoiding geographical determinism. Second, at the micro level, the work of Michel Foucault. Like the French geographers, Foucault's best work builds out from an account of particular circumstances. With his concept of power-knowledge and his notion of surfaces of emergence for discourses and forms of social control, it is possible to think about the conditions for, and the effects of, the micro spaces of power, such as churches, fortresses and prisons.

Rather than as a negative critique, this theoretical approach can best be seen as an antidote to many of the current theorizations of space. It tries to do something different, instead of merely criticizing and opposing other approaches. Thus, for example, ideas that are highly influential in both architecture and social theory, like those of Gilles Deleuze and Felix Guattari or Paul Virilio, are not ignored and are sometimes used here, but do not organize the analysis. Deleuze and Guattari's *A Thousand Plateaus* is at once too generalized to aid a detailed account of many of the complex spaces considered here; it develops grand themes that play across the whole of human history, and yet is also unhelpful and often wrong in its specific accounts. It is a curious mixture of abstraction and empiricism. Thus two of their key general themes of de-materialization and de-territorialization are shown here to be exaggerated and misleading in relation both to war and to modern politics. The emphasis on networks as against hierarchy and themes like nomadology and the war machine is shown to be excessive: here, networks are generally nested in hierarchies, nomads stick to riding camels and raiding, and the war machines run on coal and petrol.

The book takes the form of a series of 'essays', that is, attempts to cope with the vast range and wide scope of the subject of space and power through a series of strategically chosen 'cuts' through the material that examine certain topics and themes in depth. Given the type of analysis chosen here, to attempt to do otherwise would be all but impossible: even an inadequate survey would run to hundreds of pages. The method is chosen because other approaches offer generalized accounts that are either too parsimonious, in that they fail to grasp the level of detail at which the phenomena are constructed and have determinate effects, or they amount to an abstracted vocabulary that redescribes the phenomena but adds little by way of explanation or new material.

The book is divided into three parts. The first considers political institutions. Chapters 2 and 3 argue that two core institutions have been central in modern European history: the sovereign territorial state and the self-governing city. They form a couple, and explain why territorial governance could be at once *exclusive*, through delimiting the range of political actors that can operate within a territory and establishing both strong boundaries and the rule of law, and *inclusive*, seeking to identify citizens with the regime and thus making them a resource of power. It is argued here that territorial sovereignty remains central to both democracy and the rule of law, and that it is not being subverted by trans-territorial actors and processes as many modern social theorists claim. However, the city conceived of as a coherent place with effective governance is being threatened by various social and spatial processes, and this helps to undermine the ongoing viability of democratic participation within modern states. The apparently local politics of the city has thus been a key support of national democracy and of collective action generally.

In Part II, the spatial dimensions of war are considered, from the conflicts of tribal peoples through to war in outer space. Chapter 4 examines the basic spatial divisions that structure war, like land and sea, and also the different forms of social organization from tribal societies through pre-modern empires to the modern state. Chapter 5 analyses frontiers of conquest and settlement through four contrasting experiences: the Christian reconquest of Spain, the Ottoman occupation of the Balkans, the Spanish conquest of Mexico, and the European frontier of settlement in North America. Chapter 6 considers how material conditions and technology have shaped and constrained forms of war from the *longue durée* of pre-modern agricultural societies with small surpluses and poor communications, to the nineteenth-century industrialization of war and the communications revolution based on steam and the telegraph, and on to the transformations of

motorization and airpower. Chapter 7 examines the role of information in modern war. It begins with an account of the key technology of
the information age, radar. Radar is shown both to have major
material constraints and to take definite spatial forms. The chapter
goes on to consider information and war today by considering the
concept of the Revolution in Military Affairs (RMA). It demonstrates
that while war is being transformed by information technologies, it is
not becoming information-centric, and thus the enduring basic features
of war as a form of human conduct subject to limited knowledge and
uncertainty endure.

Part III shifts from the macro-spatial to the micro-spatial level and
to distinct dimensions of power. Chapters 8 to 10 examine how space
is organized to facilitate power through forms of rationalization of
structures. The examples of buildings chosen are the Renaissance centrally planned church, the geometry of which was designed to mirror
the divine order and to convey an experience of that order to the subjects who entered it; the panoptical prison, where space is rationalized
according to the demands of the inspection principle and the programme of the reform of prisoners' conduct based upon it; and, lastly,
the artillery fortress, where the bastioned trace provided interlocking
fields of fire that covered the whole external space of the town or
citadel.

The book thus interweaves a variety of discourses around the fields
of architecture, politics and war. It is based upon a long period of
teaching these topics at the Architectural Association, both in the
Graduate School and in General Studies. Chapters 8–10 were published in *AA Files*, although they have been revised for this book, and
chapter 10 has been updated to cover the post-1945 period. Chapter
2 was given in a lecture series in Copenhagen sponsored by *Byforum*
(Urban Forum) and has been rewritten for the book. Chapter 3 was
given at the conference 'Habitus: A Sense of Place' in 2000 in Perth,
Australia; it was published in the proceedings but has been extensively
changed and expanded to fit the themes of the book. Chapters 4–7 are
new and hitherto unpublished.

2

Cities, Globalization and Governance

Europe has created two distinctive and very durable political-spatial entities: the self-governing city and the sovereign territorial state. They form a couple. Cities have been – and still are – one of the key foundations for effective and legitimate government in modern states. The European city and state have been replicated across the world since the sixteenth century. The widespread adoption and retention of these political forms is not just a function of colonial legacies. On the contrary, those post-colonial societies that have been most economically successful and best governed have made those institutional inheritances work well and have developed innovative policies on the basis of them.[1] In this chapter we shall consider the future of the city as a political entity. In the next chapter we shall examine the future of the other part of the couple, the sovereign territorial state.

Both of these political-spatial entities, city and state, are now widely perceived to be under threat from a variety of forces. Most of these forces are perceived as trans-territorial, acting across and to marginalize political frontiers and economic boundaries. Not the least of these forces is cultural and economic globalization. The measure of the success of the city and the modern state as political-spatial forms is that neither is seen as being challenged by alternative emerging *political* institutions; rather, their demise is seen by optimists as the retreat of politics before markets or the Internet, and by pessimists as the collapse of governance. The solutions proposed for such a collapse of governance mostly involve spatially scaling up existing political processes to the global level. Global problems and processes, it is argued, now require governance institutions on a global scale. This has been the claim of advocates of world government from supporters of the League of Nations in the 1920s and 1930s through to today's cosmopolitan democrats. Can we thus scale up inclusive and accountable government? It is unlikely, because it ignores the role of a limited territory, controlled by one authority and bounded by clear borders, in sustaining the projects of building cultural, religious and national identity and, on that basis, creating inclusive polities.

Institutions operate on a definite scale. That scale is not given as a natural constant, but is dependent on the prevailing forms of political belief and legitimacy. Modern European empires, for example, were global and incorporated many heterogeneous peoples. Despite this, they were able to function for a considerable time if they had both a strong and relatively cohesive metropolitan state at their core, able to impose its rule, and also a principle of legitimacy to justify that rule to at least a section of the subordinate population. However, once the prevailing principle of legitimacy changed, for example from dynastic loyalty to nationalism, or once the demands for full inclusion within the imperial polity on the part of colonial settlers or subordinate peoples became pressing, then such empires began to break up. Austria-Hungary is an example of the first process. The revolt of Britain's American colonies is an early example of the second. Extensive forms of rule that are not based on legitimate territorial polities have yet to emerge and are unlikely to do so. No clear principle of legitimacy has been devised for institutions of supra-national governance, other than inter-governmentality and the support of the contributing member states, and no credible scheme of popular and democratic inclusion in such super-national institutions has so far been developed.

Similarly, scale affects city government too. Cities cannot grow beyond a certain size as free-standing city-states, nor can they easily sustain extended trading networks in the face of competition from other larger territorial powers. Thus these two European innovations, city and state, worked because they effectively matched appropriate spatial scale with effective political processes. They were strong because they achieved a sufficient measure of political inclusion, that is, the identification of a substantial part of the population with the regime.

Here we shall consider the past and the future only of Western-style cities. This is not to deny that there have been other non-European forms of developed urbanism: Cairo, Tenochtitlán or Tokugawa Edo are obvious refutations of such a proposition.[2] However, they had very different forms of social and political institutions. Our purpose here is not to survey the different historical forms of urbanism in different cultures. That would be a project that required the avoidance of 'Eurocentrism'. Here, we are looking at the legacies of the dominant political forms that developed in Europe and spread from it. Other considerations are not relevant to the problem in hand. The themes of the future of the city and the distinctive nature of Western cities do, however, require that we define what we mean by the term 'city'. First of all, the city is a concept.[3] It is not just – or even – a dense concentration of built environments: for that we have the concept of the 'urban' and the word 'town'. Cities are not just large towns. The city can only be fully understood as a political institution. It is defined by its role in governance. As an institution it has a substantial degree of political autonomy and a salient role in political and social life. Those attributes are not possessed by, for example, the substantial exurban agglomerations that have grown up around highway intersections in the United States, or the vast shanty towns attached to cities in developing countries. Neither of these has a coherent government or a civic life.

The future of the city is thus relatively distinct from the wider issue of the future of urban environments. Indeed, those wider forms of urbanism may subvert and threaten the city as a political and social institution. In this chapter we shall also consider how the widely postulated processes of 'globalization' are changing the economic and thus the political functions of cities. This involves two key questions. First, does the city have the prospect of an enhanced salience as the city-state in a new global market economy? Second, is the city now faced with marginalization in the face of increasingly trans-national market forces and the growth of virtual means of social organization through information and communications technologies?

The City as a Political Model

To consider the city as a form of governance we shall have to leave the future for the moment and go some way back into the past. The city has shaped and defined our understanding of political community. The concept of the city has been, with the sovereign state, one of the two key institutional poles of Western political thinking. The city is by far the older of the two. The concept of the modern state was not fully developed before the sixteenth century, whereas the city has provided the key model for government since classical Antiquity. Central to our imagining of political possibilities has been the Greek ideal of the *polis*. This is a self-governing community in which the ruling citizens have effective control over every aspect of their public lives.[4] The city is identified with freedom: as Aristotle says, the citizens govern and are governed in turn. Democracy was by no means the political ideal of the majority of Greek thinkers, but tyranny and autocratic rule were generally despised. Despite modern liberalism's invention of the liberty of the moderns as freedom in private life, we have never lost our aspiration to this aspect of ancient liberty as collective control.[5]

The ideal of inclusive governance became salient as never before with the development in the eighteenth century of the concept of representative government in the modern state. Enlightenment theorists scaled up the notion of the self-governing community from the city to the state. This intellectual rescaling could work because both the *polis* and the democratic nation-state are based on the idea of political homogeneity: rulers and ruled shall be alike, and they share a common culture and way of life. Rulers and ruled differ only in their *political* functions as magistrates and citizens. It is this that makes governance in common possible. Of course, neither in the Ancient World nor in the Modern could such homogeneity be realized. Thus, for example, women, slaves and metics did not count in the formal political life of Athens. Women and servants were governed in and through the household into the twentieth century in many Western representative governments. Inclusion could and has been expanded as the social beliefs defining who is capable of autonomous social life have changed. Both the ancient city and the modern nation-state have been quite different from forms of imperial and monarchical power in which rulers frequently differed in language, religion, ethnicity and culture from the populations they ruled. Such non-inclusive forms have predominated in European history since late Antiquity. Through that long period, self-governing cities were the main carriers of the ideal of the inclusive polity.

The notion of the inclusive and self-governing community reached its apogee in the 'Keynesian' welfare states of the 1960s. We came to believe that society could be fully ordered by good governance and that it could include all, substantively as well as formally. The members of the modern community were to be united by common welfare rights.[6] Since then, this ideal has appeared to be under threat with the growth of supra-national economic and political forces.

In the modern conception of representative government, the city and the state formed a couple: they were the two key *loci* of a division of labour in governance. Cities were the crucial subsidiary governments within the state, the anchor points of a relatively autonomous 'civil society'. Without lively, self-governing cities, democracy threatened to degenerate into centralization and the tyranny of the majority. Cities were the great municipalities that provided the economic and cultural strength of the state. Urban life afforded the spatial concentration necessary to facilitate collective action, and thus the basis for political parties, labour unions and other associations. These are the secondary associations vital to the maintenance of political plural-ism.[7] City councils were the school for national political leaders.

Cities have always had hinterlands. The concept of the 'city' has never been exclusively urban, but involved a specific relation between town and country. Thus the Greek *polis* was a city-state. It combined the urban centre and its rural hinterland in one interdependent entity. The Greek city was the political and religious centre that turned the surrounding countryside into an integrated community. Likewise, Italian Renaissance city-states included a *contado* – although the rural population were not included in governance and were subjected to the rule of the urban patriarchate.

Developed governance has always been urban. Large cities and dense networks of lesser towns are both a sign of and a resource for political centralization. Cities like Rome and Constantinople (which at their peak both had a population of 1 million people) could not exist without drawing on the resources of the entire Mediterranean world.[8] Denied the political scope of empire, both cities shrank to a mere fraction of their former size. The Mediterranean world was a society of cities, dependent for its cultural superiority to the surrounding barbarian peoples on its urban social organization. Cities hegemonized the countryside through the resident landowning elites who formed their governing class and who funded urban life through their donations.[9]

If one were to generalize about the city in classical Antiquity, it would be to claim that it was first and foremost a cultural and religious centre.[10] Its political role as a *polis* stemmed from the fact that it was a community linked by common rites, ceremonies and practices. Although trade and crafts were significant, they were secondary to these defining functions of the city. Citizens accumulated wealth in part to play a major role in public life. This was not only true of Athens and Rome, but also of provincial cities throughout the Roman Empire. Thus the ancient city was a consumer, rather than a producer of wealth. It relied on extracting from the rural world supplies of food and labour by means other than market exchange. Thus Rome depended on the state-organized grain supply from Libya and Egypt. It also relied on war at the frontiers with the barbarian world and on its elites' rural *latifundia* for the supply of urban slaves. There was an immense contrast between the lives of the urban elite of Roman cities and, for example, an Egyptian peasant. The bulk of the rural masses had little part in the advanced civilization that their crops and labour sustained. Hence Ancient civilization was vulnerable when faced by a serious barbarian threat, as we shall see in chapter 4.

Such highly developed pre-industrial urban life was fragile. It was heavily dependent on politics. In the case of Rome, it imploded when imperial rule failed to provide external security and when the elites abandoned the towns, turning instead to rural patron–client relationships. This led to accelerating social disorganization and localization, to the loss of great cities, to the shrinkage of the surviving towns, and to the loss of resources for governance provided by urban culture and trade.[11] Forms of governance based on the local rule of non-urban elites, like European feudalism in its heyday, were chronically weak and prone to internecine conflict. Hence the mutually reinforcing role after the eleventh century in Western Europe of the growth of trade and self-governing towns and monarchical centralization. Monarchs relied on the cities for the economic basis of their efforts at centralization. Cities accepted this partnership in exchange for security of trade and the greater influence that extended commerce brought.[12] Medieval cities in Italy and Northern Europe were based on trade and commerce, and were run by an urban patriarchate derived from merchants and guild masters. Thus they were very different from the cities of Antiquity, even if they often drew upon them for their ideals and practices of urban self-government.[13]

This partnership between free cities and sovereigns was unstable. From the newly centralizing monarchies, like England, France and Spain, emerged the political project of the modern sovereign state. If the city offered the model of the self-governing community, the concept of 'state' adapted the idea of sovereignty developed by Roman imperial lawyers to the confines of a definite territory, rather than a universal empire. The modern state is a sovereign body exercising exclusive and lawful control over a definite territory, and recognized as such by other states outside its borders.[14] The formation of the modern state involved the concentration and centralization of the powers of governance, appropriating them from local elites, free cities, and trans-territorial institutions like the Church and city leagues. Thus major cities like Barcelona and La Rochelle were at the centre of localist and religious revolts against this process of centralization, and institutions such as the Hanseatic League became marginalized as territorial rulers sought to limit the power of cities to act politically across borders.

Other major cities were crucial in promoting political centralization and thus achieved control of economic centralization for themselves as a result. Without the concentrated money markets and trading networks of Amsterdam and London, Dutch or English power could hardly have existed.[15] Cities thus redefined themselves in a new alliance with sovereigns as semi-autonomous subsidiary partners. The concentration of territorial power and the consolidation of the states system after 1648 boosted both national and international trade. This enhanced the political and economic role of key cities, and promoted the growth of certain major cities at the expense of others. In the early-modern period, mercantilist economic doctrines made sense. There was a limited volume of long-distance trade into Europe, based on key commodities like spices and sugar. States and key cities fought to control and to centralize this trade and could only prosper initially at the expense of their rivals.

Only after the widespread commodification that accompanied the agricultural and industrial revolutions did the logic of ever-expanding commerce make sense. Before that, trade was confined in the narrow envelope of demand set by the dominance of most European societies by semi-subsistence peasant production. Long-distance trade was vulnerable to capture and monopolization: it depended crucially on the organizational capacity and military competence of the competing states and cities.[16] Until the widespread growth of wage labour, the invisible hand was well hidden.

The strengthening of the major successful cities in turn laid the material foundations for the struggle for representative government on a national scale. Urban forces, both elites and masses, were in the vanguard of this development in England and France. This process gradually turned the sovereign state into a full political community: states became national and not merely territorial, and political community extended to dimensions wider than religion.

It is widely believed that this historical sequence of the consolidation of territorial power based on state and city is now being reversed. Supra-national processes are seen as undermining the power of national states and their ability to maintain territorial governance based on inclusive political communities. Global market forces and global culture are held to be beyond national control, as are climate change, terrorism, health crises like AIDS, and mass migration. Some commentators believe we are returning to a world of complex and competing agencies of governance as in the Middle Ages.[17] Then, as we shall see in chapter 3, there was no clear separation between national politics and foreign affairs. Distinct institutions competed to control affairs across different territories.

Today a variety of agencies and bodies (financial markets, international organizations such as the IMF, trans-national companies, global media and virtual networks, a 'global civil society' composed of NGOs, and international criminal and terrorist syndicates) appear to be doing the same thing. As states grow weaker, so more forces act across their boundaries to govern within their territory. The city and the state have provided our models of self-governance. States seem to be threatened, and opinions are divided as to the prospects for cities.

It is obvious that we have no ready-made models of trans-territorial governance to replace the state-city couple. Most of the modern forms of trans-territorial power listed above are inherently non-inclusive. They would involve a return to rule by elites that are not like us and do not need to involve us. Control by markets, trans-national companies and exclusive networks violates our basic expectations about self-governance. These organizations are also inaccessible to local collective action – unlike the elites of cities and nation-states. This is true even of well-meaning NGOs like Greenpeace. To Icelandic or Norwegian coastal whalers, Greenpeace represents a foreign elite seeking to force locals to conform to international standards that they do not share.

We have few ideas about how to ensure democratic governance in supra-national institutions.[18] It is difficult to find an adequate political vocabulary to describe the EU, for example, let alone provide effective remedies for its democratic deficit. The EU fits none of our conventional constitutional and political categories. It is obviously not a unitary state, nor is it a federal one, but its common institutions and laws have more powers than a confederation. The EU is created by treaties and yet it is not just a treaty organization. It depends crucially on the input of member governments, but it does not simply comprise intergovernmental cooperation. It is a permanent association of states with certain functionally specific but powerful institutions of common governance. It is difficult to see how those institutions, the rules and policies of which take precedence over national laws in their areas of competence, can be democratically controlled, whether by political action within individual states, or by common institutions like the European Parliament.

The history we have sketched indicates why the state matters to the city and the city to the state when both are seen as inclusive governing institutions. A trans-territorial and exurban social system is hard to imagine. Since Antiquity accountable governance has been linked to the growth of cities and trade, but within the borders of a definite territory.

Threats to the City

The city is seen as under threat from a variety of social forces. These forces challenge the economic viability, the spatial coherence and the cultural coherence of the city. They would, if the postulated effects were fully realized, produce an exurban, post-public and culturally heterogeneous future. Let us consider those factors in turn. They are:

1   the communications revolution;
2   exurbanization – the merger of city and countryside;
3   cultural pluralism;
4   globalization;
5   a self-destructive flight to the cities in the developing world.

The communications revolution

Cities have always been shaped by transport systems and communications media. Until the nineteenth century the carriage of bulky goods by land beyond short distances was difficult and prohibitively expensive, thus tending to limit both markets and the economic scale and scope of towns. The Mediterranean world functioned as an integrated whole in Roman times because of the possibility of sea travel across its centre. Likewise, cities in Northern Europe in the Middle Ages grew on seaborne trade and river trade. Most major cities in medieval and early-modern Europe were ports or were on navigable rivers. The ones that were not, like Madrid or Berlin, were mostly creations of pure political will. Cities were also limited in size by the constraints of internal travel. Even the largest, such as London or Paris, were 'walkable' cities.

In the nineteenth and early twentieth centuries two revolutions in transportation transformed the economic scale of cities. First, railways, steamships and telegraphs created an explosive growth in cities as they both promoted long-distance trade and opened up rural hinterlands. London became the first mega-city in the world because of its role as the centre of world commerce and finance. Chicago grew explosively in a few decades after 1850 as the centre for the vast hinterland of the American West, linked to it by railroads.[19] Throughout the 'neo-Europes' that were brought into existence by inward investment and international trade, such as Australia or Argentina, cities like Melbourne and Buenos Aires also grew with incredible rapidity. City growth was thus promoted by early 'globalization', which was itself driven by the new means of long-distance communication. Second, the transport revolution within cities made possible massive city growth because the new means of local transport facilitated suburbanization.[20] Railways, streetcars and underground trains rapidly expanded the possible spatial scope of the city. To begin with they did not subvert the city spatially or institutionally. Suburbs tended to be incorporated within city governance and to be oriented towards the commercial centre. London, New York, Paris and most medium-sized American cities expanded their boundaries to include large parts of the urban area. Communications favoured growth, but also promoted political centralization and collective action.

This latter effect is not apparently obvious in the case of the new revolution in information and communications technologies. The Internet makes spatial dispersal combined with social complexity a real possibility. Digitalized media have broken the spatial limits of communications costs and networks. The real marginal cost of a telephone call or an Internet hit is close to zero. Digitalized information can be almost infinitely replicated without diseconomies of scale or problems of scarcity. Telecommuting and e-commerce, at least in theory, make possible an elaborate division of labour mediated by cyberspace and fibre optic cables rather than by the physical propinquity of bricks and mortar. The need for spatial concentration in order to have organizational and cultural sophistication seems to have been transcended. Thus the principal economic reasons for concentration in cities to achieve spatial economies of scale and to coordinate divided labours are apparently *passé*.[21]

It may be possible to live in Montana and to conduct business in New York and Tokyo, to be linked across the globe by virtual networks, but this presupposes plugging into the ongoing non-virtual world by electronic means. In fact the development of information and communications technology has produced the further concentration of the financial, creative and cultural industries into key cities.[22] The main reason for this is that communication networks are no substitute for social networks. To some considerable extent, the medium and the message are still distinct. Social networks require real nodes where people can still interact in complex and non-programmed ways. That is why people still need and want to go to the office. This is also the reason why IT, advertising, fashion and financial firms continue to concentrate in 'post-industrial' districts.[23] Just as Alfred Marshall argued that nineteenth-century industrial districts in manufacturing existed largely because of an 'industrial atmosphere', that is, the sharing of tacit knowledge, access to current information, and the chance to plug into a complex and recombinant division of labour, so modern industries still cluster together in crowded environments like Silicon Valley, Wall Street, or London's Soho.[24] This is unlikely to change, and the more innovative and fast-changing the industry is, the more likely it is to cluster.

There is another powerful reason why this is so: labour markets. The chances of getting and changing a job are far greater in such districts, where one is much less dependent on a single employer. Equally, the opportunity to hire and keep the best people is greater in a big city than in a remote suburban 'campus' – only a few major firms like

Microsoft can afford to risk this option. Cities are unlikely to be killed by it. The paradox is that clicks require mortar: either expensive locations like New York or, in the case of e-commerce, real fulfilment networks, warehouses, roads and trucks.[25]

Exurbanization

This does not mean that all cities will thrive or that forms of non-urban agglomeration will not jeopardize urban values. The first phases of suburbanization were based on public transport and linked dormitory suburbs with central business districts. Two phenomena have threatened those central cities and have acted to constrain their growth, especially in the United States. The first is white flight and tax flight. The movement of blacks from the South to the North during the two world wars led whites to flee city areas and inner suburbs towards more distant and 'safer' outer suburbs. Alarm about crime and racist fear for property values meant that central business districts were surrounded by rings of poor districts with decaying housing. As the tax base stagnated and city taxes rose, so outer suburbs resisted incorporation and more residents fled beyond the city boundaries. Thus were created the divisions prompted by suburban affluence and inner-city poverty – with areas like East St Louis, Camden, New Jersey and the South Bronx becoming ruins devoid of jobs or public services. Even if the economic decay of central business districts has been reversed or slowed, the problems of fragmented governance where cities are too small and where regions are governed by competing authorities are still all too real in the US. The affluent self-governing suburban township is a form of exclusive governance, where locals are willing to subsidize first-rate services for themselves and to zone out the poor.[26]

The other problem is exurbia proper. The growth of edge cities, post-urban built environments, and 'boomburgs' has created phenomena that have few of the political attributes of the city.[27] An ideal-typical example is the growth of a complex of shopping malls and office facilities around a major highway intersection. Housing developments then cluster around the new agglomeration that has no corporate existence. It may cross at least one county boundary; it will have no coherent planning and no common public space; its core facilities, the malls, will be private. Such post-urban phenomena are based on the road system, cheap petrol, and a high density of car ownership. Workers commute to jobs in a suburban network in complex ways, not into the central city. The response to this is the 'New Urbanism', which actually means heritaged housing developments. This is carried to extremes in the Disney Corporation's 'Celebration', which plays on the nostalgia for small-town America in a replica development.[28]

The result is what Ed Soja has called 'city-full non-cityness' – lots of built environment but no sense of a coherent place, let alone a common civic life.[29] Collective action tends to wilt in such dispersed commuter exurbs, above the most local and self-interested level. High rates of geographical mobility plus highly fragmented patterns of work and commuting mean that people have fewer opportunities to associate. This seems to me a key cause of the decline of voluntary action in the United States that can be set alongside Robert Putnam's chief villain, television.[30] That seems more symptom of isolation than cause.

European city and state planners still have the option to resist the worst aspects of such exurbanization.[31] It is not that such phenomena are unknown, but in the main Europe's cities are spatially coherent places with effective municipal governments. The threat in America is that large parts of the country have become a decentred and post-public world beyond effective governance. In the exurbs most of the key 'public' space is actually under private control in office complexes, malls, and closed and gated housing communities.[32] There is precious little public realm left. This trend to private government is reinforced by the policy of 'reinvention' of public government, in which the local public authorities privatize most of their collective services and put them out to competitive tender.[33] The combination of the growth of private governance at the expense of public authority and the privatization of the services provided by public authority leads to a threat to the political role of the city part of the city-state couple. Without a strong civic life, national politics is undermined and democracy is weakened. The associational base that supports formal national politics shrivels. The political class is then drawn from a narrow stratum of political professionals and the public becomes more indifferent to politics. Of course, these phenomena have other causes too, but the role of urban structures is significant.

Cultural pluralism

The city-state couple has been founded on a degree of social and cultural homogeneity. Democracy requires that both the people and their rulers be sufficiently alike that the electoral losers will tolerate the victors taking office. Parties represent different interests, not incompatible cultures or communities. Nation-states were founded on such processes of homogenization: through education, military service and cultural policies populations were turned into Danes, Germans or French.[34] Such 'national' cultures were not merely the product of formal state policy. They were also created by voluntary action in civil society. Think of the English Boy Scouts, or the role of Catholic voluntary associations and rural improvement societies in shaping a distinctive Irish nationalism in the later nineteenth century, or the role of Grundtvigism in building modern Danish identity.[35]

Cities also played a central role in this homogenization. The massive urbanization of Britain, Germany and America in the 'long' nineteenth century from 1815 to 1914 took people from diverse rural cultures and placed them in a common urban setting. Urbanization promoted assimilation and individuation. Cities created their own distinctive culture and forms of social organization, integrating people into a common public and voluntary civic life. The intense poverty and social dislocation chronicled by Engels in his *Condition of the Working Class in England in 1844*, for example, were overcome by a huge effort on the part of ordinary urban dwellers to rebuild their lives. Friendly societies, the Cooperative movement, trades unions, religious associations like the Methodist Church, football clubs and cycling clubs transformed a grim existence into a vibrant civic life.[36] Much of this has been lost in Britain by de-industrialization and the ruin of old working-class communities since the 1960s.

Cities offered both cultural assimilation *and* greater individual freedom. They were part of the process of building relatively homogeneous societies in the democratic West. Since the 1960s many major Western cities have changed their character radically as a result of three processes. The first is post-colonial migration. Major cities like London, Los Angeles, Sydney and Toronto have become cosmopolitan and pluralistic, accepting people from a wide variety of cultures, ethnicities, languages and religions. The second is the growth of lifestyle communities, the most obvious of which is the new tolerance extended to gays and the formation of gay 'villages' in cities like San Francisco and Manchester. The third is the decline of old community-based associations in the face of greater individuation, privatization and consumer choice.

The result is that cities have ceased to be melting pots in the sense of assimilating incomers and acculturating the majority of them by the second generation. Current experiences are more complex. Many come to cities like London for the cultural diversity and freedom. In other cases communities differentiate themselves and keep or build distinct identities. This is the case both with ethnic groups, such as

Bangladeshis in the East End of London, or lifestyle groups like gays. Cultures also hybridize and cross-fertilize. The result is that educational and cultural policies become problematic in such major cities. It becomes harder and harder to push the old 'national' culture and less and less clear what that is. The very scale of diversity and hybridity also makes policies of pluralistic integration such as 'multiculturalism' difficult. Services like health care are also hard to provide, since groups have such different expectations and needs.[37]

This can be positive. Living in a large cosmopolitan city gives people great freedom and the opportunity to choose between diverse cultures and lifestyles. It also means that people have complex and changing cultural loyalties. Furthermore, many people have conflicting loyalties and supra-national interests and identifications. In both state and city it becomes harder to create a 'thick' common cultural script. The common civic life becomes a thin core of those largely formal and procedural values that the majority share.

Cultural pluralism can also be negative: groups can reject it – both migrant groups who seek to maintain distinctive identities and rejectionist local groups who resent diversity. One can set against London places like Oldham or Bradford in northern England. Here, white and migrant communities lead exclusive and increasingly mutually hostile lives; both feel victimized and powerless and both seek to express their frustrations against each other.

It is hard to combine diversity and democracy. Singapore, for example, has worked hard to create a common identity and to ensure the rights of the Chinese, Indian and Malay communities at the same time. It remains an authoritarian and far from democratic city-state. The old ideas of political community from the *polis* to the nation-state found it hard to accommodate diversity or conflicting loyalties. We need to build thin but strong – and not just formal and procedural – civic and national identities that the vast majority can share without feeling either excluded or that they have to compromise their own values. Civic nationalism can be combined with cultural pluralism. This has been relatively successful in new nations like Australia; whether it will really work in other nations with traditional thick scripts of what it is to be British or German, for example, remains to be seen. In the same way that it is difficult to achieve citizen identification and democratic participation in supra-national bodies like the EU, so it is problematic to accommodate the existing idea of the nation with the diverse peoples and cultures that now make it up. Cities helped to build nations in the past, but their diversity challenges them today. Our traditional political models are not helpful in this respect, since they require strong cultural homogeneity. New ones, however, such as multicultural urbanism and civic nationalism, are not well developed and are fragile.

Globalization

The word 'globalization' means many different and incompatible things. In *Globalization in Question*, with Grahame Thompson, I have tried to counter some of the more widespread and pernicious myths associated with this contested and complex concept.[38] However, even if one adopts the common-sense meaning that most people share when they use the term, that is, processes of growing international interconnectedness, then there are still some major questions to answer. International financial markets, foreign direct investment and foreign trade have all grown substantially since the 1970s. Have these increasing flows undermined distinct national economies and replaced them with ungovernable global market forces? Do international financial markets threaten the policy autonomy of nation-states? Do international competitive pressures mean a 'race to the bottom' in which welfare states and public services will be reduced to the lowest common denominator that international business is willing to tolerate?

There are good reasons for scepticism about the supposed demise of distinctive national economies or the policy autonomy of the nation-state. If investment and trade were truly globalized then the Japanese economy, for example, would not remain in the peculiar and singularly intractable mess that it is. Japan's problems are not due to the pressure of the international financial markets but to its absence, along with the intractable crisis of its peculiarly national banking system and structure of corporate governance. If there were a 'race to the bottom' then, for example, the Danish welfare state would be impossible. Instead of going over the globalization debate yet again here, let us concentrate on a strong version of the globalization thesis that foregrounds the role of cities, and also on a theory of new emerging patterns of governance that emphasizes the decline of the territorial state and the rise of networks. The proponent of the first hypothesis is Kenichi Ohmae, and of the latter, Manuel Castells.[39]

Ohmae believes that global market forces have reached a scale where national economies and economic governance by nation-states no longer exist. He sees this as a good thing. States only distort markets and use political power to impose sub-optimal outcomes on consumers in order to benefit special interests. The true governors of the new economy are trans-national companies that are now free to efficiently allocate resources across the globe as economic advantage dictates. However, public authorities do have a role to play. States are in decline, but alongside trans-national companies, and constrained by markets so that the scope for political distortion is limited, the governments of city-states and city-regions are the new providers of the collective services that industry needs.

Pace Ohmae regional governments, city-regions and industrial districts are indeed important, but only as part of a division of labour in governance that includes the nation-state as an effective going concern. The true city-state is vulnerable politically and could only thrive in an environment where national power had really and completely given way to markets. City-states are vulnerable because they have international economic scope, but a very limited territory under their direct governance. They need other powers to enforce the property and trade rights on which they depend. City-states like Florence or Venice faced this constraint in the past, that is, they did not have the territorial base to raise the military force sufficient to sustain their far-flung commercial and financial empires.[40] The two genuine city-states in the modern world are Hong Kong and Singapore. Both were colonial creations and have depended for their survival on British support and on their convenience to their powerful neighbours. Britain supported Singapore after it broke from Malaysia and guaranteed it against Indonesia. Hong Kong was a convenient outlet for Communist China, and China accepted its semi-autonomous position with distinctive institutions both as the price of getting the British out, and because of the economic flight from the colony that would have resulted from a more complete Beijing takeover. These two Asian entrepôts are unlikely to be joined by other politically autonomous cities.

The reason why true city-states, rather than world cities or city-regions embedded in nation-states, are not more widespread is also the reason why trans-national companies have not and will not become major institutions of governance. There are very few truly trans-national companies, that is, ones that are really multilocational and with a cosmopolitan management. Most major companies are in fact *multinational*: they have a legal and economic base in one of the major developed nations from which they operate internationally through subsidiary and affiliate companies abroad.[41] States are a good bargain for companies, and that is why companies stay national. The vast majority of multinational companies are located in the US, Japan or the EU.[42] Thus they have major governments to protect their overseas interests and to act on their behalf if they are threatened. Modern multinational companies are the beneficiaries of an interspace of economic exchange between the major economies created by public policy after 1945. Without states and the constant pressure that they exert to ensure access to markets for 'their' companies, to make legal rule inter-operable and the international political environment relatively stable, MNCs could not exist on the scale they do. They are dependent on politics.

Major states in developed countries have several advantages for companies and cities: an extensive territory that they police and, therefore, a better balance between economic salience and the scale of governance than either cities or companies; cooperation with other major territorial states to ensure the reciprocal protection of companies' and citizens' rights; a large tax base to provide defence and services; skilled legal, diplomatic and trade policy personnel to represent interests externally; and the ability to work with international agencies in shaping supra-national governance. Companies, unlike states, are relatively fragile and short-lived institutions.[43] The average life span of a major corporation as an autonomous entity is forty years. Companies are even less able to provide their own protection than are city-states. September 11 has proved how dependent the market system is on the force and stability provided by states. Ohmae over-estimates the power, scope and efficiency of markets and, therefore, downgrades the governance capacity and the positive role of states.

Manuel Castells paints a picture of a new, far more flexible and unstable system of governance in which institutions and territoriality count for much less than they have done since the formation of the modern state. He calls this the 'network society'. In it people will be able to act virtually and trans-territorially using networks of private power to exercise functions that have hitherto been public. This network power may be for good or ill and more or less coercive, acting through, for example, NGOs or criminal syndicates. People will be able to live in one place and operate economically in another. This will enable the rich and successful to shed the tax burdens of welfare states, and live in the international equivalents of the prosperous suburban communities that have opted out of the inner cities in the USA.

The problem with this vision is that networks are either a form of 'soft' power that depends on collaboration, or they rely on forms of coercion that are exclusive and unregulated.[44] Network governance works as an addition to the public and territorial governance of the state, but is a poor substitute for it. States, if they are successful at legitimating themselves, balance inclusion and coercion. Major states are still the key *loci* of governance in the modern world because they operate on a large scale: they both govern their own substantial territories, and they coordinate with other states and supra-national agencies to ensure wider and trans-territorial governance.[45]

For a similar reason the state remains the lynchpin of a division of labour in governance between city/regional, national and supra-national levels. The state shares power 'above' it and 'below' it, with international agencies and with subsidiary governments at regional and city level. Thus the idea that we might return to a situation of parallel and competing powers like that of the Middle Ages is improbable. Modern economies require a much higher level of stability and, therefore, more effective coordination in governance. A division of labour between agencies, rough and ready though it is in sharing competences, exists to prevent competition in governance. 'Gaps' in governance mean that governance capacity drains from the system like matter being consumed by a black hole. Too many ungoverned marginal zones, like tax havens, failed states and terrorist enclaves, threaten the working of the international economy. September 11 has shifted public priorities in the developed world from market freedom to security. This is likely to involve a tightening of the rules on tax havens, money laundering and parallel markets. It also means that cracking down on terrorism encompasses acting against coercive and illegal networks more generally.

Governance has changed. States share power with other agencies, private and public, sub-national and supra-national. But states remain salient in a way that other institutions do not. States alone, if they are democratic and constitutional, have the capacity to legitimate other agencies and to hold them to account. Thus the major states of the G7 continuously underwrite agencies like the IMF or WTO, as well as formally donating sovereignty to them by treaty. States have a place in the governing councils of such agencies and thus can also render them accountable to domestic publics through national democratic means. This is not to imply that such democratic controls are used effectively or that the policies of major states and international institutions are unproblematic, simply that the decline of the state has been grossly exaggerated and that it remains the dominant political actor across national borders.[46]

If the state is not threatened with marginalization, then this is good news for the city. Globalization, were it to happen on the scale the supporters of the strong globalization hypothesis assert, might mean the flight of the rich from all but a few world cities to wealthy international ghettos and tax havens. The breakdown of territorial state power would make life harder for city governments, themselves territorial. Instability brought on by chaotic national and international governance would threaten cities with the effects of distant financial crises and with crime and terrorism beyond control. The negative effects of globalization would be sufficiently serious that we should be glad that the phenomenon has been greatly exaggerated.

The flight to the cities

The fact that globalization has been exaggerated does not provide grounds for complacency. The benefits of the new division of labour in governance are largely confined to the developed world, as is the provision of services by effective national and city governments. The current policies of the major states and agencies like the IMF and World Bank, promoting free trade and opening economies to investment, are unlikely to transform the major developing countries. Throughout the developing world, especially in Africa and Latin America, people have for decades been fleeing an impoverished countryside for the cities. This is particularly evident in Brazil and South Africa. Cities like São Paulo have drawn rural migrants to *favelas*, shanty towns, where they find neither adequate housing and services nor employment.[47] Brazil is now 80 per cent urbanized. City governments are overwhelmed by this influx. The staggering levels of inequality in countries like Brazil frustrate growth. Education, public investment and promotion of effective demand – the preconditions for growth and for the employability of the urban masses – are sacrificed to policies aimed at protecting the financial stability of the wealthy and foreign investors. There are exceptions: for example, in the city of Porto Alegre a determined effort has been made to include the poor in municipal government and to plan services and investment fairly. Most governments at national and city level are, however, overburdened, negligent or corrupt.[48]

The largest cities in the world, the true megafauna of modern urbanism, are anti-cities – if we consider the city as above all an effective political institution. São Paulo, Cairo and Lagos are in one sense the future of modern urbanism: sprawling chaotic cities full of shanty dwellers. Their very growth, driven by uncontrolled rural migration, renders them all but ungovernable.[49] They represent a Third World version of exurbanism: they are also decentred and post-public. When we consider the future of the city, we have to bear in mind that most urban dwellers on the planet will not live in stable civic environments. Architects and planners are prone to taking particular cities, such as Los Angeles or Las Vegas, as models of the future of urbanism. Perhaps we should see Cairo as more typical of the future, in the sense that such cities will be the largest and fastest growing on the planet. Such a prospect is disturbing, because Westerners have tended to see urbanization as progress and the city as a force for order.

3

Politics and Territory

We still tend to think of politics as defined by the spatial container of the territorial state.[1] Politics is, of course, a much contested concept: it has many different meanings and possible spatial locations. Think, for example, of the diametrically opposed but equally compelling definitions of 'the political' offered by Bernard Crick and Carl Schmitt.[2] Think of the spatial implications of usages like 'the personal is the political' or 'office politics'. Yet despite this contestation, both academic and popular notions have given a salient role in determining what politics is to the governments of territorial sovereign states. It is such states that are typically held to have the capacity to define who else may govern – and how – within their territory. Thus they set the limits of possible politics. Such government (and especially that of states that attempt to *include* their own citizens in the polity) is therefore exclusive by nature: it controls the rights of external actors' access to its territory, and it denies certain activities and organizations political legitimacy.[3] This dominant model sees politics as state-centric and every inch of the globe as the territory of a state. We know that states differ hugely in their governance capacities, size and institutions: from continental-scale states like the USA to small Pacific island statelets like Vanuatu. We also know that the number of states has quadrupled in the last fifty years, to some 190, and that the capacity of many of these new states for exclusive governance is little more than a fiction. Yet political science has remained resolutely state-centric, focusing on politics within the container of the nation-state, and leaving politics beyond the border to the sister discipline of international relations.

The widely perceived phenomenon of 'globalization' has led many commentators to question both the continued salience and the very viability of the nation-state. They see economic and social processes escaping from territorial limitations and becoming truly global; that is, they become supra-national or trans-spatial, taking place either without relevance to borders, or in cyberspace. The consequences for politics are held to be twofold. In the first place, politics disappears as markets and electronic interchanges replace the need for more than basic local regulation. States become like local authorities in a global market system. Markets and the Internet will come to absorb the coordinative function of states. In the second place, politics becomes redefined as a cosmopolitan planetary system based on supra-national entities like the UN, and orchestrated by new global political forces such as NGOs. In the first case, politics is an irrelevance: it just gets in the way of more efficient, trans-territorial forms of social organization and resource allocation. In the second case, it becomes a cosmopolis, a world political community, but one which must rely, if it is in fact possible at all, on political processes quite different from those of the nation-state.

Globalization is a highly contested concept and the scale and scope of the phenomena grouped under it can be strongly questioned, as we saw in chapter 2. Yet the concerns about the eclipse of the nation-state stemming from this currently fashionable concept do help to remind us that the nation-state is a highly specific historical form. It developed between the sixteenth and seventeenth centuries in Europe. The rise of the modern state not only changed the territorial landscape of Europe: it also transformed our imaginative landscapes. Since the seventeenth century, we have come to see political power as inherently territorial. Politics takes place within the institutions and the spatial envelope of the state as the exclusive governor of a definite territory. We also identify political territory with social space, perceiving countries as 'state-societies'. This is not, as some modern social theorists would have us believe, a conceptual error. It is a fact of political transformation, as sovereign territorial states reinvented themselves as nation-states. Rulers and ruled became alike, and together they shared a distinct culture and institutions defined at least in part in opposition to those of other nations. Such differences were shaped in and by the conflict of states that has been inherent in the states system since its formation.

Territory and Political Power before the Sixteenth Century

Clearly, politics has not always been identified with a power that claims to be the exclusive ruler of a given spatially and culturally coherent territory. Pre-modern states and other political entities were seldom spatially homogeneous. Rather than a rigid spatial demarcation of governance rights, different agencies governed different domains of life across the same territory and competing claims to rule involved a complex pattern of enclaves and exclaves. Rulers and ruled were often ethnically, culturally and linguistically different. Part of our difficulty in thinking about politics, power and territory is that our political ideas have been shaped by what we might call a 'double territorialization'. The actual construction of exclusive territorial rule has been reinforced by a reinterpretation of the past as if it too conformed to modern models of politics. The Renaissance thinkers who tried to conceive of the modern state, like Niccolò Machiavelli or Jean Bodin, tended to return to Greek and Roman models. They thought of post-feudal politics as a single political community with a single source of legitimate government, and in which those who participated in politics shared a common culture. Thinkers like Machiavelli tended to identify the contemporary Italian city-states with the republics of Antiquity. Likewise, Bodin compared the power of the French monarchy with the Roman *Imperium*. This identification was made unexceptional by the general Renaissance practice of recovery of classical cultural models.[4] It hid the distinctiveness of the modern territorial state.

But Antiquity was actually very different in the relationship of space and politics. The Greek *polis* created an enduring model of the self-governing political community. The Greek city-state was, indeed, territorial and it was defined by a common culture. Yet the city-state was the exclusive ruler of a *small* territory, defined by the ability of the members of the governing class to meet in common and, therefore, by the distance that could be walked in a day. The culture of the city-state was doubly exclusive, of those in other cities, and of the large proportion of the population of the city who were not political participants: women, slaves, and resident aliens. City-states were limited by a definite and symbolically significant territory, which they neither could easily nor generally wanted greatly to extend. Their military power was restricted by their relatively small, free adult male population. States could either grow by founding sister cities in the form of colonies, as the Greeks did in Sicily and Asia Minor, or they could subordinate others in the form of a tribute empire, as Athens did the cities of the Aegean. That empire depended on the Athenian fleet, its maximum size of about 300 *triremes* determined by the number of rowers in the free population.

When protracted war stretched Athenian manpower and public financing by the gifts of its wealthy citizens and residents to the limit, as it did during the Peloponnesian War, then the limits of the Greek *polis* were revealed. Greece above the level of the city-state was a cultural entity, not a political one. Greece was doomed once it was confronted by a major power, Macedon, that had absorbed its culture. The common elements of Greek society, the games and the great religious sites, did not provide a lasting basis for political institutions above the level of the city-state. The relationship between politics and territory established in Greece was thus quite unlike that of the modern state. The modern state developed the military, administrative and ideological capacity to absorb the different self-governing cities and local powers into a common and legitimate system of rule. The new unified states were thereby able to expand outside the core political territory and to create overseas empires.

Rome had also been able to do both of these things. It expanded by incorporating Latin cities within its own political system and eventually by extending the rights of Roman citizenship to all qualifying free men. The empire at the height of its power at the end of the first century AD was a network of self-governing subordinate cities, of tributary kingdoms, and of tribes living by their own customary laws. Rome's empire was, however, conceived as universal. It was without fixed boundaries and saw itself as potentially capable of expanding to include all the known world, as the surrounding kingdoms and tribes were conquered and civilized. Rome recognized no legal or cultural limits to its expansion – no political community had a right to exist except as subordinate to it. It was thus quite unlike the modern state, which as a condition of its own existence recognizes other states as part of a common states system governed by certain rules of interaction between sovereign powers. Rome's only partner in the ancient world was Persia. But Rome's relations with the Parthian and Sassanian Empires were complex and *de facto*. Persia was never accepted as a legitimate partner in a stable international system.

The difference between Rome and the early modern empire-building states was that the latter were part of a competitive states system. Rome was a state without recognized territorial limits. Because of this, it was simultaneously powerful and weak. It was powerful because until the latter part of the fourth century AD, it faced only disorganized barbarian tribes on its frontiers, with the exception of that with Persia. It concentrated on exclusionary frontier defence. It was weak because, confronted with no strong system of rival states, it faced no defining external threat that imposed a constraint on its own institutions. It was thus able to allow the military basis (and the political rationale) of citizenship to atrophy. A militarily demobilized and politically inactive free population had little interest in – and no right to – the control of higher politics in the empire. When military disaster threatened, the mass of citizens was no longer a resource to be drawn on, as it had been many centuries before during the campaigns of Hannibal.

Moreover, Rome's armies had become the principal source of right to rule: political power grew from the point of a gladius. Armies on the frontier repeatedly rebelled in favour of a new candidate for/usurper of the imperial purple, and precipitated a civil war. Rome was undermined by these wars and the barbarians were emboldened to raid deeper into the empire as the frontiers were left unguarded. In the absence of a real states system, Rome was a lone superpower without an external reality check on its internal policies and practices.

Early-modern political theory looked backward to envisage sovereignty and political community. But both of these things were embedded in something new, a system of competing states that recognized each other as such. Other types of regime had little place within early-modern political theory, except as that against which it defined itself. The Ottoman Empire was from the later sixteenth century onwards widely perceived as a form of essentially arbitrary power, against which Western sovereigns could be seen as rulers bound to respect both the laws that they had made, and the fundamental constitutional laws of the state.[5] Thus, for Bodin, the French king was sovereign; he gave orders but did not receive them. He was an absolute monarch who controlled both legislative and executive power. But he was not a tyrant because, although he could make and change ordinary laws, he could not tax without the agreement of the *Estates Général* and had to abide by the Salic Law, which prescribed succession by the first-born male. Like Rome, the Ottoman state conceived of itself as a universal empire. It was committed to imposing the rule of the Sublime Porte and Islam wherever the force of Turkish armies could carry. It was only in the eighteenth century that the Ottoman state began to make normal treaties with other states, rather than temporary pacts or truces. Even in the mid-nineteenth century, when it accepted the logic of mutual recognition, it was not really accepted by other European states as a full member of the international system. Turkey was seen as a problem, a terminally weak and declining regime, and its boundaries in the Balkans were seen as illegitimate and subject to rollback by at least some of the Great Powers.

Other pre-modern forms of rule had an even less explicit relationship between a definite space and politics. Nomad confederacies, like the Mongol Empire, were non-territorial. Mongol rule recognized neither spatial limits nor the right to existence of subordinate powers, let alone legitimate independent rulers. Mongol rule relied on free movement over the steppes of Eurasia, on a military community fed by its own sheep and horses that moved with it. The Mongols incorporated other nomadic tribes within their confederacy, but their ruling elite was defined by clan membership and by a tribally exclusive shamanistic culture. Whether Mongol rulers were nominally Muslim, Christian or Buddhist, the key nomadic clan rituals defined the exclusive culture of the core of those who controlled the state. Mongol rule was thus both culturally exclusive and non-territorial. The rulers lived in a facsimile of a nomad camp, even when it was a permanent city like Karakorum with thousands of imported artisans providing goods for the court or, as in Beijing, where the nomads created a miniature steppe in the form of a park at the heart of the imperial city.[6]

Early-modern political theory tended to ignore and downplay the institutions that the modern state displaced, precisely because they were decentralized, non-hierarchical and weakly territorial. It was only well after the transition to territorial modernity, in the eighteenth century, that historicizing discourses invented the concept of 'feudalism'. This does not mean that 'feudalism' was an illusion, even if the ideal-typical characterizations of latter authors ignored the variety and complexity of medieval institutions.[7] Feudal forms of government that had developed after the decline of Roman rule in the West were also non-territorial in their conception of the basic form of authority.[8] They were based on personal ties between lord and vassal. The fief was a gift of land in return for obligation and service. It was contingent on where it was located: territorial rights derived from personal obligations and could be changed. The unfree population was tied to the land by labour service and had no part in governance. Feudal elites, however, served with their lords as dynastic acquisitions, conquest or crusade dictated. Norman nobles, for example, could be found ruling in England, in Sicily, in the Holy Land, and on the Baltic coast. Typical of medieval feudal states were borderlands where rule and title were ill-defined. Medieval Europe steadily expanded across such shifting frontiers – raiding, settling and conquering as the occasion arose. After the year 100, in the Baltic and in Spain, Christian power steadily expanded against pagan tribes and Muslim rulers respectively. In the Balkans, by contrast, the Ottomans expanded by similar processes against the Byzantine Empire and the various kingdoms of Serbia, Hungary, etc. Such moving frontiers existed within Europe before they became typical of the neo-Europes of North America, Argentina or Australia.[9] We shall discuss this more extensively in chapter 5.

Medieval states lacked not only exclusive control of a given territory by a single ruler, but also a clear and coherent division of labour in governance. Powers competed to control the same spaces, claiming forms of territorial or functional rule that were ill-defined in their scope and rights. Kings and great nobles held fiefs within each others' territories. Realms were not homogeneous, but a patchwork of enclaves and exclaves in which rulers held power by the random logic of dynastic inheritance. Different entities ruled in the same space, often making contradictory claims upon the ruled. The Church claimed not only functional rule over religious matters and over clergy, and the right to raise revenue by taxing the laity and to have its own law, but it also disputed temporal power. The Pope claimed universal dominion over Christendom, as did the Holy Roman Emperor. Popes claimed the right to invest secular rulers in office, with the threat of veto, and hence to exercise hierarchical control. Kings, for example the French and English, in turn demanded the right to appoint bishops. Not only was the Pope a secular ruler in the Romagna, but prince bishops elsewhere ruled their dominions and possessed armed forces.[10]

Cities were territorially coherent forms of government, but their very autonomy helped to limit the coherence and power of wider territorial forms of rule. Cities enjoyed extensive powers of self-government, either granted as particular liberties or privileges by monarchs in return for money or military aid, or appropriated *de facto*, as with the Italian city-states in respect of the empire. Cities raised taxes, possessed armed forces and their own system of justice, and made treaties with rulers. Leagues of cities, like the Hanseatic League of northern trading cities, acted as powers in their own right. The Hanseatic League's cities coined money, donated armed forces to the common purposes of the League as defined by its ruling institutions, made commercial laws, enforced trading privileges, and dealt diplomatically with rulers.[11] It had most of Bodin's marks of sovereignty, except territoriality. The cities were drawn from territories that would later form part of Germany, Poland, Sweden and so on. The Hanse obtained exclusive trading privileges from rulers and the right to establish its own trading factories, with extraterritorial rights for its members. The League was a quasi-polity with common decision-making institutions and rules: its members were the participating cities. Within the League certain cities, chief of which was Lübeck, were the main sources of its financial and naval power.

In medieval cities the guilds enjoyed functionally specific governance of their particular trade and its practitioners.[12] Guilds determined entry to the trade, training, the quality of work and prices, thus regulating the production and sale of goods and the number and character of the labour force. They also imposed codes of honour and settled disputes between members. Frequently, they formed the basis for town militia companies and religious confraternities. The guilds were typically controlled by the leading guild masters. For the ordinary journeyman, such functional governance was more important in ruling their lives than any other form of governance. Guilds also served in many cities as the main route of representation to the town council. Guilds thus also played a wider political role outside the economic governance of their trade.

Within the Ottoman Empire, the *millets* system of self-regulating religious and merchant communities allowed the subordinate peoples of the empire a measure of control of their own affairs, according to their own religious laws.[13] Christians and Jews had to pay additional taxes and were subject to other liabilities, but as religions of the Bible they were legitimate communities and had some rights to self-government. Ottoman cities were typically divided into closed quarters where the different religious laws prevailed. Throughout the medieval world, Muslim and Christian alike, laws thus depended on status. Priests, serfs, guild members and so on had different rights and were subject to different laws. Rulers and the ruled might be unlike in culture, ethnicity and rights. The nobility and peasants they ruled often had little in common. These are examples of the parallel governance by different groups within the same territory, but also of the common functionally specific governance of people across distinct spaces.

Bodin's various marks of sovereignty – to give orders but not to receive them, to make laws, to administer justice, to coin money, to tax, to raise armies, to deal with other rulers – were complexly distributed across territory before the sixteenth century. Various agencies could do these things, including raise armed forces and enter into relations with other rulers. The Hanseatic League, the monastic military orders like the Teutonic Knights or the Hospitallers, mercenary forces like the Catalan Company, city-states, prince bishoprics – all these bodies acted much as later 'sovereign' states would claim exclusively to do and often across the same territory. Late medieval society was complex and political power was distributed differentially across it, creating multifaceted relations between space and politics.

The Sovereign Territorial State

From the sixteenth century onwards, starting with the centralizing late medieval monarchies of England, France and Spain, states across Europe struggled and eventually succeeded in becoming the dominant powers within a definite territory to which they laid claim.[14] This is not the place to rehearse in detail the reasons for the rise of the modern state, or to look too closely into the temporality of the process with its numerous challenges, crises and conflicts.[15] Suffice it to say that this dual process of state formation and the creation of a system of states has two defining characteristics.

First, *exclusion*: all entities that are not exclusively sovereign are gradually de-legitimized and eventually expelled from the international system. Thus the Hanseatic League, the monastic military orders, the Church as a pan-European institution and the city-state are all either eliminated or marginalized. Both the papacy and the Hanseatic League, having previously been major powers in the politics of the Germanic lands, had no effective part in the Treaty of Westphalia of 1648 which ended the Thirty Years War. Likewise, the Hospitallers, having played a vital role in resisting Ottoman advance in the Mediterranean at the siege of Malta in 1565, became an increasingly honorific irrelevance in the European system, until removed by Napoleon. The Holy Roman Empire, itself a ghost after Westphalia, lingered on, ever more marginal in relation to the member states, until abolished by Napoleon in 1806. Exclusion is thus a process that takes place primarily at the international level. It also means the redefinition of the authority and the capacities of local and functionally specific governing powers within centralizing states.

Territorial states did not prevail because they had no effective opposition or because they faced only fragmented and weak local powers over which they were able to assert a monopoly of the means of violence. They had competitor institutions in the race to supplant the late medieval complexity of forms of governance. Such competitors were territorial, wealthy city-states such as Florence, and trans-territorial, city-leagues like the Hanse.[16] Thus few, for example, would have imagined in the early fifteenth century that Sweden would come to displace the Hanseatic League as the dominant power in the Baltic. Sweden was a small and relatively poor country. It rose through mobilizing its slender resources by means of the organizing power of the state.[17] Territorial control enabled it to conscript the manpower it needed for its foreign wars. Foreign possessions became a vital source of revenue. The League, by contrast, became ever more marginal as the territorial powers in which its cities were embedded strengthened their control in order to face their own external competitors. The cities of the League were increasingly parts of other polities, whereas in the medieval period they had been almost autonomous within loose-textured realms.[18]

Second, *mutual recognition*: states acquire powers over their societies to a substantial degree because they recognize each other as exclusive rulers of a definite territory. A central aspect of such recognition is non-interference, with states refraining from acting directly within the territory of another state. During the religious wars of the sixteenth and seventeenth centuries, such intervention had become normal practice, with states aiding religious dissidents in other countries either for reasons of ideological affinity and/or for reasons of balance of power. France and the German lands were torn apart by religious civil wars, fostered in part by external powers. The Treaty of Westphalia established the principle of non-interference in domestic religious conflicts, thus enabling states to begin to assert control over their societies. Until they did so, confessional loyalty tended to take priority over loyalty to monarch or state. Once a stable relationship between religion and territory was established in Germany, with states being recognized as either Reformed or Catholic, the process of building political or territorial loyalty of the population could begin, incorporating religion as part of state identity. The control of internal violence allowed states to turn the aggression of their peoples outward, towards other states. Hence the succession of wars from the late seventeenth century into the early nineteenth century, ending with the peace of Vienna in 1815. States used wars to build forms of identification between rulers and ruled. Where this was successful, as in Britain, state, regime and nation came to be defined together in one form of legitimacy. Where this was less successful, as in France, state and nation were brought together after the fall of the old regime.

Without territorialization and exclusivity, there could not subsequently be political nationalism. Why should rulers and ruled be alike if political institutions were distributed by function and status, and different institutions competed to rule the same territory? How could subjects or citizens identify with a territory if it did not have a definite link between its symbolic and spatial features? Nationalism typically claims not just an ethnos/national group, but also a territory that this group should inhabit as its homeland as of right. Without the prior existence of the sovereign state claiming a definite territory, it is difficult to see how nationalism might arise. Typically, nationalism begins as the project of rulers seeking to harness people to states. Then rival projects follow, demanding political rights for all members of the nation, or unification of states into a nation-state, or the secession from states in the name of the right of peoples to self-determination.[19]

Without territorial nationalism, it is difficult to see how there could now be democracy. Representative government is not new and has existed, for example, in quasi-polities of heterogeneous composition: feudal estates or the councils of the Hanseatic League were 'representative' in that delegates spoke for statuses or cities. People expected such delegates to be different from one another – to speak for the particular interests of their estate or of their city. Democracy – where the government is chosen by the abstract majority vote of the people – is quite distinct from this traditional representation. People have to feel sufficiently like their neighbours for a simple majority decision to be acceptable. Nationalism provides a basic cultural-social homogeneity that enables people to trust majorities.

Where such homogeneity does not exist, the introduction of democratic procedures simply exposes the conflicts of the wider society, as in the former Yugoslavia. 'Nations' are seldom homogeneous enough to begin with to suffice for political purposes; they are made up of *ethnoi*, the local customs and *patois* of various *pays*. A 'nation' is seldom, however, a purely political creation. It has foundations out of which a national culture and institutions are made by a variety of processes: from teaching a uniform language to the opening up of the country to national commerce through new roads and railways. Equally, nations do not emerge naturally: the 'people' have to be chiselled from the bloc of local customs and particularities by political projects from above, using state power, and from below, by patriotic organizations in civil society.[20] Given such a network of 'nationalizing' cultural and social institutions, state and society merge. The continuation of such politics of nationalism and the wars that are its inevitable outcome, as nations define their differences and establish their territories in conflict with others, leads to the unity of politics, culture and territory.

Such a unity gives state borders a special salience. Borders existed before the modern state, but they were mainly zones of control, like the Roman *limes*, or shifting lines of conquest and colonization between rival civilizations. As Lucien Febvre has shown, the modern concept of *frontier*, that is, a clearly demarcated line marking the external boundaries of internally coherent and adjacent state territories, did not really exist before the sixteenth century.[21] This notion is an early modern coinage that is coincident with the creation of the concept of state sovereignty and the attempts to construct such territories in practice. Before the fifteenth century state boundaries had little special significance as against other boundaries. In the medieval period there was no developed concept of the state as legally and socially superior to other forms of organization. Realms were merely one of the many bodies that could claim to be *Universitates*, that is, with the right to full corporate existence and the right to govern their members.[22] Boundaries between realms were seldom clearly marked, or they were ill-defined marchlands, zones in the hands of local lords who often had shifting loyalties.

Where well-marked boundaries existed in the Middle Ages, it was mostly to define the limits of *property* rather than political entities as such. Thus the boundaries of manors and Church lands were typically well-defined, whereas those of feudal states were not. Only when the sovereign territorial state was well-established did the detailed demarcation of external frontiers become both possible and necessary. Mutual recognition and frontier definition went hand in hand. When states accepted the legitimate existence of others as exclusive governing powers, it mattered crucially where the rights of each began. It takes both adjacent states to agree on a frontier line and to mark it. Only in the eighteenth century did most states have the material and administrative resources to survey, to map and to mark their frontiers.[23]

With the modern state, the frontier becomes not a disputed region or a zone of control, but a line. Then we expect things to be socially and culturally different on one side as against the other. The frontier is marked and policed: that is a secondary effect of exclusive governance of territory and of peoples being defined culturally. Within those EU states that are signatories of the Schengen Agreement, borders now matter less and less, in some cases less than borders between US states. Once, such frontiers were closely guarded: now they are often imperceptible. The reason is not merely because the states in question are no longer in conflict, but because it is increasingly difficult to tell the peoples of adjacent states apart.

As we have seen, the formation of exclusive control within the state's territory owed a great deal to the fact that states were members of an international system. The modern state evolved not merely *pari passu* with the system of states, but to some considerable degree as an effect of it. War was also a central fact in producing identification with the state, creating the territorialization of populations that served as the foundation of nationalism. From the beginning, however, states did not just compete: they also cooperated, and from the earliest times their interactions were governed by norms. This normatively governed system created a radical disjuncture between the space governed by the states system and its rulers, and that beyond, the civilized and the uncivilized. As Carl Schmitt realized, international law created the conditions for the control of the 'non-civilized': 'A nation that was not civilised . . . could not be a member of the community of states. It would be regarded not as a subject but as an object of that community's civil laws. In other words, it was part of the possessions of one or another of the civilised nations, as a colony or colonial protectorate.'[24] By the late nineteenth century, European states had extended the states system to the whole of the Earth. They had converted most non-European territory into colonies and had reduced China to a series of spheres of influence. Colonial control created new spatial patterns in Africa, the Americas and Asia, divisions based on European conquest and political entities that were artefacts of conquest. Most of the states created by de-colonization are thus marked in their very territory by the impact of European conquest.

The modern states system created the principle of no territory without a state, and in the nineteenth century this standard was vigorously applied: there was a gradual squeezing out of marginal areas and political entities that did not conform to the norms of modern statehood, like the pirate enclave of the Dey of Algiers.[25] The sea, however, was another matter. States did try to claim the sea. The Treaty of Tordesillas, concluded by the Pope between Spain and Portugal in 1494, imagined that the globe, including the sea, could be divided like a land barrier. Neither country in fact could exclude the French, British and Dutch from raiding and trading. As we shall see in chapter 4, control of the high seas depended not on borders, but on the effective capacity to trade, and on the dominance of one fleet over others. Naval conflict and wars on land each followed a different logic. In the early seventeenth century the Dutch theorist, Hugo Grotius, developed the notion of the seas as commons open to all to trade and to use. He argued that law was based on fact, not *fiat*: the seas could not be monopolized, nor did the passage of one ship diminish the utility of the sea to another.

The Creation of an International Economic Order

The principal political projects of legitimation that emerged in succession from modern territorial statehood – dynastic absolutism, nationalism and representative democracy – all depended on a certain spatial order, that is, on a claim made by a given form of rule over a place. Dynasticism by right of inheritance, nationalism by the established co-residence of a people with distinct attributes, democracy as the will of the nation, link power and place together. The interstate order, however, was never limited in this way. From medieval times, states had sought to foster and control commerce, with trade bringing money and thus the sinews of war in train. As we saw in chapter 2, in the mercantilist period in the seventeenth and eighteenth centuries, states sought to annex and monopolize trade in efforts to concentrate long-distance trade in their ports and in their ships. They attempted to control access to trade through monopoly companies like the Dutch VOC or the English Hudson's Bay Company. During the eighteenth century, these projects of monopolization faltered as private traders sought to enter these markets.

Adam Smith provided a rationale for free trade in *The Wealth of Nations*, and the origin of a new political principle: commercial liberalism. In the nineteenth century, under British naval and commercial hegemony, a new international economic order was erected, based on the freedom to trade and the right of citizens freely to engage in private actions across the borders of their states. Commercial liberalism was the only doctrine that could build a genuine *international* order, something that went beyond the interaction of states at their borders in diplomacy and war. The new liberal sovereignty existed above all to promote the freedom of private individuals to trade and, therefore, on the redefinition of the role of the state in facilitating such commerce. The liberal state was thus committed to definite international norms and therefore used its power to enforce freedom to trade. Hence the forced opening to trade of China and Japan that refused such freedoms. Hence the stigmatization of states as backward when, as in the Russian Empire, the free movement of people and goods was prevented. The 'long' nineteenth century (1815–1914) created a world free-trading system based on growing levels of international trade, investment and migration. In 1914 Britain, France and Germany had attained merchandise trade to GDP ratios broadly comparable to those of today; Britain and France had levels of capital export to GDP not exceeded today, and the whole Atlantic economy experienced levels of mass migration that dwarf those of today. Between 1800 and 1930, 40 million Europeans migrated permanently overseas. The world created by commercial liberalism was unlike the world of today, which is controlled by borders, passports and visas to a degree that in the nineteenth century was regarded as particular to barbarous regimes like the Tsar's.[26]

The nineteenth century was the first great age of 'globalization'. The liberal politicians in the major commercial states, far from being threatened by such developments, and like politicians and international technocrats today, saw it as their role to promote and protect free commerce. Liberal sovereignty implies a world of other states bound by rules of international civility and a system of free exchange by private individuals across the borders of states. The liberal state is thus inherently internationally oriented: its exclusive control of its territory is designed to promote an open commercial system within and without. Liberal sovereignty is state power applied to promote commerce, whether in the form of compelling reluctant 'partners' to trade, as in the Opium Wars the British fought in China, or in the domestic social policies designed to force workers to participate in the capitalist economy, as catalogued in Karl Polanyi's *The Great Transformation*.[27]

Liberal sovereignty and international trade were not the only forces at work in nineteenth-century international politics. The world trading system existed in parallel with the interstate system of Great Power politics centred on continental Europe. In the period after 1815, the major powers had cooperated to maintain the post-Napoleonic order.

The unification of Germany between 1864 and 1870 changed the balance of power on the continent. The new Germany was half trading state and half continental hegemon. Although Germany imposed protective tariffs on both grain and industrial goods, it joined the Gold Standard and became a major exporter whose national interests were tied to foreign trade. After the fall of Bismarck, the conflict between the two aspects of Germany's foreign position was exacerbated by a policy that downplayed cooperation between the conservative powers in Europe, ending the loose alliance that had linked Germany, Russia and Austria-Hungary, and which antagonized Britain through naval expansion and an imperialist *Weltpolitik*. Conflict tended to replace cooperation between states, and Europe divided into two rival alliances. The only supra-national order capable at this time of being erected on the basis of territorial sovereignty was the interstate alliance committed to mutual support in case of war.

British hegemony was exercised over the global financial and trading system, not over the policies of the continental powers. It was an economic primacy, backed up by naval power, not an overall military dominance like that of the USA today. The *Pax Britannica* worked to the extent that European states were willing to play by the liberal economic rules and in the absence of a general European war. In the end conflict came not through international economic competition, but because of rival nationalisms and the Great Powers' struggle over spheres of influence. Germany was pivotal in making the resulting war a world war: the combination of seeking dominance in Europe, naval expansion, and *Weltpolitik* ensured that England was forced to join France and Russia. The effect of the First World War was to destroy both the liberal international order and British hegemony over it. The two distinct principles that organized international politics – competing territorial states and a liberal international order – had proved incompatible. They could only be made compatible after 1945 because the majority of states outside the Soviet Bloc accepted the logic of liberal sovereignty under US hegemony: the US had the capacity to play both roles, setting the rules for the world trading system and prevailing over the other powers to assure existing borders.

This was only possible because the main opponents of international liberalism, with the exception of the Soviet Union, were comprehensively defeated and destroyed. This was by no means a foregone conclusion. After 1918, and especially after 1929, the system based on liberal sovereignty nearly foundered as the defeated and frustrated powers of the First World War sought through neo-mercantilist economics and authoritarian nationalist politics to create an alternative order based on the state control of large economic areas (Haushofer's *Grossraumwirtschaft*). The defeat of the fascist powers gave the USA a far stronger position than that which Britain had enjoyed after 1815. The USA confronted the Soviet Union militarily in the Cold War, but also in a process of institution-building. Two projects for the international economic order competed after 1945: American hegemony based on commercial liberalism, and Soviet hegemony based on administered trade and satellite states. Commercial liberalism proved far more capable of creating an international economic order in which states had a measure of autonomy and citizens were free to trade. The Soviet order crumbled precisely because it was not genuinely international. It relied on the Russian domination of satellite states and the forcible control of movement of citizens in each Communist country and of trade within and beyond the Bloc.

Globalization

What most people mean by 'globalization' is the continued development of the international system of commercial liberalism. This system remains *international*, not truly global, because it involves high levels of trade and investment between distinct national economies centred on major states. It survives because the policies of the major states support it and US military hegemony undergirds it. A global economy based on supra-national market forces has not developed. Instead, most major companies continue to sell about two-thirds of their products and keep the bulk of their assets in their home country/region.[28] Despite the integration of short-term financial dealing, capital markets remain stubbornly local, with about 90 per cent of investment sourced locally in the advanced countries. Migration is more highly controlled than ever. Borders function now not to exclude invading armies, but primarily to keep economic migrants out of welfare states.

If we look at globalization in historical perspective, we can argue that after the massive contraction of international trade in the 1929 Great Crash, and after the effects of two world wars in the twentieth century, the international economy is returning to something resembling its late nineteenth-century heyday. Liberal states in the nineteenth century were limited governments, but they were not weak. The expansion of the market did not undermine them. In fact, to the contrary, the first half of the twentieth century was dominated by state power, not markets. Liberal states now use their power to promote the market, but that does not mean that the market must hollow out their power. In some ways, current policies in the major states mirror nineteenth-century liberalism, promoting global free trade and domestic de-regulation within a 'sound money' economy.

It would be foolish to pursue this analogy too far. The modern world is not fully comparable with that of the *Pax Britannica*. Equally, it would be unwise to judge the capacities of the modern state by the standard of the excesses of regulation and control prompted by the two world wars and their aftermath. The powers liberal states took in this period and in the period of reconstruction after 1945 were a result of dire necessity and were generally seen as temporary. The essential differences between the governance of the pre-1914 world and now are twofold. First, a complex division of labour in governance has emerged in which states share power and governance capacity with supra-national agencies such as the WTO, IMF and World Bank, and also with functionally specific public, quasi-public and private bodies that control a plethora of things from the global radio-wave spectrum to the insurance classification of merchant ships. Second, states have chosen to associate into trading blocs like NAFTA, the EU and MER-COSUR, in which they accept free movement of goods and – in the case of the latter two – people. States are increasingly embedded in larger entities to which they have ceded certain sovereign powers; for example, members of the WTO accept its adjudication over a wide range of trade-related matters that impinge on the scope of national policy, and the EU member states under the Single European Act accept EU legislation in matters facilitating the single market as superior to those of their national legislatures and enforceable as such in their courts.

For all the changes in supra-national organization and governance, the sovereign territorial state is not being undermined, even if its role is changing. Indeed, the creation of the new complexly governed space of the international economy gives it a new salience. The first point to note is that most of the new international bodies are primarily about the standardization of rules in this new space. This space exceeds the domestic regulation of states, but it cannot be governed without them. The new standardized rules, reached by agreement between states, can only work if there are territorial agencies that enforce these rules locally and have the power to do so. Those agencies can only be – and are – states. Moreover, international rules and supra-national decisions acquire legitimacy because they have been consented to by states in international agreements and treaties. Without such consent, supra-national agencies like the WTO would either fail to achieve local compliance, and thus the rules would be void, or they would have to acquire the equivalent of state power to enforce them. Together, states and the principle of international agreement make extended supra-national governance possible and tolerable. The WTO, for example, acquires legitimacy from treaties: it has consent. Thus states have an incentive to comply locally because the agreement provides mechanisms to police default and contain freeriding. In turn, local compliance ensures that the rules are effective, thus reinforcing consent. The messy business of making and keeping trade treaties seldom looks as neat as this, but truly authoritarian government beyond the state and imposed upon it would soon fail. The anti-globalization movements already see institutions like the WTO as a supra-national tyranny and thus resist them: were that really to be so, the resistance from states would be so great that these bodies would not exist.

States are the key *locus* that ties together the various levels of governance – supra-national, national, regional and quasi-private. States, *because* they are territorial and if they are legitimate, are able to speak authoritatively for their populations and to make international commitments that are binding and that will be enforced. The forces that are supposed to be supplanting the state in a globalizing world – multinational companies, networks, NGOs, virtual communities – can do neither of these things, precisely because they are neither territorial nor inclusive. It turns out that states are better at sustaining the global order than these trans-territorial and apparently more 'global' bodies.

If states are essential to the international governance of the world economy, and if interstate agreements are central to such governance, then clearly states remain the primary *political* actors across borders. Indeed, the growing interspace of economic exchange between nations makes them more important in this role than ever before and thus vital to the interests of national economic actors engaged in international exchange. National actors need states to do things that no other agency can conceivably accomplish for them. States have become the external champions for nationally based multinational companies and for wider nationally located economic interests, like financial trading communities. National interests have become centred on the international economic domain. Free trade and financial flows do not remove the need for international action by states: rather, they reinforce it. Faced with an external threat to their interests, such as the prospect of default by an indebted nation, financial market crisis, or illegal actions by rival companies such as dumping, companies and market makers plead for national action and international cooperation to resolve the problem. Investors, bankers and CEOs do not believe that the major states are powerless. Hence the pressure to bail out Mexico in 1994, or the public orchestration of the rescue of Long Term

Capital Management. The centrality of international economic issues to national politics grows, but the major states remain powerful in respect of these issues.

We do not live in a borderless world. Borders still matter. Borders and national citizenship rules are a primary check upon migration. Migration is not limited just because of xenophobia. The great nineteenth-century flows occurred because of the vast demand for labour in the new neo-Europes, and migrants to countries like the USA or Argentina had to make do, as there were few welfare rights. Unregulated migration now would undermine both citizenship and welfare rights. This would threaten democracy, which depends on the notion of a national community. Thus a degree of exclusion of outsiders is essential to democracy, and democracy is a key basis for the legitimacy of a government's external actions. The present system of international governance could not survive without populations defined by and governed within national borders. Paradoxically, it is borders that make extended international governance work. In the last instance, nationally regulated populations with full political rights are the foundation upon which consent by states to supra-national agreements is based. In the nineteenth century there was little in the way of supranational governance, few state democracies, and limited public welfare: migration thus mattered less. Even so, mass migration produced a backlash by established populations, leading to immigration quotas in the USA, for example.

Borders and local policies of national security are now central to containing terrorism and organized crime. Markets are highly vulnerable to such shocks. International travel, equity markets, and commodity markets are all capable of extreme volatility in the face of repeated terrorist outrages, possibly leading to a wider collapse in confidence and demand. The international economy needs state power. Markets are a means of economic coordination through exchange: they facilitate the division of labour, but they are a very weak form of governance. They depend on the security and stability provided by a non-market public power. Military forces and security services are essentially national and will remain so. Without the power to tax, to legitimately compel and to override the rights of property, it is hard to provide and to control armed force. States have huge advantages in this regard over companies and markets, and these advantages stem from territorial control.[29]

Borders are not only political: they are also spatial and cultural. Distance, taste and varying institutional legacies all have real effects on markets. Distance still matters. Beyond 1,000 km there are significant obstacles to merchandise trade posed by transport and information costs. At 2,000 km the effect is a reduction of some 58 per cent in potential trade. At 8,000 km and over trade is reduced relative to that at 1,000 km by some 97 per cent. This explains why continental-scale economies like the USA or the EU work. In Europe one is seldom more than 2,000 km in radius from a circle drawn around Brussels or Milan, for example.[30] Such limits are not just a matter of distance. Evidence shows that the Canadian border has a significant, if declining, effect that has not been eliminated by NAFTA.[31] Inter-provincial trade as against cross-border trade remains larger than econometric models would predict. A world of trade blocs thus makes sense both in terms of the politics of supra-national governance and the spatial constraints of economics. It may be that we are reaching the limits of the current phase of international economic integration and inter-bloc trade growth. If that is so, then we should assume that the various other causes reinforcing the salience of borders will continue to act too.

Territory still matters. States remain the most effective governors of populations. They have an inherent advantage in funding their activities since they are more effective at taxing than are trans-territorial agencies. The vast bulk of GDP in the developed world derives from personal incomes, assets and exchanges that are nationally rooted and cannot easily evade local taxation. This is reinforced by the shift from manufacturing to services in the advanced economies. Most people remain nationally rooted. They lack the marketable skills of the international technocracy or the compelling push factors that would drive them to compete with poor and unskilled migrants elsewhere. For them, the nation remains their horizon of prosperity and their primary source of identification, a community of fate. For this reason they have a real stake in maximizing their nationally defined social and political rights. The powers to exclude, to tax, and to define political rights are those over which states acquired a monopoly in the seventeenth century. They remain the essentials of state power and explain why state sovereignty survives today and why it is indispensable to the international order.

The reason that so many voices claim the demise of the territorial state in the face of supra-national agencies and processes is because they have identified political power and governance capacity with the claims of the theory of sovereignty advanced to promote the rise of the modern state. This theory, developed by thinkers such as Bodin, defined sovereignty in zero-sum terms: any sharing of power would be a loss of power.[32] This made sense then because territorial states were abrogating the rights of trans-territorial agencies and local powers to govern in their own right. But, now, we need not believe the proposition that the state must become weaker and thus a less effective governor if it shares the task of governance with others.[33] The paradox in terms of the Bodinian doctrine is that by sharing power with other agencies and institutions, states can stabilize their external environment and thus maximize their domestic economic performance. States thereby help to create a less volatile environment in which to govern and enhance the domestic resources that can feed into governance capacity. The division of labour in governance is thus a positive asset to most well-managed developed states and is not experienced by ruling elites as a diminution of governance capacity. Indeed, for all but politicians and officials in the major states of the G7, bodies like the EU or the WTO become a wider theatre for a more interesting politics and a peaceful substitute for the dramas of the old international diplomacy.

Territorial states also remain our primary source of accountability and democracy in such a complex system of governance. National representatives to supra-national bodies remain, in theory at least, subject to domestic political pressure. Cosmopolitan forms of strong democratic governance are unlikely to develop for the foreseeable future because we still operate in a world shaped by nationalism. Citizens still identify with nation-state. States are the largest bodies that can claim any sort of primary legitimacy. International bodies are the preserve of elites, and the international technocracy needs the check of politicians directly answerable to national politics. Accountability of international agencies through national publics is at best indirect and weak, but strong supra-national democracy is just impossible. There is no global 'demos'. If democracy implies a substantial measure of homogeneity in the demos, then the world is just too unequal economically and too different culturally for the rich to submit to the decisions of the poor, or for one established culture to accept the internationalization of the norms of another.[34] Hence the unwillingness of the G7 states to give a greater say to developing nations in the core institutions of supra-national economic governance. Hence also the widespread resistance by other major cultures to international human rights norms that come in a box marked 'made in the USA'.

Some contemporary commentators, confronted with the impossibility of an international order based upon consent, the rise of systematic anti-Western terrorism and the existence of failed states, argue for a new solution to this disorder: empire.[35] For them, existing patterns of international governance are not enough and national jurisdictions are currently inadequate in scale to respond to these problems, and so their solution is based on extending the scale and power of the territorial state. This seems to me as doomed a project as cosmopolitan democracy. Empire and world government are both failed nineteenth-century projects. The modern conception of empire developed at the time when the Great Powers were in competition and sought to maximize their colonial acquisitions, often without economic logic. The old forms of domination based on trading posts and naked power were to be replaced by uniform systems of administration adapted from the modern state to colonial conditions.

Empire, even conceived in its most benign form as a civilizing mission, was doomed. It ran up against the forces of nationalism and democracy that had been unleashed in the West and that could not be kept out of the colonies. No Western empire tried to give non-white populations full citizenship rights in the imperial polity. After 1945 such colonial regimes were difficult to legitimate at either end of the chain of imperial power: democratic publics in the metropoles were unwilling to bear the costs of colonial policing and war against insurgents, and colonized peoples sought self-determination rather than a foreign rule that was at best patronizing and at worst brutal. Little has changed, except that the rhetoric 'legitimating empire' has now shifted to 'nation-building'. Western publics will not pay for extended protectorates. Client rulers will lack real democratic legitimacy and will face determined extremist minorities committed to expelling them and their foreign sponsors. Those areas seen most to need such imperial protection, like Africa and the Middle East, are precisely where powerful forces will reject both the liberal rule of law and the secularization of the political sphere that are essential to either domestic democracy or stable external Western rule.

If empire and even temporary protectorates on a large scale are unsustainable, what then? The West cannot garrison every failed state. The experience of the protectorates in Bosnia and Kosovo, and now post-Taliban Afghanistan, should be sobering enough. The West cannot intervene wherever local populations are abused by their rulers. The only option is to contain disorder and for the major powers to respond ad hoc to situations that are beyond toleration. Local rulers should be tolerated, provided they do not systematically export terrorism, practise economic subversion, engage in wholesale massacres that can be prevented, or threaten to attack their neighbours. The existing apparatus of collective security is sufficiently strong to prevent acts of unprovoked aggression and almost all major states, China, India and Russia included, have an interest in the containment of terrorism. Crises can be handled by coalitions of willing states acting to uphold the actual norms and customs of the society of states. This is a form of conservative multilateralism, providing the minimum of force necessary to sustain the current liberal international economic system and the prevailing interstate order. The current tendency towards unilateral activism on the part of the USA is not conservative regarding the system of which it has been hitherto the chief architect. In effect it is more likely to provoke disorder, instability and resistance. A degree of disorder is inevitable. However, it can be contained by active but cautious international governance orchestrated by the major states.

We thus live in a world constituted out of apparently contradictory components: territorial sovereignty and the openness necessary to commercial liberalism; nation-state democracy as the basis of international accountability; the growth of supra-national institutions and the continued viability of nation states; the ongoing military hegemony of the richest and most powerful states; and a new international terrorism that those states find hard to suppress. The territorial state will remain a central component of the new division of labour in governance, even if it no longer has quite the monopoly of governance it had when it appropriated political power from the complex division of labour in governance of the later Middle Ages. Politics is no longer exclusively territorial. On the other hand, it cannot hold together unless it is rooted in the democratic political will of territorial states that practise liberal policies, that are internationally oriented, and that submit to supra-national norms.

Part II

4

The Spatial Dimensions of Military Power

What is War?

War is one of the few great constants in human affairs. War existed before recorded history and organized states. Almost all societies have engaged in some form of combat against others. This does not imply that war is 'natural', whatever that means. It is certainly not reducible to an instinct for aggression: even if such a well-articulated instinct did exist there are plenty of other avenues for its expression. As Clausewitz (still the greatest and most profound thinker on war) says: 'War is the continuation of policy by other means.'[1] War is the organized pursuit of interest by means of force; it involves violence but it is never just a fight between angry people. War is a conduct. It is something that arises in and through structured human interaction. War happens when social groups class others as 'enemies' and take organized action against them involving force. A relation of enmity is one in which, as Hobbes says, the will to give battle is known.[2] Fighting may be episodic, but the possibility of conflict is constant. Societies can live in a state of permanent war, as may be seen in, for example, the conflicts of contiguous villages in the New Guinea Highlands.

Enmity exists because of a conflict of interest between groups that cannot be resolved except by combat, in which one group attempts to prevail in some way over the other.[3] The interests that group people into friends and enemies are various: they can be material or symbolic. Groups fight over resources, but they also fight over principles, beliefs, wrongs done to them, or as a means of defining the individual status honour of warriors or of establishing group prestige.

At its simplest, war consists of combats. Clausewitz begins with the analogy of two wrestlers, each of whom attempts to force the other to submit. From this simple initial definition he is able to construct a complex and comprehensive theory of war. His core definition is: 'War, therefore, is an act of violence intended to compel an opponent to fulfil our will.'[4] Such acts of violence are not rule-governed: war is not a game. It is complex but ultimately unregulated, reciprocal action. Each participant in the combat must anticipate and respond to the actions of the other. Hence war is inherently uncertain: combat cannot be planned. Because war involves two sides, each composed of individuals who must cooperate and coordinate, because it takes place in a context of space and time that cannot be given, and because it involves a changing physical environment, it is subject to those forms of uncertainty and chance that Clausewitz calls 'friction'. To overcome the enemy and to counter friction, fighters must be resourceful, act together and have high morale. Other things being equal, it is morale, the will to win and to accept suffering and effort in order to do so, that eventually decides the outcome. Given forces of equivalent numbers and morale, then reciprocal action, the logic of blow and counter-blow, means that there is an inherent tendency in war to ascend to extremes, to ever greater violence, the ultimate state of which Clausewitz calls 'absolute war'.[5] This state of absolute war is never attained precisely because of friction. War is action in a resistant medium, and a good deal of that resistance is associated with the qualitative spatial properties of specific forms of war.

Space, War and the Built Environment

Technology, social organization and the different forms of the physical environment all act on these basic constants in human armed conflict, and together they shape what wars are like and how they are fought. War takes different forms at different levels of social organization. These forms of war interact with space in complex ways. Space is not just a 'container' for war, an abstract coordinate system in which conflict just happens. Space is shaped in complex and qualitative ways by circumstances, and in turn its specific features condition and shape war. Space matters differently in diverse types of social organizations. It is also shaped and altered by technologies.

Some initial examples are appropriate here. There are some very basic spatial divisions that organize this discussion. These should be taken as general categories that refer to and organize our reflection on specific spatial environments that emerge in definite historical, cultural and technological conditions. They should not be taken as deter-

mining of phenomena or productive of effects at that level of general-
ity. Land and sea are very different environments.[6] It is almost impossible to stand on the defensive in the sea and await enemies. Ships have
to move and fixed positions cannot be built on the high seas. Weather
can drive ships from the sea. Leaving aside choke points and enclosed
coastal waters, the seas are capable of forming a single continuous
space across which vessels may move relatively freely. The seas have
come to form such a single great common since the sixteenth century.
Technology affects how far and in what ways ships can move over this
single great space. Oared galleys, sailing ships and steamships are all
quite different in their pattern of mobility and the constraints this
places upon them. Physical environments on land are also qualitatively different. The steppe, like the sea, was potentially a single extensive space across which nomads and their animals might move
relatively freely. Settled agricultural societies offered a surplus over
subsistence, which made complex forms of social organization like the
state possible; until the Industrial Revolution, however, they also
required the bulk of the population to work the land for most of the
year. This limited the scale and scope of the military operations they
could undertake. From the earliest times until the eighteenth century,
war on the part of settled societies was limited by poor agricultural
productivity and the low military participation ratio that resulted
from it. A limited surplus also constrained the investment in roads and
in magazines. Wars could not typically be fought in winter, at harvest
time or over long distances. This explains why, until the formation of
the modern state in the sixteenth century in Europe, nomads tended
to enjoy certain basic advantages in mobility and numbers of combatants over equivalent settled populations.

War is also affected by how space is perceived. In addition, space
is defined and shaped by forms of knowledge and symbolic significance. Thus Europeans derived a huge advantage from the change of
spatial consciousness that made possible and followed on from the
discoveries of the fifteenth and sixteenth centuries.[7] Europeans came
to see the world as a single space to be controlled and conquered.
This was perhaps as significant as the new naval technology and the
new forms of state power that enabled them to realize the novel
ideas.[8] The Chinese Empire, for all its political sophistication and
resources, inhabited a very different symbolic and spatial world.
Hence, despite their advanced ships and extensive exploration, they
turned inward towards the defence of the steppe frontier in the mid-
fifteenth century. This was the very point at which the Portuguese
and the Spaniards were mastering the technology of high seas navigation.

In the long run of human history, war has vied with religion as the foremost source of humanity's major constructions. Fortifications are an obvious example, to which we shall return in subsequent chapters. However, the spatial scale of some of the forms of defence was enormous and far exceeds the local fortification of castles and towns. The conflict between nomads and the settled and sown has produced extensive linear defence works. Obvious examples are the successive walls across northern China that reached their full development with the Ming, or the fortification of the Roman Empire, Hadrian's Wall and the *limes* on the Rhine and Danube. This should lead us to think of other systematic spatial, if not continuously fortified, frontiers like that between Christian and Muslim Spain, or the system of Crusader castles in the Holy Land. In the same way, the Mediterranean in the early-modern period can be thought of as a continuous system of fortified bases for navies, dividing its distinct basins (eastern, central and western) into distinct spheres of conflict and controlled trade, and a system of linear coastal and island defences against predation by galley fleets and pirates. These themes are further developed in this and later chapters.

We are concerned here not merely with specific built environments but also with wider spatial patterns. War organizes space in subtle ways, and not just in fortifications or battlefields. It often links together structures and places that seem to us to belong to very different orders. Thus, for example, war and the temples of the pre-Conquest Aztecs were closely linked. The annual 'flowery wars' provided their temples with the essential ingredient of their ceremonies, the blood of large numbers of captives. The temples were built for sacrifice, with captives ascending the pyramid on one side and their bodies being thrown down the steps on the other. The purpose of war for the Aztecs was to seize prisoners in individual fights; their tactics revolved around this and imposed fatal limitations on their war-making against the conquistadores.[9] Another example is that road and railway networks have been largely shaped by the needs of war. Until the eighteenth-century turnpikes, most non-military roads were little better than tracks. Inca and Roman roads provided the basis for a fast messenger service that linked the respective empires together. In the Roman case the roads were primarily for the legions, not commerce. Indeed, the burden of maintaining the roads drove settlements away from them, as villagers sought to avoid *corvée* labour. General Wade's military roads in the Highlands of Scotland after the 1715 rebellion cut the clans into controllable districts and linked the major fortresses on which Georgian rule relied. German railways from the 1850s onwards were built with the needs of military mobilization in mind.

'Primitive' War

Having provided a general introduction to our subject, we can now begin to look at the various types of spatial-conflict systems. But before we do so we must consider some of the essentials of social organization. The great divide in terms of war is that between state and non-state societies. Stateless societies have no distinct institutions of government and no apparatus of organized force under central control and separate from the rest of society.[10] Warfare in stateless societies, therefore, involves members of multi-purpose social groups such as kinship networks, or non-compulsory associations like hunting societies or war bands. People fight from social obligation or choice with their own weapons under customary or chosen leaders. Not everyone fights: some stateless societies restrict the privilege to aristocratic lineages or groups of initiated males. War is a group matter, and members decide when, how and why to fight, and how hard. The boundary between feuding within a lineage system and all-out war against outsiders or very remote kin is clear in theory, if sometimes blurred in practice. Feuding is essentially a form of social control: it is rule-bound conflict subject to community sanction and thus not war. Societies with a good deal of low-level violence may thus not be warlike.[11]

Non-state societies can be classified into three basic levels of relative complexity: band societies, tribal societies and chiefdoms. The classification used here is that of E. R. Service in *Primitive Social Organization*; it is used here only as an analytical device and should not be assumed to imply an evolutionary perspective of linear development from simplicity to complexity.[12] Band societies are made up of small groups of hunter-gatherers. Often hunter-gatherers have had high levels of material culture and can be 'prosperous' if game is plentiful (thus they may have a better food intake and more leisure time than farmers). They engage in relatively limited forms of war, not because they are the most 'primitive' peoples, but because hunter-gatherer groups are small, almost too small to fragment, and they generally have a low ratio of population to territory. Many hunter-gatherers are semi-nomadic. Hence such groups tend to come into conflict less often. Many modern hunter-gatherers, such as the Kalahari 'Bushmen', are either highly specialized or have been driven into ecological niches that are difficult for more numerous invading farmers or pastoralists to occupy.

Tribal groups tend to fight in conditions of specific spatial contiguity. Thus the Nuer of the southern Sudan, studied in the colonial period by E. E. Evans-Pritchard, were semi-nomadic pastoralists.[13]

They faced very different conditions in the wet and dry seasons. They might be crowded together on islands in the flood plain or at waterholes in the dry season. In these conditions it was essential to limit conflicts and to contain the scope of feuding among members of different lineages crowded together. Hence the strong social rules governing feuding, and the presence of a class of arbitrators, 'the men of the earth'. The Nuer, despite such imperatives of internal social control, were also fierce cattle-raiders and made predatory war on outgroups. Another example is the Kurelu tribe of the Baliem Valley in the central New Guinea Highlands. The valley was only discovered by Europeans by air in 1938 and was not subject to thorough ethnographic study until 1961.[14] The combination of fertile land, geographic isolation from colonial government and commerce, and the large number of different languages and rival groups in a small area of the Highlands, had created the conditions for intense and ongoing war between traditional rival groups. The rich garden agriculture allowed for the emergence of specialist 'warriors' and thus almost constant raiding, skirmishing and ambushes. Warfare appeared to be a continuous activity on the frontier between rival but closely proximate groups. Raiding took place across well-defined boundaries, complete with field guards and watchtowers.

The Maori of the pre-colonial period likewise fought one another from fortified settlements or *pai*. Fierce inter-tribal conflict was reinforced by ecological stress. Such warfare, already brutal with ritual cannibalism of the defeated, became devastating when the Maoris began to acquire European firearms from traders in the 1840s, and when settlers began to interfere in inter-tribal conflicts for their own ends.[15] Contiguity does not just apply to groups on land. In the case of Tahiti, conflict took place between the war fleets of neighbouring islands. The islands were rich enough to support large numbers of specialist war canoes and these were used for inter-island raids. Part of the aim of such raiding was to overthrow the enemy's sacred places or *marae* on beaches.[16]

In discussing the Maori we have clearly moved across what H. H. Turney-High called the 'Military Horizon'. There may be conflict and war in many non-state societies, but both the military organization capable of sustaining tactics and the occurrence of sustained war are less frequent. Turney-High defined the military horizon thus: 'This means that there are tribes with social control adequate enough for all other purposes . . . but which is so lacking in authority, team work, cohesion and cooperation that they could not indulge in a fight which could be called a battle.'[17] Indeed, one might say that the more effective the methods of social control between lineages for ordinary purposes, the less likely tribal societies are to cross the military frontier. The Nuer have methods for limiting conflict in environmental circumstances that often impose considerable stress and sources of tension. Likewise, the Crow Indians of the American plains limited conflict between hunting bands during the buffalo-hunting season. The hunt police, drawn from rival bands serving in succession, kept order and ensured that different bands did not fight.[18] The forms of non-state governance thus tend to limit the capacity for organized aggression.

This fusion of military force and the wider society is not true of organized chiefdoms and proto-states. Chiefdoms do have some elements of distinctive government, although chiefs do not control specialist bodies of armed men separate from the warriors of the lineages. Chiefdoms are capable of organizing the armed men of society more effectively for a common purpose. Such chiefdoms and kingdoms may evolve into states with centralized control and the creation of disciplined armed forces that act on command. Consider, for example, the African kingdoms of Zululand and Dahomey. The Zulu army was a formidable force for much of the nineteenth century, until destroyed by the British in 1879. Zulu 'regiments' were under central control and fought in organized formations under the tactical control of their generals.[19] They specialized in rapid march, decisive concentration and mass attacks in close-order fighting by disciplined groups using stabbing spears. They used a crescent-shaped formation to envelop the enemy. In many respects of organization and tactics, they were like the Roman legions. In 1879 they destroyed a substantial British force at Isandhlwana. The Zulus overcame many of the limits of pre-industrial war. As pastoralists they had more scope to mobilize large numbers for a campaign, including a substantial reserve army of older married men.

The West African kingdom of Dahomey rose to power in the eighteenth century.[20] It fought annual wars to provide captives to sell as slaves to European traders on the coast. It used the proceeds from such sales to support its military regime, including buying European weapons. The army was based on conscription, and incorporated standing regiments (including an Amazon guard of formidable women fighters) and units mobilized for the annual wars, when the agricultural cycle permitted. Conscription and taxation included systematic record-keeping and the assessment of the obligations of the localities. The annual wars were based on coordinated and concentrated surprise attacks on neighbours: superior organization made possible rapid and directed mobilization. Thus, in addition to its guns and tactical discipline, it had the strategic advantages of scale and speed deriving from its institutions. Dahomey was a predatory empire with an efficient army and a proto-bureaucracy. It might be compared in many respects to seventeenth-century Sweden, which also combined an efficient system of military mobilization with predation on its neighbours. In both cases, crossing the boundary between state and stateless societies enabled the exploitation of real advantages in military organization, including swift mobilization, concentration of force and rapidity of movement. This made such societies tough opponents, even for well-organized European armies with superior weapons.

In this first introductory section to the whole of Part II of this book, as well as to this chapter, we have defined war in general, raised the issue of its spatialization and taken our account up to and beyond the military horizon. In subsequent sections of this chapter and in later chapters we shall consider various issues bearing on war and space: some of the basic divisions of spatial organization, such as that between steppe and sown and that between land and sea; the issue of frontiers in different settings; the way that the environment and technology before the modern era limited the scale and scope of war; how railways and other technologies transformed war in the nineteenth century; and the relation between information, space and war.

Civilization and Barbarism

Edward Gibbon, in *The Decline and Fall of the Roman Empire*, written in the latter half of the eighteenth century, saw the conflict between civilization and barbarism as the basic feature and driving force of world history up to his own day.[21] Civilized empires had hitherto enjoyed no technological superiority in weapons or mobility over the barbarians, possessing only the advantages of military and political organization. Once those were lost, when empires had become corrupt and the invasions of vigorous barbarians had proved too large and frequent, defeat and decline were almost certain. This fact prevented the continuous progress of civilization. Europe had regressed from the high point of Roman power in the Age of the Flavians and Antonines. It had only really returned to something like the same degree of prosperity, security and culture in Gibbon's own day.

Gibbon did not worship centralized power: he saw in the Roman Empire's exclusive dominion of the whole of the European and Mediterranean world a source of weakness. Such highly concentrated power without check is at the mercy of corrupt and weak rulers; there can be no guarantee that wise and competent emperors will succeed one another ad infinitum. Better was the system of competing but substantial states of Gibbon's own day. The balance of power meant that no state could achieve total hegemony. If it tried, then its rivals would combine to thwart it. It was unlikely that the rulers of most of Europe's states would become corrupt and feeble at the same time: competition from other states acted as a check on really bad rulers. This system of states was secure against both hegemony and the threat of barbarian invasion because Europe had come to enjoy technological superiority in war deriving from its civilization. Gunpowder weapons and modern fortifications ensured that no barbarian horde could ever repeat the exploits of the Goths, Huns and Mongols.

The great Maghribi historian, Ibn Khaldûn, had anticipated Gibbon in his fourteenth-century work *Muqaddimah (Introduction to History)*.[22] Ibn Khaldûn saw history as organized around the conflict between vigorous and austere nomadic tribes and rich cities based on trade and agriculture. When tribes develop 'group consciousness' and combine, they enjoy the advantages of numbers and valour over the effete urban dynasty corrupted by the luxury of civilized living. The conditions of nomad life mean that the majority of them are practised and fierce warriors, whereas the majority of the settled population – farmers and townsmen – is sedentary. Moreover, the soldiers of the ruling dynasty are mercenaries corrupted by urban living. In the Muslim world, the successive waves of nomad conquest, the foundation of new dynasties, and the inevitable corruption and decline of the new rulers gave history a fundamentally cyclic form. Like the classical authors and the Western writers who drew upon them, such as Machiavelli, Ibn Khaldûn believed that all polities have a natural cycle of rise and decline, and that corruption is inherent in all social organization. History is cyclic, not progressive.

This wisdom of Antiquity, transmitted through the Arabs like Avicenna to Ibn Khaldûn, is deeply pessimistic. The reason is that this conflict between barbarism and civilization was indeed basic to pre-modern history. This history was driven by the conflict between the settled and sown and the nomadic and pastoral, between urban elites and their political culture and migratory tribes. Both the great empires of the pre-modern world, China and Rome, fought an ongoing battle to control and contain nomads and migratory barbarians within and beyond their frontier zones. From Manchuria to Hungary, Eurasia offered nomadic pastoralists an almost continuous series of habitats: semi-deserts, steppe grasslands and plains. Nomads could move across these environments with their flocks and horses. Normally, nomads were confined to definite localities over which tribes claimed common rights and within which they moved, utilizing the available seasonal fodder for their flocks. Only when pressed by ecological crisis and/or when combined under a common pan-tribal leadership (Khaldûn's 'group consciousness') were they likely to travel far or to engage in extensive raiding or systematic warfare.

This continuous space of pastoral environments meant two things. First, nomads, under exceptional conditions, could combine and move relatively rapidly over large distances. This involved clearing the steppe for their advance, as the Mongols did in their whirlwind campaign against Russia and Europe in the mid-thirteenth century. Second, population pressure and ecological change could drive nomads and hitherto settled migrants in successive waves against and across the frontiers of empires, as each group pressed against its neighbours.

Something like this latter phenomenon probably happened to the Roman Empire in the fifth century and overwhelmed its capacity for frontier management and defence. Barbarians in contact with Rome were driven to seek security inside the frontiers of the empire by the pressure of more numerous migratory peoples moving West. The Roman Empire was never directly confronted with steppe nomads, for the obvious reason that, with the exception of the Hungarian Plain, most 'barbarian' territory was a mixture of forest and lands given over to shifting cultivation. Most barbarian tribes lived by a mixture of semi-sedentary pastoralism in the forests and burn-and-slash farming. They were peripatetic rather than nomadic, willing to move in order to settle in more favourable lands. Even the Huns seem to have had only a minority of horsemen and not to have been pastoral nomads like the Mongols. Barbarians on the march usually had their women and children with them, and were encumbered by large numbers of wagons.

If centralized government had an inherent tendency to decline, and if it increased the scale of the threat to civilization when rulers became unfitted to their tasks or authority collapsed in civil war, the problem was that Ancient civilization had no option. Ancient civilization couldn't really exist without the centralization of power. Only the growth of ancient empires could provide the scale for the accumulation of the resources necessary to sustain great cities and advanced infrastructure. In conditions of low agricultural productivity and before the formation of market societies, extensive exploitation was the only option available for the creation of a large surplus. Rome and Constantinople, both with populations of over 1 million at their height, depended on the resources of the whole Mediterranean world. Gibbon's eighteenth-century Europe had no city to match either in their heyday. In 1750 London had a population of 676,000 and Paris 560,000.

The frontier between the civilized and the barbarian was never a rigid and exclusionary line. As we have seen, borders like this did not begin to exist until the formation of sovereign territorial states in Europe in the sixteenth and seventeenth centuries. The frontier was an extensive zone in both China and Rome. It included varying degrees of contact with and acculturation of the barbarian peoples. Security involved management of peoples well beyond the normally policed zone. The frontier was also a sociological process, involving regular contact and trade, the acculturation of barbarians and their admission into the empires, but also the loss of provinces and the regression of areas into nomadism and barbarism. In the cases of both China and Rome, the more the frontier turned into a defensive line and the more policy moved towards the exclusion of barbarians and limited contact with tribes beyond the line, the more fragile the frontier and the greater the threat of major incursions. Barbarians generally wanted the benefits of civilization; some were willing to become subjects to enjoy them, but others were not. Only when imperial power declined or imperial policy refused these benefits did nomads and barbarian tribes move to another option, becoming rulers of cities and subjects of settled populations themselves. It should be clear that civilization and barbarism are socio-political and not moral categories. It would be foolish however to fail to use a valid term, 'barbarism', vital to the history of the Old World, because of misplaced modern sensibilities.[23] Barbarism was used as a category by many leading contemporary intellectuals, who experienced directly the conflict between city-based government and migratory and nomadic peoples. Some, like Tacitus in his *Germania*, were highly ambivalent in their valuation of the barbarians, seeing them as a threat but also as possessed of noble qualities that civilized peoples had lost as they had become corrupt.[24] In the case of both China and Rome, the forms of interaction between barbarians and civilized empires produced striking and very similar spatial military-political patterns: elaborate systems of linear frontier management and defence.

Rome

By the beginning of the second century AD, Rome had reached the limits of its expansion which had begun in the third century BC. After its victories over Carthage and the Hellenistic monarchies, the empire was confronted by only one organized state, Parthian Persia. It faced tribal peoples in southern Egypt, who were never a serious threat, and in North Africa the frontier was the Sahara Desert and its nomadic tribes, again easily contained.[25] In Britannia, the line of Hadrian's Wall screened the bases of the cavalry forces that controlled the Pictish tribes beyond, and it also served as a means of surveillance of local move-ments. The key frontier on which Rome managed its relations with the barbarian world was that along and beyond the Rhine and the Danube.

Rome limited its attempts to control Germany after the destruction of three Roman legions in the Teutoberg Forest in AD 9. Beyond the Danube lay the forests of Bohemia and Slovakia and the plain of Hungary. The decision to halt expansion in the West was not merely a consequence of defeat; the costs of civilizing the lands beyond the Rhine–Danube *limes* were out of all proportion to the benefits.[26] The last great conquest, of Dacia (modern Romania) in the early second century, proved the point that conquest had ceased to pay for itself.

At the death of Trajan in AD 117, Rome's legions were concentrated in the areas of greatest threat: in Syria, and thus able to move against either the Persians or a revolt in Judaea, and along the Rhine–Danube line. For the first two centuries AD the empire practised strong peripheral defence. It is arguable whether it had either the institutions, like a central army staff, or the concepts to sustain a 'grand strategy', but if we are to infer one from its practice then it represented the active maintenance of the boundaries by military and diplomatic action across them. Thus, if we are to make such a presumption, then it is Arthur Ferrill rather than Edmund Luttwak whom we should follow.[27] The frontier zone was managed and monitored, but not passively defended. The main legionary fortresses on the periphery provided bases for a rapid response forward into barbarian territory or in reaction to major incursions. Hadrian's Wall as it stands gives a mistaken impression of such frontier control; it was not like the popular image of the Maginot Line as a static frontier defence. The Roman defences on the Rhine and Danube have mostly vanished, but what we know of them shows better the policy of frontier management. The *limes* were never and could never have been a continuous wall. Both rivers were not barriers alone, but means of transport, vital to the economics of efficient control. The rivers involved a system of naval patrols, watchtowers and major fortresses. Major centres like Cologne were bridgeheads for a forward policy across the rivers, not just obstacles to attack. This system channelled local movement and provided warning of major raids and invasions.[28]

In the late third century Rome was forced to pull back from its frontiers. In the 270s it withdrew from the lower Nile; in AD 282 it retreated from Dacia (conquered in AD 106), and it evacuated Mauritania in North-West Africa in AD 298. Rome was finding it difficult to afford the cost of sustaining marginal peripheral provinces. Rome's strategic position was based on its army. In the period up to the third century this consisted of around 25 legions, 125,000 citizen conscripts, plus an equivalent number of auxiliary troops attached to the legions and recruited from subject peoples within the empire. This was hardly a large force, but it consumed over half of the relatively moderate imperial budget. Rome maintained its dominance with these modest forces and in the absence of military technological superiority for four reasons. First, Roman troops fought with discipline and effective tactics under central command. Second, Roman fortifications and field defences were all but impregnable by barbarians. Third, first-rate logistics ensured that Roman armies were reliably fed by regular contractors, and were thus able to build their own roads, forts and bridges. Fourth, good strategic communications – a system of military roads, the Rhine and Danube, and the Mediterranean in the centre of the empire – allowed the movement of troops to threatened areas. Roman commanders on the frontiers were normally expected to deal with major barbarian incursions from their own resources. There was no central reserve.

By the early fourth century this implied strategy was in disarray. Constantine reorganized the empire's defences. The army was divided into a frontier guard force, the *limitanei*, and a large central reserve, expected to move to counter major attacks. The army shifted from a core of legionary infantry towards a cavalry force. Certainly from the third century onwards, Rome faced mounting barbarian challenges. The old peripheral defence system might have proved inadequate – with fatal consequences – in the absence of a large central reserve, for, once inside, major barbarian forces could only have been countered by further denuding the frontier. The new army was larger, but the way it developed ensured that Rome would suffer increasing defeats at the hands of the barbarians. The conventional view is that the army gradually became both less effective and less 'Roman'.[29] The frontier guards degenerated into second-rate troops who could be bypassed. The main army was gradually converted into a force of barbarian mercenaries, using tactics and weapons similar to their opponents. As the political vitality of the empire declined, it became harder to get citizens to accept the obligations and great hardships of legionary service. Political corruption, with the loss of civic virtue and the devaluation of citizen status, went together with military decline.

In the course of the fourth and fifth centuries the integrity of the Roman Empire was threatened as the system of frontier defence gradually broke down.[30] Barbarians began to enter the empire and settle in large numbers. In AD 363 the Emperor Julian was killed and a large Roman army destroyed by the Persians. In AD 378 the Emperor Valens was killed at Adrianople and another Roman army defeated by the Goths. In AD 410 Rome was sacked by Alaric and the Goths. Barbarians gained an ever more central role in the empire as its administrative structures and economic base declined. The distinction between Roman rule and barbarian kingdoms became less clear and the role of the frontier less obvious. Barbarians both ruled themselves within the empire and intervened decisively in its politics, making and unmaking emperors. Barbarian elites adopted many of the institutions of Roman rule and the trappings of Roman civilization. Theodosius temporarily restored the fortunes and integrity of the empire, but at the price of converting the army into a largely barbarian force. The separation of the Eastern and Western empires, initiated by Diocletian, further weakened the capacity to concentrate the resources of the whole Mediterranean under one control. When Attila and the Huns were defeated in AD 451 at Chalons, thus saving 'Europe', it was in effect a battle of two barbarian cavalry armies.

China

The Roman *limes* pale in comparison with the scale of the Great Wall of China. The remains of the Great Wall are still impressive and have been extensively restored, particularly the sections most accessible from Beijing. However, the idea of a single continuous wall existing since the earliest empire is a misnomer, as Arthur Waldron has shown.[31] The extant wall is mostly Ming in origin and dates from the sixteenth century. There have been different walls, in different places, serving different purposes at different times. In like manner it is misleading to present Chinese history as if it had been governed by a succession of similar imperial regimes since the formation of the Chin state in the third century BC. Chinese imperial history has been marked by periodic crises and by regular periods of non-Han rule. Repeated incursions by nomad forces who created their own regimes are almost as much a part of Chinese history as Han dynasties. The Khitan Liao, the Tangut Hsi Hsia, the Jurchen Chin, the Mongol Yuan and the Manchu Qing all exercised either substantial or complete control of Chinese territory.[32] Indeed, the Sung (AD 960–1126, 1127–75 in the south) and the Ming (AD 1368–1644) could equally well be seen as interludes of Han rule in an otherwise strong tendency towards nomad control.

Mark Elvin, in his ambitious interpretation of Chinese imperial power, *The Pattern of the Chinese Past*, argues that China should be viewed in the context of two issues central to ancient empires. These are summarized here as follows:

1   Ancient empires are determined in their scale by a basic relation between size and the resources that define state capacity – economic productivity, technology (civilian and military) and social organization.

2 The durability of regimes depends on their relation to their barbarian neighbours; if the barbarians can shift the advantages defining state capacity in their own favour, then imperial rule is threatened.[33]

Empires expand to meet the barbarians. Both Rome and China were 'universal' empires. Neither accepted the legitimacy of other states, neither had legitimate boundaries defined by agreement with other rulers, and both had a strong tendency to conquer their weaker and less organized neighbours. Equally, there is no given fixed line between settled and nomad. These divisions are the product of changing sociological processes and balances of power. As Owen Lattimore has shown, the shifting frontiers of colonization and ecology move with changing climate and political fortune.[34] Thus Han colonists who settled in periods of strong imperial power and ecologically favourable times might turn nomad in order to survive during a period of desiccation.

The barbarians who conquered both the Western Roman and the Sung Empires had long been in contact with civilized peoples beyond the frontier and had acquired technology and political resources from them. Consider, for example, the role of iron in the Mongol conquest of China.[35] The Mongols acquired iron arrows from the south: this made their powerful composite bows deadly at longer and decisive ranges. The Sung Empire was gravely weakened by the Chin conquest of northern iron supplies. Both the Chin and the Mongols learned Chinese siege techniques and were therefore able to occupy cities and the centres of civilized power. Among the barbarian nations, only the Huns had done this in the West. The Sung were further weakened against the Mongols by the very productive success of their agriculture, one factor in their technological superiority acting against another. Intensive rice cultivation led to a shortage of horses for the army, chiefly because of the scarcity of fodder. The Sung had created a highly productive agriculture that supported a large population, but which resulted in it being dependent on year-round labour that was thus unavailable for war. The Mongols also rapidly acquired naval technology. Thus we can see how nomad peoples were able to conquer large populations in areas not adapted to steppe warfare, and to shift the technology of civilization to their own advantage.[36]

Empires rely on interaction with barbarians to control and pacify them. This ensures that the barbarians benefit from closely controlled access to trade with their civilized neighbours. Purely exclusionary policies fail once this relationship is well-established. Barbarians are by now well aware of the riches beyond the border and will be tempted

to take them by raiding if they are excluded. To succeed, such a strategy of controlled contact requires forward defence and an active policy
of keeping the barbarians disunited: 'divide and rule'. The inherent
danger in this is that it civilizes the barbarians and thus strengthens
them, providing them with the lure of conquest if they can combine
and if imperial rule is weak. Such a policy requires a mixture of fore-
thought, regulated contact and the use of semi-barbarian methods and
tactics by the imperial frontier forces, and a system of linear control
and supervision and frontier garrisons. It is expensive and difficult:
hence the lure of either a policy of decisive advance into regions too
poor to be civilized fully, or of withdrawal and exclusionary defence.

Thus the Ming successfully expelled the Mongols, and until the
middle of the fifteenth century practised a policy of forward defence.
In AD 1449 the Mongol leader, Yesen, defeated and captured the
emperor at the Battle of Tumu. Up to this point Ming policy had been
expansionary: a forward policy in the north and the active promotion
of expensive voyages of discovery under Admiral Cheng-Ho, which
reached East Africa. Yesen's rebellion was the result of an incautious
policy of breaking off contact with the nomads and denying them
trade goods.[37]

The Ming turned from long-distance exploration (which brought
few concrete benefits for the considerable costs) and local seaborne
trade to a policy of closing the coasts and rigid frontier defence in the
north. This defensive system involved three elements:

1 The Great Wall, an elaborate system of new linear defences
   designed to exclude the nomads by fortifying the key passes
   through which nomad forces would have to invade, providing a
   barrier to movement and giving warning of attack along the whole
   frontier.
2 Military colonies, in which soldiers were settled as farmers at strategic points along the frontier where they would be available as
   reserves in the case of a major incursion, but also would be able
   to support themselves and thus limit the cost of frontier defence.
3 The Grand Canal, which ensured the security of food supplies to
   northern China and the new capital, Beijing; this allowed the productive lands of the south to be used to sustain northern defence
   without exposure to a sea voyage.

The Wall was part of a system of rigid linear and essentially passive
defences. It excluded and abandoned the key region of the Ordos
Desert that in climatically favourable times could serve as a massing
point for nomad armies.

Both Lattimore and Elvin emphasize the crucial role of northern nomad neighbours and interaction with them throughout the course of Chinese imperial history, and also the shifting and relative nature of the frontier. The Great Wall was a relatively late move to contain the nomads once and for all. It failed when the Ming were outflanked and defeated by the Manchus.

Both the Roman and the Chinese Empires were very big relative to the sophistication of their communication technologies. Both relied in large measure on water transport to move grain from the most productive regions to the cities and the periphery. Neither could exist as large integrated political entities without the bonus of relatively cheap water transport and the ability to use political power to mobilize surplus grain for urban populations and military uses. Both relied on irrigation for the higher productivity of their agriculture: the Nile was used for this in Egypt and the water transport for rice cultivation in southern China depended on the great rivers, the coastal route and the Grand Canal. The Roman Empire relied on the transport of Egyptian and North African grain across the Mediterranean and the use of the Rhine and Danube. Both imperial systems had very long linear land frontiers on their exterior, away from their waterborne core, and active barbarian/nomad pressure on the periphery for much of their existence. Thus they faced very different problems from the subsequent seaborne/gunpowder empires that arose in the West from the sixteenth century onwards. Gunpowder, coastal forts and naval superiority limited the costs of extensive seaborne empires. The Western empires were based on trade and commerce (even if in the form of extracting rents from markets) rather than on the occupation and rule of large territories. They had no extensive land frontiers to defend against barbarians. Neither Rome nor China was a market-based imperial system, even if there were extensive commercial relations within them.

The Mongols created an extensive empire that covered most of Eurasia, from China through Central Asia to the borders of Poland. It relied on the rapid movement of steppe cavalry and it would be tempting to see the steppe as resembling a great ocean. The Mongols used a relay system of posts and riders to communicate rapidly across this large space. It was possible to go from western Russia to Karakorum in a matter of weeks.[38] But great armies could not move at will across the steppe: way had to be made for them, and having consumed the available grazing they were forced to move on or to return by another route. Mongol rule was fragile because it relied at its core on the political institutions of a tribal confederacy. It could neither build stable institutions that were not dependent on the will of tribal notables, nor include the conquered securely in the political system.[39] Kublilai was successful in China because, to a degree, he used the Han elite and their resources of governance. But this was not sufficient to insulate Mongol rule against relatively rapid rebellion and overthrow. The empires tried to civilize – or at least tame – the barbarians. Barbarians had less to offer to civilized peoples as rulers: they could not easily 'barbarize' their subjects. The most successful barbarian elites made their peace with most Roman institutions and much of Roman culture, including Christianity. Mongol power was created by a strategy of inclusion among nomad peoples; it could not do the same for the Han Chinese.

Land and Sea

In the most influential book on naval strategy ever written, *The Influence of Seapower on History 1660–1783*, Alfred Thayer Mahan wrote in 1890:

> The first and most obvious light in which the sea presents itself from the political and social point of view is that of a great highway; or better, perhaps a wide common, over which men may pass in all directions, but on which some well-worn paths show that controlling reasons have led them to choose certain lines of travel rather than others. These lines of travel are called trade routes.[40]

Mahan, a US Navy captain, influenced both Theodore Roosevelt and Kaiser Wilhelm II in building their fleets in challenge to Britain. Mahan saw 'command of the sea' as essential for a modern trading nation. Mahan's doctrine helped to set the USA on a course from being a fourth-rate naval power to world maritime dominance, a position that is now almost unchallengeable.[41]

Mahan's main claims were threefold. First, he argued that economic, political and naval power are connected. Only by ensuring access to trade and by acquiring colonies, and thus secure markets, could states grow powerful. Therefore, the struggle for maritime dominance was central to economic success and also to world power. A narrow focus on naval combat misses the point of Mahan's book: it was a political as much as a military treatise, setting naval warfare in the framework of economic competition between nations. Thus England's rise to command of the sea, the subject of the book, involved successive struggles with rivals for world trade. England had beaten first the Netherlands and then France for naval mastery and the lion's share of colonies and trade. After 1815 it then enjoyed a century of dominance of the world economy. It enforced a liberal world-trading regime through the *Pax Britannica*, with a combination of naval and financial supremacy. It was challenged from the late 1890s by Germany, which it then defeated in the First World War. The economic consequences of that struggle made the UK unable to bear the costs of naval competition with the USA. It surrendered primacy in conceding parity of naval tonnage to the USA in the Washington Naval Treaty of 1922. During the Second World War the USA became the principal naval power. It defeated its chief rival, Japan, for control of the Pacific. After 1945 it enjoyed a hegemony over the world trading system very like that of Britain's after 1815. It contained and defeated a naval challenge from the USSR during the Cold War. In essence, Russia sought to deny the sea to the USA and its allies, not to rival America for world trade. Russian strategists saw naval power in narrowly military terms and thus missed the central point of Mahan's teaching. Mahan argued that naval power and commercial power are intimately connected, and that no power can maintain commercial and political dominance without naval mastery; equally, naval power is fragile when not based on the defence and promotion of commerce.

Second, Mahan claimed that the essence of naval power was control of the sea, that is, the ability to exclude enemies from using the sea for their own purposes, trade and power projection. Such exclusion enabled the power with command of the sea to exploit it for its own commercial and political purposes. Sea control primarily involved naval operations aimed at the destruction of the enemy's battle fleet. Given such control, then enemy commerce could be all but excluded from the sea. However, the opposite strategy of commerce-raiding in the absence of effective sea control could neither defeat the enemy nor destroy his trade. Mahan assumed that the dominant power would protect its trade and shipping through convoys. He wrote before submarines were practical weapons. However, even given the sub-surface threat, his doctrine was proved by the experience of the two world wars. German submarines failed to cripple Allied shipping, despite heavy losses and the need for continuous innovation in anti-submarine weapons and tactics. The devastating success of US submarines against Japanese merchant shipping was in large measure due to the failure of the Japanese to develop effective anti-submarine warfare methods. Mahan's basic doctrine remains valid and is still accepted as the basis of US naval strategy.

Third, Mahan saw the battle fleet, able to go anywhere and to concentrate against and to pursue enemy fleets, as the key source of naval power. Bases were necessary but ancillary to this. It also meant that some states were favoured by geography and others faced difficulties in access to the sea or in concentrating their forces. Germany's navy could be blockaded in the North Sea. Russia has the problem of combining its four scattered fleets in the Arctic, Baltic, Black Sea and Pacific. In the 1904–5 war against Japan, Russia sent the Baltic Fleet round Africa to the Far East in a futile attempt to aid its Pacific Fleet, which was blockaded in Port Arthur. Even with modern technology like nuclear submarines, basic facts of geography and the qualitative features of space do matter, and they benefit some powers at the expense of others. The sea is only a great common to some.

The Invention of the Sea

Mahan's argument was powerful in its time and remains basically valid, but it rested on a set of largely untested assumptions. It treats sea power as if it were an historical constant, from which universal lessons can be drawn. Yet 'sea power' in Mahan's sense really did not begin to exist before the sixteenth century.[42] It was an artefact of two processes: the formation of sovereign territorial states in Europe and the construction of competing long-distance seaborne commercial empires by those states. Before that there were local naval and trading systems centred on particular areas of the globe. Some of these appeared not to have involved naval rivalry for control of trade. The monsoon-based trading system between the Gulf and the Arabian Peninsula and India seems to have been largely de-centralized and non-military before the arrival of Vasco da Gama.[43] The Mediterranean set severe limits on Mahanian sea power. Secure control of the sea in a narrow sea divided into semi-enclosed basins, and where the dominant form of ship was the short-ranged galley, depended on control of the land through fortified bases.[44] Naval war was primarily amphibious war directed towards capturing such bases. In the case of China–Korea–Japan, sea power was again to a great degree ancillary to land power. Chinese trade was largely coastwise and on inland waterways. Ships were used for seaborne invasions as in, for example, the Mongol endeavours to conquer Japan, and Hideyoshi's attempt to invade China via Korea in the late sixteenth century. Such warfare could be sophisticated, and involve impressive vessels, such as the Chinese paddle warships on the Yangtse or the Korean armoured turtle ships, but it did not aim at 'command of the sea'.[45]

Sea power came into existence when the seas were united into a single great common. This could not happen until the late fifteenth century. It required the unification of hitherto separate culture areas like Europe, China and the Americas through the processes of the age of discovery. This had two preconditions. First, from the mid-fifteenth century several European centres developed strong multi-masted ships that could sail against the wind. Such ships were first used by the Portuguese and Spanish to explore and conquer islands in the Atlantic, the Canaries and Azores.[46] Without such ships intercontinental trade was just not possible. Medieval European sailing ships were slow single-masted vessels fit only for coastal trade. Galleys, used for high-value commerce and warfare, could not make long journeys away from land. In 1291 two Genoese merchants, the Vivaldi brothers, attempted to sail beyond Cape Bojador in North-West Africa and disappeared. Their galleys had to stop frequently to take on water for their large crews and in the Mauritanian Desert they had no chance of doing this.[47]

China had impressive seagoing ships. From 1405–39 Ming fleets were sent into the Indian Ocean in seven great expeditions.[48] Some of these ships were 400 feet long and numbered crews in the hundreds. This would have made them bad vessels for Atlantic exploration. They were just too big and could hardly have fed their crews during a crossing to the Americas. Long-distance ships had to survive for weeks out of sight of land. The Portuguese ships were not only seaworthy: they also had great guns. Effective cannon were developed in the 1450s in Europe. This meant that, rather than large crews, they could use firepower to defend themselves and impose their will. Europeans had the advantage of seaworthy ships and guns, something no other culture area had in combination.[49] Chinese cannon were feeble compared to the largest European cannon.

The second precondition was navigation. Europeans developed and adopted techniques of navigation by celestial observation and dead reckoning that enabled them to navigate out of sight of land.[50] These techniques, which involved borrowing the mathematics of the Arabs and Iberian Jews, were not available until the latter half of the fifteenth century. Equally important was the gradual discovery of how the wind systems in the North and South Atlantic worked. These systems enabled the Spaniards to sail to and return from South America in different seasons, and allowed the Portuguese to sail far out into the South Atlantic round the Cape of Good Hope.

These technical innovations were accompanied by and reinforced by a revolution in spatial consciousness that we alluded to before. Europeans linked the three great continental systems of Asia, Europe and the Americas by long-distance sea routes, and in so doing not merely unified the globe, but achieved world dominance through sea power. The Portuguese created the first real seaborne empire. This extensive trading empire was based on brutality and superior violence, not superior economic efficiency. The Portuguese destroyed their competitors and then sold protection to native traders. Thus they profited both by monopolizing long-distance trade to Europe and extracting rents from controlling local trade in Asia.[51] They did not attempt large-scale territorial conquest, but relied on sea control backed up by a network of fortified bases. Local rulers could easily have bested them had they attempted extensive conquests on land. Only when Asian rulers developed effective navies, like Aceh, were they able to resist the Portuguese.[52]

In the case of the conquest of Mexico and Peru, the Spanish easily overthrew the Aztec and Inca Empires, replacing their rule over widespread territories and large native populations.[53] These were societies without extensive seaborne trade or ships; Spanish naval power enabled the conquerors to exercise territorial dominion. Unlike the Portuguese, who annexed existing trade patterns to themselves and opened up new trade routes to Europe, the Spaniards extracted wealth, chiefly silver, from Mexico and Peru and shipped it to Europe. Both were rent-seeking and sought to monopolize trade. Neither was a true trading empire in Mahan's sense and neither could keep control of the sea, despite large populations of seafarers. They were unable to make trade and sea power interact positively. Overseas trade did not invigorate local commercial societies in the Iberian peninsula; indeed the reverse.

It was Holland and England that combined the use of the sea for long-distance trade with domestic economic transformation. In both countries naval power, local trade in Europe, long-distance trade and colonies all interacted to create a seaborne commercial system. Trade, new financial markets and the economic foundation of military power all interacted – commerce and war reinforced one another. Holland and England expanded at the expense of the Iberian empires, and then England deliberately fought the Netherlands for dominance at sea.[54]

Such maritime superiority relied on the sailing ship. Wind was free and ships could move anywhere in the world at low cost, operating independently of land for long voyages. Sailing ships were skill-intensive. Maritime power depended on populations of experienced seafarers. Ship-handling and navigation were skills that were refined by their use. England developed a real advantage in both commerce and naval war because of the sheer scale of its maritime activity. During the Napoleonic Wars the British blockade of the French fleet meant that such skills atrophied among the French sailors and gave a considerable practical superiority to the British. The advent of steamships changed this. Steamships were not dependent on the wind. They could keep to planned schedules, whereas sailing ships were often becalmed. However, they required coaling stations and were dependent on travelling between ports where fuel was available. Moreover, steamships required fewer ship-handling skills. The value of a large population of sailors dedicated to the sea declined. This made it possible to catch up with the dominant power by investment and technical training. Thus, after the 1898 Navy Law, Germany was able to create a fleet that rivalled Britain's in competence in less than two decades.[55]

Land versus Sea

Steam did not just transform sea travel, but also revolutionized land travel in the form of railways. Land transport could now become an economic rival to sea transport. Mahan had a contemporary rival too, the British political geographer Sir Halford Mackinder. In 1904 Mackinder, in a paper called 'The Geographical Pivot of History' read to the Royal Geographical Society, argued that the period of maritime dominance was at an end. Railways had made it possible to open up the great continents, especially Eurasia.[56] The seas had become a great common to supplant the role of that of the steppe and did so precisely at the point when the military power of steppe nomads was waning. Now the world was integrated by land transport as much as by sea commerce. Railways altered the vast advantage of the relative cost of sea over land transport, and could now compete in both cost and speed with maritime trade even after the steamship. The basis for modern power was great industry and large populations. Whoever controlled the heartland of Eurasia controlled what Mackinder called the 'World Island', and whoever controlled that, he believed, controlled the world. Thus the future belonged to the two great continental powers, Russia and the USA. Political strength was now based on industrial strength, and, without an industrial base equivalent to a great continental power, modern naval strength could not exist. The era of pure sea power was over. In these circumstances the 400 years of naval experience of the Columbian era counted for little.

In a way, both Mahan and Mackinder now show their late nineteenth-century limitations. Pure 'seapower' is an antiquated notion, although to be fair to Mahan he was always clear about the interaction of economics and naval power. However, the concept of great autarchic continental heartlands has proved even less convincing. Russia's GDP is currently smaller than that of the Netherlands, which has less than one-tenth of Russia's population. The USA is not a purely continental power, but the centre of a great industrial, commercial and financial informal empire. It is powerful because it combines a continental-scale economy with dominance of the world trading system, much like the British Empire in the nineteenth century. Air travel and air power have changed things much less than one might expect. At one level aircraft are just like ships, except they cannot match ships' capacity to carry bulky cargoes. Most goods that are traded intercontinentally are still moved by sea. Shipping is vital to the world economy, whereas air travel is secondary. Air power and sea power have turned out to be closely connected. The two greatest naval powers, Britain and the USA, were the powers that achieved air superiority in the Second World War.[57] The USA has retained it ever since. The combination of air and sea power enables the USA and its allies to dominate the world's air- and seaways and to move their forces wherever they wish. Since the collapse of Russian naval power, the US Navy has no rival and its carrier battle groups and cruise missile-equipped ships enable it to project power deep inland. Mahan is thus closer to being proved right.[58]

What has changed is that the dominant maritime power no longer uses its strength to monopolize trade and exclude others. In the early nineteenth century Britain discovered that its commercial hegemony meant that there was no advantage in excluding others from the great common in peacetime.[59] Britain had the largest and most efficient merchant fleet and monopolized the financial infrastructure of world commerce. It was thus to its advantage that world trade grow as quickly as possible. Local monopolies limited trade. In the mid-nineteenth century Britain adopted free trade at home. It repealed the Corn Laws in 1846 (which offered price support to British wheat farmers). It withdrew the privileges of trading companies like the East India Company, and in 1849 it repealed the Navigation Acts, which limited access of non-British ships to its ports. It used its navy to open the common, not to close it. After the failure to reconstruct the institutions of the world trading system in the aftermath of the First World War, and as a consequence of the economic dislocation following the Great Crash of 1929, states returned to the old logic of trying to corner trade. The 1930s were a decade of competitive protectionism, in which all major states attempted to build autarchic trading blocs and spheres of influence.[60] After 1945 the USA sought to re-create an open world-trading economy and use its power to underpin it. Thus the *Pax Americana* has operated much as Britain's hegemony did before 1914, and depends on naval–air power.[61]

A Mediterranean Exception

We have already mentioned that naval war in the Mediterranean did not follow the logic of Mahan's command of the sea.[62] This was not because warfare in the narrow seas was backward. In fact the style of war changed and intensified in the fifteenth century: from 1450 onwards there was a new 'arms race' in the Mediterranean. The hitherto dominant sea powers, Genoa and Venice, were in relative decline. If the classic notion of pure 'seapower' has any meaning, then these two states embodied it. Since the Middle Ages they had built up extensive trading associations supported by a parallel network of fortified ports. From the mid-fifteenth century their dominance was challenged by the growth of the naval power of two large land-based states, the Ottoman Empire in the Eastern basin and Spain in the Western. Genoa and Venice both used sailing ships for bulky goods and galleys for war and high-value goods. Galleys cruised between fortified harbours that were at most a few days apart.[63]

After the conquest of Constantinople in 1453 the Ottomans became a major naval power. From the 1520s they started to expand their fleet. They began to roll up Venetian bases and to raid the coasts of Italy. Galleys were used like landing craft to transport armies to sieges. Warfare at sea was a mixture of raiding, sieges and occasional pitched battles in coastal waters. Galleys fought in line abreast and could manoeuvre independently of the wind. Battles were more like the clashes seen on land, designed to culminate in hand-to-hand fighting from the vessels as platforms. Sea control was impossible without dominance of the surrounding coasts. The Christian response to the Ottoman advance was to fortify extensively the coasts of Italy with elaborate defences of major ports and a system of coastal watchtowers.[64] Such fortifications were very much like linear defences on land. The Spanish response was to attempt to conquer the Muslim bases in North Africa, Tunis and Algiers, from which the pirates – who formed a major part of Ottoman naval power – operated. In return, the Ottomans eliminated the remaining major Christian bases like Rhodes and Cyprus in the Eastern Mediterranean, and sought to seize Malta and to establish a bridgehead for an attack on Italy.

In 1565 the Ottomans failed to take Malta from the Knights of St John after a closely fought siege. In 1571 a major Ottoman thrust westwards was heavily defeated by the allied Christian forces at the Battle of Lepanto.[65] Mediterranean galley warfare could not be decisive at sea alone. The sixteenth century saw the construction of huge galley fleets, out of all proportion to previous experience. These fleets were so large that they could no longer be manned by free professional rowers, as Venetian galleys had been. Instead, Christian and Muslim captives were forced into slavery. The galley was not an obsolete type in the prevailing conditions of Mediterranean war. The Spaniards, who were well experienced with broadside-armed sailing ships, built up their galley fleet in the middle of the sixteenth century. Galleys could operate in narrow seas and calms; they could land troops on beaches, and they could easily run for cover in bays and under the guns of forts. They could do things which sailing ships could not, and also evade such vessels. Because of these features, as galley fleets became more dominant, they reinforced the interaction of sea and land war. If Mahan's logic applied, then Lepanto ought to have been decisive; the Turks' main battle fleet was destroyed. The Ottomans lost 160 galleys at Lepanto, but this did not end the Ottoman threat. In 1574, 280 Ottoman galleys retook Tunis. By the late 1570s there was an effective stalemate in the Mediterranean. Both the Ottomans and Spanish were limited by fiscal and logistical problems, in part brought on by the costly and indecisive nature of galley-siege warfare. Spain then was forced to turn its attention to the revolt in the Netherlands and subsequently to its struggle with England. As the goals and methods of warfare changed in the Mediterranean in the seventeenth century, so the galley was displaced in relative significance, and the narrow sea became a part of a recognizably Mahanian naval world by the late seventeenth century.

The Mediterranean shows in an exaggerated form a feature of the interaction of land and sea, the existence of straits and semi-enclosed waters. Such areas constitute 'choke points' through which shipping has to pass, such as the Straits of Gibraltar or of Hormuz, or enclosed bays. Thus battles are fought again and again in the same place, like Actium 31 BC and Prevesa AD 1538, both conducted with galleys off the Adriatic coast of Greece, and the numerous battles in the Gulf of Corinth.

Land and sea do differ in certain basic ways. However, neither is a constant: the salience of both and their relative value alter through time with changing technology, cultures and institutions. The sea did not mean the same thing before and after 1500. The Mediterranean had a very different military–naval–commercial system in 1400, 1550 and 1700, and this affected the role and nature of the sea. Qualitative differences and geographical configurations affect the role of the sea and the power of states which border it: thus Denmark was long able to raise revenue from tolls in the Sound, while Russia's exit from the Black Sea is held hostage by the passage through the Bosphorus and Dardanelles. In this sense we can only talk about spaces like the sea historically and specifically.

5

The Frontier, Conquest and Settlement

So far we have considered frontiers in two different contexts: as the mutually recognized and demarcated borders of modern sovereign states, and as the linear systems of external regulation whereby premodern empires at the limits of their expansion contained their barbarian neighbours. These two meanings of frontier are distinct, as they involve different institutions and spatial forms. However, they have two things in common: the frontier as a means of control of populations, and the frontier as a source of threat. Modern states used mutually agreed borders to gain control over their peoples, and across the frontier were other states with which one might well be at war in the future. Imperial frontiers were designed to keep barbarian tribes at bay.

There are other meanings of frontier, chief of which are the varied experiences of the frontier as a moving line of conquest and settlement between different peoples. From the year AD 1000 onwards, Western Europe was enlarging by processes of internal and external settlement. On the one hand, it was expanding locally to link scattered settlements by felling forests, draining marshes and pushing into the uplands, and, on the other, pushing forward new settlements in Eastern Europe, in Ireland, in Spain and in the Balkans and the Holy Land.[1] From the thirteenth century onwards, the Turks expanded into Anatolia and into the Balkans. Christianity and Islam advanced at each other's expense, with one driving back Muslim settlement in Spain and the other imposing Ottoman rule in the Balkans.[2] Here we shall concentrate on those two rival enterprises of conquest, before going on to consider the frontier in the Americas.

These diverse experiences of expansion and settlement can be grouped together into a third conception of the frontier, in addition to the two outlined above, by using Frederick Jackson Turner's concept derived from European settlement in North America. This backward reference from America to Europe enables us to see the earlier situations as 'settler societies' driven forward by the possibility of expansion into under-occupied lands, and also by displacing native peoples and rulers. Turner wrote his classic essay 'The Significance of the Frontier in American History' in 1893 at the time of the Chicago World Columbian Exhibition.[3] Chicago had grown from a village in the 1830s to the metropolis of the West with a population of 1,100,000 in 1890. The occasion of Turner's reflections was the report by the superintendent of the US Census for 1890 that there was now no clear Western frontier line: the whole area had been broken up by pockets of settlement. Turner saw the closing of the frontier as the end of one of the fundamental driving forces of American history. US history had been shaped by the existence of land open to settlement to the West and a shifting frontier as pioneers moved forward in successive waves. The frontier shaped the character and institutions of the American people, strongly reinforcing the trend towards freedom and democracy. The ability to move, to escape local control, enabled ordinary citizens to shape their own destiny and to enjoy freedom. It can be argued that something similar influenced Spaniards and Turks as they pressed forward and displaced their opponents.[4]

Turner has been strongly criticized and his thesis has produced extensive debate. Among his critics have been major American historians such as Richard Hofstader and D. M. Potter.[5] Turner has been challenged for the imprecision of his thesis and also for the ideology surrounding it. His ideas are now anathema to politically correct US historians who loathe the Manifest Destiny foundations of the thesis and the marginal role he gave to the indigenous peoples and their sufferings in the course of western expansion. It is still worth separating the argument from the ideology and accepting that, despite the imprecision, there is a real point in the significance of the frontier. It is obvious that Turner did see the western course of empire as the displacement of those who used the land inefficiently by superior and more vigorous settlers. Even historians basically sympathetic to Turner, like William Cronon, have emphasized how the frontier in the railway era depended not so much on rugged do-it-yourself settlers as on the organized expansion of large capitalist enterprises and the urban financial speculation that funded them.[6] In a sense, the various objections are beside the one major basic point. The existence of exploitable land to the west *was* a decisive feature of American history from the colonial era onwards. Turner also articulated prevailing values: people came to believe in Manifest Destiny and thus they made it happen. However repellent it may be to us, the displacement and the massacres of the indigenes did not alter the settlers' own experience of freedom.

Before the railway era, the frontier depended on politics and military control and also on land speculation, but it still required settlers willing to take the risk of pushing beyond the mountains into the Ohio basin. The key point that Turner makes is the effect on the manners and institutions of a society defined by a shifting line of settlement.

Spain and the Balkans

Castile and the Ottomans were both 'societies organized for war'. They were driven to expand across a frontier against densely settled enemy societies, not sparsely settled tribal peoples. The two processes of conquest and settlement had five fundamental features in common.

First, a coherent narrative that sustained the process of expansion through decades and centuries, enabling efforts to be re-focused after reverses and periods of accommodation. In the Castilian case, the ideology of Reconquest had become firmly established after the great victories of the eleventh century. In the case of the Ottomans, the legitimacy of religious war and of the Gazi tradition made raiding and the taking of booty a road to righteousness. Crusade and *jihad* in these specific local forms were rival enterprises in legitimation.

Second, expansion in both cases was organized by a carefully modulated combination of central power and local action. Raiding across the frontier was an almost continuous process and the frontier peoples and military forces were adapted to it: they acted on local initiative in both offence and defence. This was supplemented by major campaigns and large-scale wars. In a sense both the Castilians and the Ottomans acted on their advancing frontier in a similar way to Ibn Khaldûn's nomads. Like the Bedouin, they were kept vigorous by an ongoing practice of cavalry-raiding. In fact, the Castilians copied both the Muslim strategy of raiding and many of the military institutions of the Muslims, as we shall see.

Third, their enemies, by contrast, increasingly played the role of the corrupt urban dynasty in Khaldûn's narrative. The Muslim states in *al-Andalus* tended towards luxury and corruption, except when reinvigorated by stern religiously inspired regimes from the Maghrib. Such weak regimes relied too heavily on mercenaries and on paying off their opponents. In a different way, the ruling nobility of the Balkans were weak and their rule fragile. Often different in ethnicity and culture from their peoples and highly exploitative of them, they had little but the armed force of a narrow elite to counter the Turks.

Fourth, the divisions of opposing rulers were exploited in both cases. Christians fought as allies and mercenaries in the quarrels of

Muslim rulers. Both the Castilians and the Ottomans were also careful to establish tribute states and protectorates, thus providing opposing rulers with the opportunity to adopt a subordinate position and minimizing the need for formal conquest. Indeed, the tribute money, *parias*, paid by Muslim rulers to Christian princes, could be a real short-term disincentive to further war and conquest for those monarchs. The religious dimension to war in both Spain and the Balkans did not mean that the participants acted from blind hatred or that they had no common culture. Raiding was probably no worse than the local wars of feudal lords in the eleventh century in France, or the cross-frontier cattle raiding where there was no religious dimension, such as between medieval England and Scotland.

Fifth, conquest had to pay for itself. Commoners and nobles alike expected to receive grants of land and privileges in Castile. Likewise, booty and the prospect of new military tenures were central to participation in the Ottoman enterprise of conquest. In both cases the advance of the frontier was driven from the edge and was a mass phenomenon. And in both cases the common people and adventurers were active participants rather than mere followers of elites. The frontier offered them real benefits and a degree of freedom, defined as the absence of subordination rather than backwoods democracy.

Ottoman Advance

The Ottoman Turks advanced steadily from Anatolia into the Balkans, with the principal exception being the period after their defeat by Timur the Lame. In 1352 they moved to occupy the Gallipoli Peninsula and thence by 1357 to subjugate Thrace. In 1361 they captured the key European city of Adrianople, thus isolating Constantinople. In 1396 they decisively defeated the crusade organized against them at Nicopolis; in 1448 they destroyed the Serbian aristocracy at Kosovo; and in 1526 they defeated the Hungarians at Mohács. They had advanced their rule from central Asia Minor to the margins of Central Europe in just over 200 years.

Modern Balkan ideologues, especially among the Serbs, portray the Turks as brutal invaders who prevailed by sheer force of arms over noble resistance by Christian peoples. This is self-serving nonsense. Many Balkan Christian nobles were culturally alien to – and extremely exploitative of – those they ruled, and Ottoman rule in its early phases was relatively mild by the standards of the day. Ottoman advance was driven by continuous raiding, slowly salami-slicing the frontier. The Ottoman frontier forces included many volunteers and irregulars as well as local Timariot cavalry. The forces were led by *Uç-begis*. By the fifteenth century there were three *begs*, one on the right in the lower Danube and Moldova, one in the centre towards Belgrade, and one on the left wing in Macedonia.

Those outside the rule of the Sublime Porte were fair game for pillage. Raiding created strong pressures for local Christian rulers to submit. As Halil Inalcik remarks:

> Yet it was the frontier *begs* who played a crucial role in pushing the Ottoman borders forward . . . Under their pressure, many of the Balkan princes and lords readily accepted Ottoman overlordship to spare themselves from the continual raiding of the frontiersmen. Once the lands had become tribute-paying territories, their non-Muslim inhabitants assumed the status of *ahl al-zimma*, i.e., protected subjects of the Islamic state in accordance with Islamic law.[7]

Ottoman society, far from being closed and corrupt in this period, was highly mobile and willing to exploit talent from all quarters. Elements of the core Turkish population were prepared to seek new lives and the prospect of prosperity on the frontier. Ottoman rulers welcomed successive waves of Christian renegades, Jewish and Morisco refugees from Spain, and Old Believer victims of Christian persecution by the Orthodox in Russia.

The Ottomans cleverly exploited the divisions between Christian rulers and between noble elites and local populations. As a result of the Fourth Crusade of 1204 most of the Byzantine lands in the Balkans 'were partitioned among Frankish barons'.[8] The Balkans were a confused patchwork of feudal states. Hungary and Venice, the principal external Christian powers, were unpopular because they were Catholic and local populations were Orthodox. The Sultanate was careful in this context to act as the protector of the local Orthodox Church. This often enjoyed the support of clergy and local lords. In contrast, the Christian elite generally favoured Western military intervention and were willing to accept Catholicism as the price.[9] Byzantine authority had been replaced by feudal lords who imposed severe burdens on the people in the form of taxes and labour service. They were also often different from the people ethnically, culturally and in terms of religion. Rapacious and remote from their subjects, the Balkan rulers had little prospect of raising mass resistance against the Turks.

Ottoman rule was by contrast 'modern'. In effect it displaced feudalism by centralized rule, and thus reduced the burden of arbitrary local exactions. *Corvée* labour and servile obligations were abolished in favour of simplified and initially lighter taxes. Even the levy of Christian children taken as slaves and to be raised as Muslims was not as appalling as it sounds to us. State slaves often occupied privileged administrative and military positions as vizirs and janissaries. Local Christian communities enjoyed the right to rule by their own customs and to be governed by their own religious authorities in return for an extra tax, the *cizye* or poll tax on non-Muslims.

Thus the rotten fabric of Christian rule in the Balkans collapsed, as the common people mostly stood aside and many of the elites accepted Turkish overlordship as the best bargain available. The Turks enjoyed until the end of the sixteenth century a relatively efficient and certainly not more unfair system of rule, superior in many ways to their direct Christian rivals. Islam consistently attracted Western converts and the Ottomans followed a policy of limited religious toleration (they were harsher against the Shiite Safavids in Persia). They also enjoyed experienced and numerous cavalry forces ideal for raiding, and thus for expanding the frontier.

This is not an apologia for the Ottomans, simply an explanation of how they were able to prevail over Christian states and rule large Christian populations. One should also remember that it is essential to distinguish between the institutions and practices of the Ottomans as a rising power, and those that gained them an odious reputation in the period of their corruption and decline. As the empire weakened, it shifted to increased numbers of mercenary troops and to higher taxes to finance a system that was no longer expanding or profiting from conquest. Also, by the end of the sixteenth century, the Ottomans had expanded to face areas where the people did not loathe their rulers in the way many Balkan peasants had, and where they were willing to fight in defence of their religion. In the Austrian borderlands, the rump of Hungary and in Croatia, the Turkish forces encountered determined resistance. From the seventeenth century onwards along this frontier, the Hapsburgs created a system of defence in depth. This included powerful fortresses like Komorn, designed to deny the use of the Danube to the Turks, but also institutions like military colonies to resist the processes of raiding that had hollowed out the Balkan states.[10] The Austrians built up forces of light cavalry and sharpshooters committed to combating Turkish raiding by Timariot cavalry and irregular infantry.[11]

Castile

Muslim Spain lasted for some 800 years, from the first invasion in AD 711 to the conquest of the last Muslim state, Granada, in 1492. It is impossible here to examine the whole of the Reconquest: we shall concentrate on an ideal-typical presentation of institutions and practices related to the frontier in Castile from the eleventh to the fourteenth centuries.

The Muslim conquest of Visigothic Spain appears to have been relatively easy. The first invasion force amounted to no more than 7–12,000 men.[12] The rulers of Visigothic Spain were at odds with each other and ineffective. A divided aristocracy, some of whom tried to use the invaders to realize their own political objectives, ruled over a disarmed population. Visigothic Spain appears to have been a relatively centralized state, with few local institutions or military resources. With the exception of a few Christian enclaves in the north, Spain fell into the hands of the Muslims once the Visigothic elite was decapitated.

The first centres of resistance in the north shed the burden of the old Visigothic aristocracy, and a new system of central direction and localized initiative was built up. Castile avoided the classic forms of Northern European feudalism. It was a military society based upon incentives to those at all levels of society who were willing to shoulder the burdens of defending and advancing the frontier. Social mobility was based on function. Rather than parcel out the land by granting benefices to nobles, conquered lands were divided up on the basis of those who accepted military duties as horsemen or foot soldiers, as *caballeros* or *peones*. Elena Lourie emphasizes the distinctiveness of these institutions well: 'Since land was not in short supply, to encourage the growth of this essential arm in the military organization of the state, it was only necessary to grant them privileges.'[13]

Between the northern Christian enclaves and the wealthy societies of *al-Andalus* lay a large, sparsely populated area, much of it semi-arid plateau with poor grazing. It was into this area that the Castilians made their first major advances in the eleventh century, taking Toledo in 1085 and pushing south of the Tagus. To secure this large area the Crown was forced to create a series of strongly fortified and self-governing towns, the functions of which were to serve as centres of resistance to major Muslim raids and to supply support to nearby villages through their own municipal cavalry. Villages were expected to provide local defence through their farmer infantry. The towns enjoyed grants of privileges by the Crown, *fueros*. They were the centre of a class of mounted commoner knights, *caballeros villanos*, who formed the basis of the frontier cavalry because they could provide their own horses, and thus they enjoyed a social status based on capacity as opposed to descent.[14] The towns of central Spain, like Ávila or Salamanca, were therefore based on a military labour aristocracy rather than a mercantile urban patriarchate as in most of urban Europe.[15]

In the early decisive phases of the Reconquest, local frontier-fighting was central and it promoted both social mobility and freedom. Servile obligations were inconsistent with the harshness of life on the frontier and the necessity of military service for as many males as possible. Towns and settlers both enjoyed a degree of liberty unusual for the common people in medieval Europe. It has been claimed that 'a whirlwind of liberty shook the frontier of the valley of the Duero'.[16] The frontier drew enterprising spirits from the interior. In an under-populated land, it forced the Crown and major lords to grant frontier privileges to each successive wave of advance and to maintain rights and incentives further back in the chain to keep people from the lure of the frontier. For the minor aristocracy and the commoner knights, war and raiding provided opportunities that were not equalled by normal economic activity: thus the advancing frontier fed on itself. El Cid rightly claimed: 'he who stops in one spot will see his fortunes diminish'.[17]

The frontier could not be expanded by do-it-yourself frontier warfare alone. Major royal campaigns and periodic crusades that brought the nobility of Europe to fight in Spain moved the frontier forward in huge leaps and then created serious problems of settlement and defence to stabilize the new conquests.[18] The crusade of 1212 led to the great victory of Las Navas de Tolosa and a significant southward shift of the frontier, biting deep into Muslim Spain. The advance from the Tagus to the frontier of Granada required new institutions. Chief among these were new monastic military orders – the principal ones being Alcántara, Calatrava and Santiago.[19] Calatrava was founded to hold an apparently indefensible isolated outpost; it was subsequently defended by a garrison of dedicated warrior monks.

Such major advances opened up large areas of Spain: La Mancha, Extremadura, and parts of Andalusia and Murcia. These could not be settled piecemeal. They were either depopulated or had large existing populations of Muslims, Mozarabs (Christians who had adopted Moorish customs) and Jews. The Crown made substantial grants of land to the great families of the old nobility and to the military orders. The effect was to create huge estates based on extensive pastoralism – cattle- and sheep-ranching. In such areas free men were marginal and hence rose relations of patronage and clientage, with the *behetria* as a form of semi-feudal obligation.[20] As the Reconquest succeeded, it promoted hierarchy and social closure, reducing the role of lesser knights, free farmers and urban militias and brotherhoods. Increasing relations of dependence and social distance made Spain a less mobile and flexible society, creating the preconditions for the highly stratified and static society that followed the creation of a unified monarchy and the expulsion of the Muslims and Jews. For some time, as we shall see in a moment, the existence of a new frontier in the Atlantic and the New World offered new opportunities for the class of military adventurers formed in the Reconquest.

The Reconquest was as much a process of contact between civilizations as it was a war between rival religious societies. Spanish culture benefited massively from its contact with what was unquestionably a superior civilization. Here we are less concerned with the general process of cultural hybridization and transfer than with the specific military and institutional borrowings central to frontier warfare. The very idea of Reconquest had much in common with the Islamic concept of *jihad*, except that in the Muslim case those who submitted to rule by Islamic authorities had the right to practise their religion, whereas the Spaniards tended to try to force conversion or to expel. The very idea of organized raids eating away the frontier was derived from Moorish practice – the *cabalgada*. The heavy cavalry of Northern Europe might be decisive in set-piece battles, but they were less than effective in frontier warfare. For that the Castilians adopted the style of *al jinete* riding, with lighter equipment and a different saddle, bit and stirrups. The military orders, like Calatrava, seem to have been copied from the Muslim institution of the *ribats* – fortified monasteries built from the eighth century to defend the frontiers of Islam. As Elena Lourie points out, the majority of the Spanish orders were very unusual in terms of European monasticism in that, like the *ribats*, they were purely military institutions with no wider social functions.[21] The Templars and Hospitallers had combined military roles with aiding pilgrims and social welfare. The Muslim rulers seem to have tried less in the way of reciprocal military adaptation: local Andalusian rulers tried to utilize Christian mercenaries and buy off the Christian rulers. The toughest rulers came from the Maghrib – the Almohads and the Almoravids – and they tended to bring Moorish military forces and styles of warfare with them.

In the long period of the Reconquest, cross-border contacts were common. Organized war was not continuous. In contrast, raiding and rustling across the frontier was more or less constant. Elites enjoyed close contacts: thus El Cid fought for Muslim rulers against Christians. The Nasrid rulers of Granada were for a time vassals of the King of Castile and required to attend at Court and to fulfil military obligations against other Muslim rulers.[22] The management of a frontier marked by conflict but also by exchange required cross-border institutions. There were four: truces, ransoms, trade and arbitration. Truces of some frequency and often of long duration existed between Castile and Granada. The Muslim state paid protection money, *parias*, and was thus able to avoid attack. The process of raiding meant that captives were inevitable. On both sides ransoms were a valuable source of revenue to locals. Kidnap and ransom were so common that a class of professional ransomers, *al faqueques*, grew up to facilitate the release of Christian captives. Trade also continued across the frontier. Granada and Castile engaged in a division of labour, with the former producing high-value agricultural goods like dried fruits and sugar, and textiles like silk, and the latter cattle, olive oil and wheat. This trade was regularized and overseen by customs officials. Lastly, on both sides there were specialist judges to arbitrate cross-border disputes: on the Christian side, *alcaldes entre los cristianos y los moros*, and on the Muslim side, the *al-quādi bagna-l-mulūk* or 'judge between Kings'.

Such institutions indicate why we cannot treat the *Reconquista* as simply the purging of alien others from an essentially Christian Spain. Christians and Moors were familiar others. For most of the period of the Reconquest they were, in a sense, different parts of the *same* society. That society was shaped by their mutual interaction: by economic exchange, by extensive cultural contacts and borrowings, by the continuous contacts and raids across the frontier, and by the major wars that punctuated the gradual subordination of the elements in that complex society to each other. Spain had to be created out of that complexity: a unified Christian state that dominated the peninsula was a political project that emerged late and was in constant re-adjustment down to the seventeenth century. Then it came close to its final form when the revolt of the Catalans failed and Portugal succeeded in reasserting its independence.[23] Christians and Moors shared a common experience of both conflict and cooperation down to the fall of Granada in 1492. Then the terms of interaction became more and more one-sided, with the religious purges and expulsions that continued until the expulsion of the Moriscos after the savage repression of their revolt in 1570.[24]

The Conquest of the Americas

In 1492, not only did the Christians conquer Granada and expel the Jews, but Columbus started the process that led to the conquest of the Americas. This was not a contact of familiar others like that in the Iberian peninsula: the territories, languages and customs of the peoples of the Americas were wholly unknown to the Europeans. Neither was the conquest slow: even by the standards of the time, it was rapid and brutal. The Spaniards quickly conquered their core centres of colonization in Mexico and Peru, the former in 1519–21 and the latter in 1531–36. The initial numbers of armed Spaniards involved were tiny, around 400 with Cortés and a mere 180 with Pizarro. Such conquests verge on the incredible and depended crucially on the peculiar character of the Aztec and Inca Empires. Both empires had established hegemony relatively recently, ruthlessly subordinating other indigenous peoples, but by the early sixteenth century neither showed any capacity to respond rapidly and vigorously to an external challenge. This was because of the political structures and forms of social order on which these extensive regimes had come to depend. Both empires were highly centralized and hierarchical; power was concentrated in the hands of an all-powerful emperor. The rulers legitimated their rule through rigid, ritualized and traditionalist societies that encouraged conformity and passivity in the subordinate populations. Both empires had expanded to the point that they faced no urgent external challenge. The rulers were not confronted with any serious threat that would have shaped their capacities for prompt and practical action against real rivals, and yet both empires were seething with discontent and faced rebellion and civil war.[25]

Confronted with a wholly alien challenge, the Emperors Montezuma and Atahualpa had no idea how to respond: both were indecisive and could not assess the real aims and capacities of the strangers. Both tried to fit the strangers into the categories familiar within their own culture with, for example, Cortés being received as a returning god. Cortés and Pizarro, confronted with an equally strange world, were not so disabled. They had a narrative of conquest and plunder into which to fit such exotic societies, and one that did not forbid effective means–ends calculation. Cortés clearly recognized the need to understand Aztec society, even if he interpreted it through his own categories, and he used his translator Donna Marina as an effective intermediary.[26] The failure to comprehend the threat the Spaniards posed can be summed up by Atahualpa throwing away the Bible given to him by a priest, who told him that the written characters would speak to him; neglecting the metaphor, Atahualpa held it to his ear but responded with disgust when he could hear nothing.[27]

The Spaniards coped better with otherness because, in a sense, they were indifferent to it and thus not awed by it. Although amazed by the size and cleanliness of the Aztec capital, Tenochtitlán, compared to Seville, the largest European city they were familiar with, they never doubted their right to seize it and in the course of their siege destroyed it utterly. In that sense their arrogance and ignorance worked for them.

Less developed New World societies were far harder to take over, precisely because they were less centralized. The Spaniards found

Yucatan hard to conquer. They were repelled in 1517 and did not impose their rule effectively until the latter part of the sixteenth century.[28] In 1521 Ponce de León was unsuccessful in his bid to colonize Florida and died in the attempt. Pánfilo de Narváez again failed to take Florida in 1528, as did Hernando De Soto yet again in 1539.[29] De Soto was no incompetent: he had been one of Pizarro's key advisers. The difference between Mexico and Peru and these cases was a mixture of social organization and terrain. These repulses prove that the Spaniards' victories were not primarily due to technology; the warriors in Florida were no better equipped than the elite of Aztec knights. In Mexico the conquistadores found themselves in an ordered landscape of streets and cities, guided on established roads to the capital city of a hierarchical state. In Yucatan and Florida they were faced by an enemy that could flee into the forest. The very high level of material civilization of both the Aztecs and the Incas counted against them. The Spanish in effect 'decapitated' highly centralized politics and gained a key advantage from the ensuing interregnum.[30]

However, even this success in removing the head of a rigid social organization based on unquestioning obedience would have availed the conquerors of little on its own. In Mexico the native recovery of initiative in order to mount an effective military response was rapid. The Aztec elite were not long bamboozled by the idea that Cortés was Quetzalcoatl returning, and they were determined to expel and destroy the Spaniards. Cortés' flight from Tenochtitlán on 1 July 1520 nearly ended in disaster. The Spaniards were able to succeed for two reasons other than ruthless leadership and military skill: native allies and disease. Without the help of the Tlaxcalans, who had long resisted Aztec hegemony, Cortés could not have hoped to prevail or to successfully encircle and besiege Tenochtitlán. As in the *Reconquista*, the Spaniards were able to exploit the divisions between different groups to their advantage. Even then the siege was a close-run thing and might not have succeeded had not the Aztecs been gravely weakened by a smallpox epidemic. European diseases to which the natives had no immunity dramatically reduced the indigenous population of the Americas in the sixteenth century – in Mexico by not less than a third and perhaps by more than a half.[31] Disease did not just kill: it destroyed the capacity and will to resist. Thus Quitláhuac, Montezuma's first replacement as emperor, died along with many of the elite. The Spaniards were relatively immune to the disease, and thus appeared to enjoy the mandate of heaven.

The regimes that the conquerors established after their initial victories were truly a product of the 'decapitation' of the Aztec and Inca hierarchies. In effect, the conquerors placed themselves at the head of the old social order. In Mexico the new order relied crucially both on indigenous allies and on local native rulers. Conquerors and the Mexican elites intermarried and the Mexican aristocracy became part of the new system of rule. In a way the conquests were a form of accelerated circulation of elites, with the Spaniards acting as the orchestrators of regime change and as elite forces in a fashion similar to the US operation 'Enduring Freedom' in Afghanistan in 2001–2.

If the conquest of the Americas involved a context very different from that of Muslim Spain, the practices and institutions of the *Reconquista* provided the experience and the means to operate in this very different environment. The New World came to serve as a 'frontier' for Spain. El Cid's advice that social mobility could not be had by staying put behind the frontier held even more strongly in the Spain of 1492; there was little prospect of gaining social mobility or new fortunes in a rapidly ossifying society. The fate of Cortés in Spain would have been at best to be an obscure provincial lawyer, and Pizarro might well have ended his days as a crippled veteran of Spain's Italian wars. Even so, few Spaniards risked the rigours of the journey and the uncertainties of the New World. And those who did mostly wanted to settle in established colonies and not become embroiled in new ventures like the colonization of La Plata.

In their progress down the peninsula, the Spaniards had created a mental and institutional 'kit' for conquest. They had experience of ruling large subject agrarian populations after the Aragonese conquest of Valencia and Murcia in the thirteenth century. The conquest of the Atlantic Islands such as the Canaries and the Cape Verde Islands gave the Spanish and Portuguese experience of long-distance overseas colonization.[32] In the Canaries the Spanish fought and exterminated the native Guanches. In Madeira and the Canaries the Iberians created plantation economies producing cash crops and worked by slave labour.[33]

Cortés, on landing in Mexico, created the municipality of Villa Rica de la Vera Cruz, thus generating an alternative source for the legitimacy for his actions than the now hostile Governor of Cuba. The new 'magistrates' and 'town councillors', his collaborators, appointed him Captain General. Cortés had thus put his limited knowledge of Spanish law to good account.[34] The closest thing to a basic law, *Las Siete Partidas*, provided for citizens forming a municipal council where necessary by agreement, rather than by a royal grant in advance. The self-governing town as a political–military formation had been of key importance to frontier defence and expansion in Spain. Towns were also to be central in the colonial institutions in the Americas.[35] Spanish America was an essentially urban civilization in contrast to Anglo-America.

In the sixteenth century the Crown and the settlers struggled over the forms of government, the social institutions and the rights of the conquered in the Americas. The violence and ruthlessness of the conquistadores and the legalism and religiosity of Charles V and Philip II constantly clashed. The Crown, the Church and the lawyers were trying to govern at thousands of miles' distance and with few instruments. Spain's empire was a largely privatized affair, depending on royal grants of privileges to colonizers who were to furnish their own arms and ships. It often slipped completely out of even the most tenuous control, as when Cortés, en route to Mexico, disobeyed the orders of the Governor of Cuba. The Crown took the view from the early sixteenth century that the native population could not just be enslaved; if they placed themselves under royal protection as subjects of the king they had the right to life and property.[36] Hence emerged the *requerimiento* which, in Castilian legalese, required those to whom it was addressed to submit to the Crown, the Pope in 1494 having granted Spain dominion of all lands west of 370 leagues from the Cape Verde Islands. If they did not submit they were rebels, at war with the king, and thus without rights. The requirement legitimated conquest even in the ludicrous circumstances of being read at some distance in Castilian to uncomprehending natives. As Patricia Seed points out, such legitimation was required not merely to satisfy a legalistic Court, but also to establish a claim to rightful rule against other European powers.[37] As a justification it was unusual and quite unlike the Portuguese claim by right of discovery, or the English claim by established settlement. The requirement also involved unconscious borrowing of the language and forms of the Islamic proclamation of *jihad*.[38] Thus was Spanish thinking shaped by the long experience of the conflict with Islam, down to recapitulating the forms of Māliki jurisprudence. In the case of the Ottomans, the poll tax on unbelievers who submitted to Islamic rule was generally applied, with the right to religious self-government in the case of Christians and Jews. In practice Spanish rule meant exploitation and precious little protection for the native population of the Americas.

The adventurers who conquered Mexico and Peru did not come as 'settlers'; they came to find treasure and to rule as 'lords' over native populations who worked for them. In the context of rapid conquest and massive population loss, the Spaniards had to create a viable form of rule both politically and at a micro-social level. For the former they relied on allies and native elites; Spanish rule was exiguous and the numbers of settlers, officials and clergy very small. For the latter they created a system that gave the conquistadores control of the key local resource – native labour. The Spaniards had conquered densely settled societies: the Indians worked the land and could not easily be displaced. Hence the colonists created the system of *encomienda*, a form of bastard feudalism, in which the Crown gave Spaniards rights to extract tribute and labour from the natives in return for participation in conquest and continuing military service. The *encomenderos* thus sat at the peak of a largely self-governing indigenous society, acting as extractors of tribute and labour. This system evolved into effective possession of land and thus to the direct control of scarce Indian labour in the *latifundia*. The evolution of the hacienda as a core socio-economic institution increased the land under direct control by a Creole landlord class who in effect set the terms of colonial rule. Royal officials sent from Spain could do little but adapt to the practices of the local aristocracy.[39]

If the Americas functioned as a kind of frontier for Spain in the period of the Conquest, then colonial Spanish America also had a frontier. In northern Mexico, in Chile and in Paraguay, the Spaniards faced the challenging combination of indigenous peoples who were not under control, taxing environments and slender resources. Spain's remote frontiers in the Americas were not dynamic: they did not attract settlers. Military posts were few in northern Mexico and existed mostly to protect the missions which were the main Spanish institution to control and acculturate the local tribes. Spain's northern frontier was fragile, and was eventually threatened by the more dynamic Anglo-American settler societies.[40]

Thus, if there were Turneresque elements in the *Reconquista*, there were few in Spain's colonial societies in the Americas. The Spaniards did not expand and settle in the Americas on the same scale as the Anglo-Americans did. For the indigenous population, after the horrors of the Conquest and the epidemics, this meant at least that native peoples continued to exist – exploited and semi-acculturated – but able gradually to recover their numbers and to shape a hybrid culture, even if in a subordinate way. The situation of the indigenous people faced with Anglo-American dynamic expansion by settlers across the frontier was far worse. Tim Flannery puts it well: 'The implications of the English frontier for the Indians were to be dire, for by and large these settlers viewed Indians not as valued trading partners or a resource to be exploited, but as competitors.'[41]

The Frontier in North America

European occupation and settlement of North America differed considerably from the Hispanic conquests and the colonial societies they created. There are four salient distinctions.

1. First, the conquests of North America were staged and relatively slow. This gave the indigenous peoples time to interact and a large period of some 150 years, between the early 1600s and the end of the Seven Years War in 1763, when the Indian tribes could act between the rival settler societies as a power in their own right and not solely as the objects of colonial control.

2. Second, the European powers – England, France, Holland and Spain – competed for control, seeking to expand at each other's expense, and central to such containment of their rivals was control of the frontier.

3. Third, the English and Dutch came to occupy the land, whether as farmers or as the owners of slave plantations, whereas the French primarily sought to control the fur trade, entering into partnership with the Indians to do so.

4. Fourth, in both the English and the French cases, the state came to have a far more direct role in the colonies than did the Spanish; mutual rivalry between colonizing nations promoted greater metropolitan military participation and tighter European political control of colonies.

At the onset of the Seven Years War in 1755 there were some 1.5 million settlers in the English colonies on the Atlantic seaboard from Maine to Georgia, and others were already crossing the Allegheny Mountains into the upper valley of the Ohio. It was in the mutual interest of the French and the Indians to block further expansion. The French sought to control the key waterways with forts – Frontenac, Niagara, Duquesne, etc. – blocking British access to the Great Lakes and the Ohio. With a system of trading posts they sought both to profit from the fur trade and to acquire the military support of the Indians of the *pays d'en haut*. The British frontier, being linear, shallow and more than 1,000 miles long, was difficult to defend. Indian raiders could easily carry out massacres close to major cities like Philadelphia. Settlement depended not merely on do-it-yourself trappers and farmers, but on the organized military defence of the frontier. Until the Seven Years War, the British frontier was fragile and depended on treaties with the Indians. The British colonists had created a structure of alliances with the Iroquois Confederacy, the Covenant Chain, in 1677 and this persisted until the Seven Years War. By keeping neutral between the European powers, bargaining for both trade goods and gunpowder, the Iroquois preserved their own lands and their domination over their indigenous neighbours. Indian society by the 1750s was part of a wider society of colonial contacts: by now the Indians were dependent on iron goods and European weapons. Without gunpowder, they were militarily weak. They could survive only by manoeuvring between the European rivals.

The British task in breaking out of French encirclement was difficult. In order to do so, organized military forces had to be moved into the interior. This involved building roads through the forest, secured by chains of fortified posts. Northern New York was defended by the road from Albany to Fort Edward, and Fort William Henry against the French threat from Lake Champlain. The French position on Lake Ontario was countered by Fort Oswego and a difficult passage through Fort Bull and Fort Stanwix back to Albany. In the case of the Ohio, the British effort to eliminate Fort Duquesne, which controlled access to the river, depended on building a road from Fort Cumberland to the Monongahela. Armies moving on such roads were vulnerable to ambush, as happened to General Braddock's force of British regular troops in July 1755. Braddock's defeat unleashed devastating Indian raids along the whole frontier, collapsing the frontier in Pennsylvania where the colonists had relied on making peace with the Indians and had no organized defence. Isolated farms were vulnerable, however vigorous the settlers, and even substantial communities like the peaceful Moravian religious settlement at Gnadenhutten, were wiped out. The frontier was thus salient in the affairs of the British colonies. Although provincial legislatures were inclined to neglect frontier defence, different relations with the Indians, combined with the campaigns of the French, gave them little option but to support extensive and expensive military operations to secure them. Similarly, the British and French metropolitan governments were forced to send larger and larger numbers of regular troops to America.

The effect of complete Anglo-American victory in the Seven Years War was to eliminate the French as a rival for control of the interior of the continent. This started a new and ultimately irreconcilable conflict between the colonists and the government in London, the two parties hitherto held together by the need to contain France. The issue was the West. The experience of the Cherokee War and of Pontiac's Rebellion in 1763 convinced the metropolitan British administration of the need for a limit to westward settlement. This required a clear resolution of the land rights of the Indians, with territory reserved for them, and a clear frontier line dividing colonists and indigenes. The British Royal Proclamation of 1763 confined the colonists to the Atlantic side of the Appalachians. Britain sought both to avoid an expensive series of Indian wars and to limit the powers of the colonial assemblies, subjecting them to greater metropolitan rule and requiring them to pay more for their own security. The issue of how to control the frontier led directly to the conflict over who was to have power over British North America. On the specific issue of limiting settlement, it pitted the major land speculators who were influential in some of the colonial assemblies and the mass of land-hungry colonists against the metropolitan government's policies. The creation of British hegemony, and the need for London to secure it at modest cost after the large expenditures of the Seven Years War, was set against the possibility of extended colonization of the continent now that the French barriers to westward expansion had been eliminated. The frontier was thus central to the American War of Independence. The colonists' victory led to the creation of a single government that soon acquired the mission of westward expansion. Against that government, without European allies, the native tribes had no chance. They ceased to be a balancing power in European conflicts, and thus became at once both militarily weaker and an obstacle in the way of American settlement.[42]

The colonies that achieved their independence in 1783 each differed in nature. Although united in opposing the British and seeking to expand westwards, they wanted the West for varying and incompatible purposes. The southern colonies had a social and property system shaped by slave labour and large plantations. The northern colonies relied on free labour and family farms. Both became strongly committed to western expansion: the planters because of the burgeoning demand for cotton and, secondarily, soil erosion, and the free settlers because of domestic population growth and a steady flow of migrants. Given expansion, the two systems implied competing property rights. In a free competition to settle western land, the planter class was bound to lose to the more numerous free settlers once the Atlantic slave trade was made illegal. The character of western expansion depended crucially on which labour system would triumph, slave or free.

The planters could not prevail by economics, and thus had to rely on politics. To settle the question, the planter class needed to control political power and thus Federal policy over land settlement. In the Missouri Compromise of 1819 the South secured the right of slave property up to 36 degrees 30' north. To maintain its political position the South needed at least an equal number of slave states to free in order to control Congress. This was achieved, firstly, by slaves being counted as 60 per cent of a free man for purposes of determining the number of representatives in the House and, secondly, by the fact that, irrespective of population, each state had two places in the Senate. In the 1850s the balance between free and slave states became precarious after the admission of California as a free state. The planter interest sought redress with the aid of their Democratic Party allies in the North through the Kansas and Nebraska Bill of 1858. Kansas became a battleground between the slave interest, abolitionists and free settlers. The conflict over the forms of property escalated as slave owners sought legal protection for their rights over their slaves in free states. By 1859 the issue of slavery had become explosive for economic and political, rather than human rights, reasons. Only a minority of northerners were abolitionists, and cities like Baltimore and New York depended heavily on the South's export trade. What tipped the balance was the fear of a political and economic system distorted to secure the rights that the slaveholders could not obtain by any other method than an armlock on state power. To a great degree, the Civil War was about how the frontier was to expand and in whose interest. The midwestern states, Illinois, Ohio, Wisconsin, etc., produced a large proportion of the volunteers for the Union armies.[43]

In the 100 plus years between independence and Turner's essay, the West was settled and the 'frontier' in this sense closed. If America ceased to have a frontier by 1890, the New World remained a frontier for Europe. Western expansion had involved the Europeanization of America in a double sense: replacing native peoples with much denser settlements of Europeans, and displacing native plants, animals and landscapes with imported European ones and also with tamed varieties of native plants, like maize.[44] America literally became a different country. The transformation of the countryside and rapid industrialization made America an attractive home for European settlers, even as 'push' factors like famine in Ireland, Tsarist tyranny and Swedish unemployment drove people to take ship. Into the 1920s the New Worlds created by the European discoveries served as a release valve for Europe. Some 60 million people left Europe to settle abroad in the century after 1815, relative to population the greatest mass migration in history.[45] Most went to the Americas. It was this mass migration that created a true 'Atlantic Economy'. It evened up labour costs and led to a substantial degree of price convergence by reducing the labour surpluses that drove down wages in Europe and the labour scarcity that drove up wages in the USA in the period after independence.[46] For Irish peasants, Sicilian day labourers or Polish Jews, it was a frontier, a new chance, even if that didn't mean settling on the prairie but working in a New York sweatshop or being fleeced by Henry Frick in his steelworks. Europe's 'West' was thus very different from Turner's. The USA industrialized and urbanized rapidly after 1860, and most new migrants ended up in towns and factories. However, migration still acted as an escape for individuals and thereby performed Turner's most basic function. Even if the frontier did not play a central role as a 'safety valve' in America, it functioned as such to the donor societies in Europe and thus helped to promote social stability.

We now have no equivalent of the frontier as a line of settlement. Migrants and refugees are trying to escape economic and political conditions as bad as the worst in nineteenth-century Europe. But they find immigration controls, border police and settled societies that barely tolerate them in menial and poorly paid work. For the poor and oppressed of the twenty-first century, the frontier is closed.

Forests, Mountains and Natural Frontiers

In chapters 4 to 7 we are looking at the interaction between politics, war and fundamental spatial divisions like land and sea, steppe and sown, earth and space. None of these spatial divisions are given effects. The sea did not become one common environment until the sixteenth century. The steppe ceased to matter when horse nomads lost their particular military advantages with the advent of effective guns. Spatial forms matter, but in complex and socially conditioned ways, as specific qualitative environments. For this reason, as we have seen in chapter 2, the chosen general theoretical framework to define space is the possibilism of Vidal de la Blache and Febvre.[47] This avoids both the determinism of some of the old political geographers and the hyper-abstraction of much modern philosophy and social theory. Because of this insistence on the specific character of spatial effects I have avoided a general discussion of what might appear to be two equally basic and consequential divisions: that between mountain and plain and that between open land and forest. The reason is that there is a vast range of specific qualitative environments within these two very general categories of spatial division.

Forests vary hugely in their physical qualities and in the social meanings attached to them. Tropical and temperate primary forests are very different environments. In medieval England and France, 'forests' and 'fôret' came to mean a highly regulated space of controlled hunting and harvesting of wood products, not dense primal woodland.[48] Likewise, mountains have varied greatly in how they function in relation to the societies within them and in the plain. In the Mediterranean region, mountain and plain are closely connected and linked by transhumance. The Pyrenees, far from being a barrier, linked communities on either side in networks of pastoralism, smuggling and trade. Thus mountains are often not obstacles, nor do they necessarily harbour different and isolated societies.

Forests function in our social and political myths and imaginings in very different ways.[49] They can be seen as alien and liminal zones, a threat to the cleared and settled. They can also be seen as a haven of primitive freedom, beyond the control of settled agrarian states. Thus forests have been seen as a source of Teutonic liberty from Tacitus onwards to the mythologizing of post-1870 nationalist Germany. Forests have been seen as a hiding place for guerrillas from Robin Hood to the Viet Minh and NLF. Forests, of course, did not defeat the Americans in South Vietnam: rather, it was the presence of a supportive sponsor state in the North and a long border open to infiltration. In Malaya, without such a sponsor and with more difficult infiltration routes, Communist insurgency was contained.

Forests, mountains and rivers have all functioned as pegs on which to hang the notion of 'natural frontiers'. The notion of natural frontiers as defining the 'proper' territory of a state is a myth that developed primarily to sustain the projects of the creation of sovereign territorial states in early-modern Europe, and the claiming of territories as 'homelands' during the era of nationalist politics from the nineteenth century onwards. The notion of France as defined by the Atlantic, Pyrenees, Mediterranean and Rhine might appeal to Louis XIV, but would have seemed laughable in the early fourteenth century when the French kings struggled to assert their authority outside the Île-de-France. Likewise the boundaries claimed by the 1848 Frankfurt Diet for Germany – along the lines of the song *Deutschland über Alles* – from the Belt to Memel and the Rhine to the Adige, were never exactly those of any state, including Hitler's Reich. Febvre's critique of the notion of natural frontiers and, secondarily, their location in specific natural features, is devastating. Geographical features could never serve as inherent natural frontiers because the social and political meaning of 'frontier' is not fixed, as we saw in chapter 3. As Febvre points out, one cannot read the concept of modern linear frontiers back into ancient boundaries because they functioned in a different way as zones of transition.[50]

6

War, Environment and Technology

Pre-modern Logistics

The mid-fifteenth century in Europe saw the onset of three transformatory revolutions in technology: effective guns, printing and long-distance navigation. These were complemented in the early sixteenth century by two major institutional/cultural revolutions: the attempt to create exclusive territorial states and the Protestant schism. The result of these changes was not an orderly transformation of society, an increase in governance capacity or improved living standards. That is to treat revolutionary technical/social change from the standpoint of nineteenth-century ideas that identify material advances with progress. The outcome was a century and a half of chaos and conflict. Changes interacted in unpredictable and often contradictory ways. Printing made large-scale literacy possible and thus reinforced Protestantism. It put the Bible into the hands of the people. It also made 'how to do it' manuals possible, undermining traditional monopolies of elite knowledge. Loading a musket was broken down into a series of steps, each illustrated by woodcut pictures: this enabled rebels and militias to train raw recruits by simple drill, undermining the old mercenary-skilled warrior artisans such as the *Landsknechts*.[1] The new navigation that made possible the plundering of the mines of Potosi created a flood of silver: this fed the wars of the Hapsburgs and contributed to the destructive inflation of the sixteenth century that impoverished the common people. The resulting unemployed and vagabonds became the cheap – but far from cheerful – cannon fodder of the new mass armies. State formation was both advanced and retarded by these processes of chaotic change. States were undermined – indeed virtually destroyed – by the religious civil wars. They were broken by the costs of interstate war, and bankrupted and undermined by rebellion.

The Military Consequences of Economic Backwardness

Only in the latter half of the seventeenth century did states begin to stabilize their domestic governments and to create an orderly system of international relations.[2] Underneath all these revolutionary changes the basic structures of life remained much as they had since the twelfth century across much of Europe. Only in the Netherlands and in England were the basic socio-economic conditions transformed. In both countries rural society was revolutionized by production for the market, and the major towns like Amsterdam and London were transformed by long-distance trade.[3] Water transport was crucial to this revolution: rivers and canals, coastal shipping, and overseas trade. The fundamental continuity of physical conditions elsewhere meant that many of the military changes that seemed revolutionary had little effect. States raised armies that grew larger through the sixteenth and seventeenth centuries, only to find them waste away in illness, desertion and through lack of pay. It was impossible to concentrate any great numbers in one place for any strategic purpose; armies tended to shrink back to the size of those in the Middle Ages during the course of an extended campaign.[4] This propensity towards stagnation in war and to the fragility and corruption of the state, due mainly to economic backwardness, was reinforced by the tendency of the new weaponry to indecisiveness. The new gunpowder weapons favoured the defence in the field: entrenched soldiers with handguns were difficult to defeat, and the latest fortifications designed to cope with artillery were even more challenging to besiege than the castles of the pre-gunpowder era.

The physical and economic conditions that limited the nature of war are as follows:

1. Low agricultural productivity. In most of Europe yields had not improved since the innovations of the eleventh and twelfth centuries and were not to do so until well into the eighteenth century, and in many places not until fertilizer became cheap in the nineteenth.[5] The seventeenth- and eighteenth-century agricultural revolutions in the Netherlands and England passed most of Europe by, since they depended on the development of market-oriented and capitalistic agriculture. This stagnation of productivity, due both to sluggish social relations and to a worsening climate, set a severe limit on the surplus that could be extracted from a locality, and thus the number of troops that could be garrisoned in it. Even in wealthy regions like Italy or the Netherlands, a province would find it hard to feed 20–30,000 troops (the absolute minimum number necessary for an extended siege of a major town) for a long time. Supplies were exiguous at the best of

times; the provision of troops imposed hardship on the peasants in normal times, and close to intolerable suffering in the case of the frequent famines caused by bad harvests. Armies could not long remain concentrated in these conditions.

2. Poor roads were universal, even in the most developed countries. Look at almost any Dutch landscape painting: the roads are dirt tracks in the most sophisticated country in Europe.[6] Roads, where they existed, did not have all-weather surfaces. Hence they became bogs in winter rains and rutted dust bowls in the summer heat. In either case, they presented formidable obstacles to heavy guns and supply wagons. Land transport was vastly expensive compared to water for a good reason. Armies could not move quickly, nor could they operate for long far from a local source of supply.

3. Maps, as we understand them, were all but non-existent.[7] At best there were itineraries, which listed towns and major features on the route to a destination. Geographical knowledge remained poor: in the sixteenth century the world was perhaps better mapped than Europe's localities. Most frontiers were ill-defined marchlands between major kingdoms, not rigid well-demarcated lines.[8] The border as we know it is an artefact of the successful consolidation of the system of states, and was only fully delineated with markers and customs posts in the eighteenth century in most cases. We forget how hard it is to plan and to coordinate an extensive campaign in the absence of maps. Armies relied on experienced conductors who knew the terrain and its resources. This was the case even in the days of Marlborough and his army's march from Flanders to the Danube in the early eighteenth century. Only in the mid-eighteenth century did systematic mapping based on surveying begin, with the Ordnance Survey in Britain.

4. The period from 1500–1800 is now known as the Little Ice Age.[9] Across Europe winters were hard and the growing season shorter. This reinforced the limits of poor agricultural technique and backward infrastructure. It exacerbated the long-run tendency for armies to be unable to keep the field in winter. Cold, wet and scarce food meant that those that did were gravely weakened by hunger and disease. They also needed to find secure winter quarters, preferably in a fortified town. The campaigning season was therefore short, from spring to early autumn, and this reinforced the tendency of war to indecisiveness. If a besieging army did not take a town by the time of the winter rains, it typically had to retreat.

The Early-Modern State

It is often claimed by historians, sociologists and political scientists that the revolutionary change to effective gunpowder weapons either led directly – or contributed significantly – to a revolution in state power and government organization.[10] This has three elements: the cost of the new weapons favoured larger and more efficient states that could raise the taxes to pay for the new armies; the new weapons made old fortifications, castles and town walls, obsolete, thus undermining local power, and the cost of the new fortifications also increased the need for a large tax base; and, lastly, the competition between states forced them both to exploit the new technologies and to increase the size of their armies, again putting a premium on large states with effective taxing powers. This account of the 'military revolution' of the sixteenth and seventeenth centuries is naive.[11] It fails to take into account the chaotic nature of social change in this period, for example, the role of religious dissent in undermining the effectiveness of governments in achieving a monopoly of the means of violence. It ignores the side-effects of the new technologies themselves: the new weapons led to indecisive warfare, making it easy for rebels to defend themselves, and allowing small, wealthy states to fortify themselves against attack. It also ignores the physical and social conditions that resulted in massive 'friction' and degraded war into disorganized local struggles, involving ill-fed and unpaid armed bands.

If the gunpowder revolution really had led to the modern state, then we should have an impressive example of systematic technological determinism. Technology did have major effects on the conduct of war, but social and political change was pushed in very different directions at once by that technology, and was also over-determined by the environment. If the thesis is valid that the changing technology of war acted like a selection pressure in favour of the 'modern' state, then we should have a lot of explaining to do. Why did the Netherlands, faced with the Eighty Years War with Spain, remain so de-centralized? It looks more like a survival of medieval pluralism than a state organized for modern war. Why did the Ottomans, often claimed to be an example of a pre-modern state that became unable to adapt to the modern world, prove such a formidable opponent? It was the organizational equal of its Christian rivals, at least until the beginning of the eighteenth century. It was arguably better – and certainly no worse – at supplying war in the sixteenth century than European states.[12] Why did Poland, with a weak polity and almost no central army, survive against the Swedes, Ottomans and Russians until it was encircled by three great powers and partitioned in the latter half of the eighteenth century? Why, too, were most of the major states so much more ram-shackle than the thesis of competitive evolution in the context of the new technologies suggests?

The answer is that the technology of war was not unidirectional in its effects; like physical conditions, it tended to limit war and favour the defence. Hence the two great powers of the era, the Ottomans and Hapsburgs, were both thwarted in their bids for dominance in Europe. The Ottomans were checked by the fortifications of Vienna in 1529 and at Malta in 1565, and the Spaniards were entangled in the inde-cisive Italian wars and frustrated by the network of fortified towns and inundations in the Netherlands. Moreover, the ambitions of ruling elites were well ahead of the ensemble of social conditions and admin-istrative possibilities. Aspirations to 'absolute' monarchy were thwarted by the realities of power.

A quasi-feudal agricultural economy limited the tax base and also, therefore, limited the physical administrative resources of states. Most states in the period 1500–1700 were fiscally fragile, including the Spain of Philip II (who, despite the gold of America, was twice forced to declare himself bankrupt).[13] Similarly, France faced periodic fiscal crises and resorted to desperate measures like the profligate sale of offices. Had there been an early-modern Standard and Poor, it would have rated the paper of all states except Holland at below junk grade. States, there-fore, sought to minimize the financial risks of war and offload costs on to others. Most army units were raised by military entrepreneurs under contract to the state. States relied on soldiers buying their own food out of their wages and arranged for private contractors to supply the armies. It was often the case that the contractors failed to supply in ade-quate quantities or at acceptable prices. The state also often neglected to advance the money for the soldiers' wages. They were then forced to live on expensive credit. Even the relatively well-organized Spanish Army in the Netherlands experienced mutinies over intolerable arrears of pay.[14] The seventeenth century was the heyday of privatization and was well used to market failure thwarting political objectives.

The effect of these constraints was to force states, once they entered into combat, to seek to live at the enemy's expense. This could be dif-ficult. By the early seventeenth century northern Italy, the Netherlands and the northern French borderlands were all well fortified.[15] Dense fortified belts of towns limited mobility and forced large numbers of troops to remain in prolonged sieges. In the areas of greatest conflict, fortifications came to form a network of defended places offering a degree of mutual support and compelling the attacker to invest in or mask more than one place. Huge numbers of troops were employed as navvies digging earthworks. These networks show how space is qualitatively organized and forms distinctive patterns. Thus, for example, the four fortified towns of the 'Quadrilateral' in the Po Valley provided mutual support and sufficient land in the area bounded by them to feed a garrison that could not be defeated. This remained a crucial part of Austrian rule in Italy until the 1860s.

The typical way of living at the enemy's expense was called the 'contributions system'.[16] This was widespread throughout Europe, but became systematized in Germany during the Thirty Years War (1618–48). Armies organized requisitions and billeting, imposing a number of soldiers on each household, with an obligation to feed them on pain of severe penalties. If the soldiers merely marched through an area and were not too numerous, this system just about worked. But they had to keep moving and couldn't go back, because if they did both they and the civilians would starve. Thus Gustavus Adolphus was forced to lead the Swedish Army into Bavaria after the victory at Breitenfeld in 1631, rather than push on to Vienna and a decisive blow against the Imperialist forces. He went there because that was the only place where he could hope to feed his troops. Movements of armies were therefore often dictated by socio-spatial constraints, rather than by military considerations.

A prolonged siege tended to strip an area bare, as did the repeated marching and counter-marching of rival armies. Armies used scorched earth tactics as a means of undermining their enemy's capacity to levy contributions. When warfare was prolonged, as in the Thirty Years War, the consequence was a broken-backed form of war in which armies scattered to live off the countryside. As a result the rural economy was driven into a downward spiral by repeated forced contributions from all sides. Warfare degenerated into little more than competitive banditry. Armies at the end of the war averaged 10–15,000, no larger than in the 1400s.

Central to the limits to transport and provisioning was the problem of fodder.[17] Armies had large baggage trains: they were towns on the move, and thus they needed sizeable numbers of animals. To supply grain for bread and as a supplemental animal feed from magazines was only possible within the state's borders, and to a lesser extent by buying supplies from contractors along the line of march. The problem of organizing fodder supply from rear bases was almost insoluble: it had to be obtained locally. It was impossible to carry enough fodder by animal transport. At a short distance from base any supply column would start to use the load it carried and would quickly consume it. Thus, even when well-organized armies did use magazines, they were still forced to forage for fodder, which was by far the bulkiest item in their essential provisions. The problem of fodder reinforced the slow movement of armies brought about by bad roads. Soldiers had to feed their horses and cattle as they went, not over-taxing them. Even in the twentieth century fodder remained a central problem for armies. In the 1920s it was the largest single item after wages in the British Army's budget. Fodder consumed much of the railway capacity supporting the German Army in Russia in the Second World War. As we shall see, despite its *Blitzkrieg* image, about 80 per cent of the local transport of the army relied on horses.[18]

We will now look at how early-modern army organization and supply worked, taking examples from the three most effective military machines of the period: the Ottomans, the Spaniards and the Swedes.

The Ottomans

We have already seen the central role of the moving frontier in the formation of the Ottoman Empire and why expansion was crucial for its finances. By the mid-sixteenth century the Ottoman Empire extended from Baghdad (1,400 miles from Constantinople) to Belgrade (600 miles from the capital). Modern historians and political scientists have read backwards from Ottoman failure, which became marked in the late eighteenth century (although the empire survived into the twentieth century). However, by fifteenth- or sixteenth-century European standards, the Ottomans had an effective state machine and army commissariat.[19] The Ottoman Army was a composite force. A large part of it derived from the Ottomans' steppe inheritance. In the sixteenth century it still consisted mostly of cavalry, horse archers supported by the quasi-feudal tenures of the *timar* system. This cavalry and the Tartar auxiliaries used powerful composite bows like the Mongols had done. In peacetime the cavalry lived on its fiefs and was fed by them. It was mobilized for war either in the Balkans or the East from those closest to the theatre of war. The other part of the army consisted of an efficient siege train with modern cannon and a force of infantry with firearms, the *Janissaries* (recruited from Christian conscript children who were raised as Muslims). Finally there was a body of six elite cavalry regiments, the *Sipahis*. This combination of hard-hitting cavalry and a capacity for siege warfare exactly reproduced the military recipe that had made the Mongols world conquerors, but also linked it to a more effective and durable form of state. It was lucky for Europe that the new fortifications were even harder to besiege.

The Ottomans used strategic magazines to provide the starting points for their campaigns. On campaign they also relied on regular wages for the *Janissaries* and payments to merchants to create market places in the theatre of operations for the army. The Ottomans supplemented these regular sources of supply from within the empire with destructive raiding across the frontier and requisitioning from their enemies. These practices served both to weaken their foes and to provide resources for the campaign. We have seen that until the end of the sixteenth century Ottoman rule was accepted by its subjects, including Christians. Imperial expansion meant that the resources of the state were growing. Thus taxes were normally not excessive and soldiers paid civilians within the empire for their food. This contrasted with the experience in Western Europe, where Christian rulers commonly used corrupt tax farmers who were rapacious for revenue and also seized contributions for the military.

In both the Balkans and the East, transport and provisioning of the Ottoman Armies was largely dependent on water routes, in the former case by sea from Constantinople and then up the Danube to Belgrade, and, in the latter, down the Tigris to Baghdad. The empire was viable militarily because it could use these two river systems to tie it together: it was built around the Aegean and Black Seas and rivers. This may seem paradoxical for a power that had risen on the basis of steppe cavalry, but then by the late fifteenth century the Sublime Porte had metamorphosed into a very different form of state, a real competitor to its European rivals. Ottoman armies were better supplied than their European opponents until well into the 1600s. In 1683 they might have taken Vienna, had they not been delayed in starting by appalling weather. Their problem in that campaign was that, behind their fast-moving screen of cavalry raiders, their siege train moved no faster than anybody else's did.

They did have one major advantage that was a legacy from the steppe: the camel. These animals could carry up to 250 kg, a bigger load than a packhorse. Camels were tougher than horses, able to cope with inferior grazing and more capable of moving over rough terrain. The roads of the empire were appalling or non-existent. Camels were crucial to the supply train and the army depended on camel herds and drivers recruited from the nomadic hinterland of the empire. Halil Inalcik goes so far as to claim that, 'The Ottoman army was able to move from the Euphrates to the Danube in one season with its heavy equipment and arms' largely because of the camel.[20]

The Spanish road

Spain had the best-organized and most competent European army in the sixteenth century. It had successfully fought a protracted war off and on from 1495–1559 against France in Italy. It had played a major role in containing the Ottomans in the Mediterranean and in North Africa. It was forced to shift its focus northwards in the 1560s with the revolt of the provinces in the Netherlands. During the long Eighty Years War with the Dutch, the Spaniards had to support and reinforce large forces in the Netherlands.[21] France was either hostile or consumed in civil war. The option of reinforcement by sea ended once the 'Sea Beggars' blockaded Antwerp, and it became quite impossible once war started with England. The solution was an overland supply route from Italy along the borders of France into the Hapsburg Netherlands. The route was across a patchwork of Hapsburg or friendly territories. Troops proceeded mostly in manageable groups, not large armies, and at a modest pace. This meant that supplies could be purchased in advance and organized to meet the marchers at each stage. 'Road' is a misnomer. The 'map' provided for commanders shows how rudimentary the infrastructure was. The roads were simply tracks or pathways and the route could be used only in the summer. The system worked. It lasted a long time and maintained the force levels of the Army of Flanders.

The Swedish military machine

Sweden was a small and relatively poor country, yet in the seventeenth century it became a great power.[22] It defeated Denmark and created a Baltic empire stretching to Poland. It intervened in the Thirty Years War in 1630 and remained the core military power on the Protestant side until the Peace of Westphalia. Sweden maintained a large force at low cost because of its highly organized conscription system (*indelningsverk*). Every commune in Sweden was required to supply an annual draft to either the army or, in the case of coastal districts, the navy.[23] Sweden had defeated the Danes and the Hanseatic League at sea and thus controlled the Baltic. It was able to use the sea as interior lines of communication from the Sound to the German coast to the Gulf of Finland. Once landed on the other shore, the army was expected to fend for itself. It was funded by subsidies from the Protestant powers in Germany and by the contributions system. Although tactically effective, the army was too small to conquer Catholic Germany in a knockout blow. What Gustavus's intervention did was to check the Imperialist bid for domination that began in 1628 and ensure the division of the German lands into separate confessional powers.[24] The army was also wholly dependent on local supplies and thus began to behave exactly like all the other parties to the conflict. Later, campaigning in Poland and against Russia, the logistic fragility of the Swedes began to tell against them and could not be compensated for by their tactical competence.[25]

Railways and Rifles

Five years can sometimes make a huge difference. During the Crimean War of 1854–5, the British and French sought to strike at Russia by besieging the Black Sea fortress of Sevastopol. The British Army suffered horribly from hunger and cold even though they were but a short distance from the sea with supplies piling up at the port of Balaclava. A short stretch of railway for horse-drawn wagons eventually helped to solve their problems. The plight of the Russians was far worse. Russian reinforcements had to march south through the Ukraine to the Crimea. Tens of thousands died of exhaustion, hunger and illness in the course of the journey, far more than perished in the fighting. In 1859, during the war between Austria and France, large numbers of French troops were rapidly moved to the battlefields in Italy by railway. It was only *after* they reached the theatre of war that the rapid French mobilization showed the chaos of their supply arrangements, so much so that the sufferings of the wounded after the Battle of Solferino moved Henri Dunant to found the Red Cross.

Until the mid-nineteenth century armies were limited to the walking pace of men and horses respectively, around 2–4 mph. Information could travel a little faster by relays of horses and, during the Napoleonic Wars, by mechanical telegraph lines.[26] The Industrial Revolution transformed these conditions at roughly the same time with railways and the electric telegraph. Railways made possible more rapid movement over long distances. This was well below the theoretical speed of locomotives and certainly no more than 10 mph for military freight trains. Nevertheless, this at least trebled the speed of movement, greatly increased the distance over which it could be sustained, and ensured that men and horses did not arrive exhausted in the combat zone. Railways cracked the problem of long-distance movement and supply that animal transport could not solve. Coal was a far more efficient fuel than fodder: a train could pull a larger load than hundreds of animal carts. Telegraphs enabled information to travel very quickly. Suitably managed, they could relay messages hundreds of miles in minutes and in considerable volumes. They were essential to coordinate railway movements. Without them, railways were not a network, but a disconnected series of local lines.

Railways had a great advantage in that they were dual-use technologies. They expanded rapidly because of their immense benefit to the civilian economy, and were mainly driven by private investment. The railway boom in the 1840s in Britain makes the recent dotcom and tech stocks bubble in the USA seem modest by comparison. In most continental countries railways were public or part-public assets, and the routing and scale of lines was dictated by military considerations. Even so, the scale of railway construction was inconceivable without the systems being able to benefit from civilian revenue. By 1850 railways were widespread on both sides of the Atlantic and telegraph lines were spreading too: by then there were 2,000 miles of wire in America. In 1858 the first transatlantic cable was laid, and in 1870 the first cable to the Far East. Communication by long-distance and intercontinental cables was expensive, but one could send a priority message to India in hours rather than months. Until the advent of the telegraph, commanders could get news no quicker than Julius Caesar. This gave generals and politicians the possibility of strategic direction of long-distance operations for the first time.[27]

Mass mobilization was invented before the railway. It had political – rather than technological – conditions. Essentially, it required governments with the legitimacy and administrative competence to call up a portion of each year's cohort of young men. Sweden had been able to do this in the seventeenth century, but on a modest scale because of the demands of farm labour. Even then the wars with Poland and Russia in the late seventeenth and early eighteenth centuries had all but bled the country dry. The French were able to do this on a larger scale after the Revolution, both because they had a big population of some 30 millions and because of the political energies released by the Revolution.[28] The *levée en masse* provided hundreds of thousands – rather than tens of thousands – of conscripts. It was only possible because the new government enjoyed a power to coerce which was inconceivable in so-called 'absolutist' dynastic states.

Mass conscription was only gradually accepted in most of Europe in the second half the nineteenth century. The French abandoned it after 1815, and did not return to general conscription until after the defeat of their professional army in 1871. By the first decade of the twentieth century the French were relying on near universal conscription, and before 1914 they introduced three-year service to compensate for their smaller population in comparison with Germany. Russia could take only a small portion of its vast manpower through annual selective conscription. The German Empire after 1871 failed to make full use of the available population or its trained reserves, as the Chief of the General Staff, Count Schlieffen, complained in 1905. Wilhelmine Germany was tax averse and also saddled with the bill for large-scale naval expansion. Nevertheless, by 1914 all the continental Great Powers had 'million man armies'. The basis for such armies was the mobilization of reserves who had served as conscripts. Without railways, these huge forces would have been pointless since they could not be conveyed to the frontier or fed once committed to battle. The military participation ratio rose greatly, but not because of a huge shift of workers out of agriculture in most European countries. Rather, it was accepted that mass mobilization would paralyse the civilian economy (thus France even mobilized munitions factory workers in 1914), but assumed that wars would be of short duration (of no more than a few months like the campaigns of German unification in 1866 and 1870–1).

Railways and mass armies created the necessity of mobilization planning.[29] Without efficient central management and meticulous scheduling, railway movements would descend into chaos on mobilization. While the railways had huge advantages in terms of both volume and speed, they imposed a certain rigidity on movements that was intrinsic to them and different from the old constraints of the premodern era. Railways required the creation of professional general staffs and the railway sections of such staffs became powerful, telling generals and politicians what could and could not be done. The German General Staff became centred on its railway movements section and dependent upon it.[30] By the time of Schlieffen, operational planning had become so sophisticated that it aimed to compensate for the inherent rigidities of railway timetables and movements and thus to maximize mobilization speed and numbers. Once the army was mobilized, Schlieffen and his successor, Moltke, intended to compensate for Germany's numerical inferiority to the Entente by shifting forces rapidly by rail within and between fronts to achieve local superiority. Initial mobilization was another matter. Once one state began to mobilize, all the others had to follow suit or risk being outnumbered in the initial battles. Thus Russia's decision to mobilize in 1914 was in effect committing the continent to war. Germany could then only have averted war by taking huge risks, given its numerical inferiority. Germany could not improvise and mobilize against Russia alone: this was not just because of the rigidity of railway planning, but also because the French were unlikely to abandon their key ally. Germany had to give priority to the planned mobilization against France and to an all-out attack in the West.

The industrial revolution that created the railway also led to a revolution in weapons technology.[31] In the 1840s armies still used muskets that differed little from those of the wars of Louis XIV. By the 1870s all armies had rifled breech-loaders that could fire several times faster and ten times further. In the seventeenth century armies had adopted linear tactics and close-order drill to maximize the firepower of the old muskets. Soldiers fought shoulder to shoulder at ranges of about 100 metres. Many of the styles and ceremonies of modern military life still derive from this period. The later nineteenth century was a period of difficult and confused evolution of spatial tactics to cope with the new firepower. A loose firing line or a swarm of skirmishers were the logical outcomes of the new weapons: both minimized the exposure of troops to fire and maximized fire effect. However, either tactic made it difficult to control or direct fire and almost impossible to deliver attacks with coordinated shock effect. Nineteenth-century tactical theorists were not imbeciles; they knew how deadly the new weapons were. Their problems were simple: uncontrolled firing could blast off the available supply of ammunition to little effect in a few minutes, and no position could be taken from long range. Troops had to cross several hundred metres of ground swept by fire before they could close with the enemy. No army solved this problem; most accepted that the eventual mass attacks on the enemy's line were just going to have to be very costly.[32]

The Industrial Revolution created new weapons, and applied management created the means to mass-produce them in the standardized form necessary for the logistics of the new armies. The 'American System of Manufactures' involved the use of standardized and interchangeable parts made by machine tools and quality-checked by accurate gauges.[33] New tools such as milling machines substituted for the handwork of artisans. This standardized mass production made possible huge volumes of rifles that were virtually alike and could accept the same ammunition. The new system had been created by a long process of experimentation by military engineers at the Springfield arsenal between the 1820s and the 1850s. It was not initially directed towards mass production but to standardization, and thus to the simplicity of supply and repair on the battlefield. It was taken up by civilian manufacturers like Colt for revolvers and Singer for sewing machines, and used to supply the large American home market. It was then imported by European arsenals to turn out weapons for the newly forming mass armies.

These social and technical innovations – railways, telegraphs, conscription, and rifles – came together in the relatively short period of about thirty years between 1850 and 1880. Unknown to most planners and theorists, although there were percipient exceptions, the conditions had been created not for a short decisive war but for a protracted war of attrition that would test the morale and productive capacity of whole societies.

It is interesting to note how these technical and social developments were prefigured in *ancien régime* and revolutionary France. First came the mechanical telegraph, developed to a high standard of efficiency by the Chappe brothers in the 1790s.[34] This used a chequer board system, where open and closed squares stood for letters. The system could be used at night with lights: only dense fog defeated it. During Napoleon's reign several lines were built and they could convey information rapidly to Paris via repeating stations. A different arrangement linked Portsmouth and London. The brothers developed their system because of the earlier failure of experiments to transmit information by means of electricity. Second, standardization was a project transferred to America from France. After the Seven Years War (1756–63) Gribeauval sought to rationalize the bore sizes and component parts of the carriages of French cannon. Following this, the French undertook a contested and only partially successful programme to standardize the parts of the model 1777 musket.[35] It was the demands of urgent mass production during the revolutionary wars that led to the abandonment of the system and the large-scale putting out of musket production to contractors and artisan methods. In the 1790s the French could not achieve standardization and mass production together with the techniques and the administrative system available. Lastly, as we have seen, Carnot introduced conscription in the crisis of the Austrian and Prussian invasion. Thus technologies have complex histories and times when their maturation and widespread diffusion is possible, whereas at other times extensive R & D and determined inventiveness produce products that existing institutions and manufacturing processes cannot assimilate.

War generally accelerates the use of technologies that are coming to maturity. There are two key spatial tendencies that are evident early on in the process of the adaptation of the industrial revolution to war:

1 War comes to revolve around communications: lines of advance are dictated by railway lines and rail hubs become central objectives to defend or to seize;
2 The 'empty battlefield', that is, a zone of fire that cannot be crossed without massive casualties: left to themselves troops take cover and fight from a distance. The old battlefield tactics of both the muscle power and the gunpowder eras relied on soldiers fighting in close order, but where this was adopted in the face of modern weapons it became suicidal.

These tendencies are evident in the first modern war, the American Civil War of 1861–65. The US rail system was built for commercial reasons; it thus provided a classic example without preconceived military planning of the logic of railway warfare. The outcome of the war against the South turned on the possession of major railway junctions and control of the Mississippi River. The Mississippi is like a single great rail line, and the steamboats that plied the river were the crucial supply line of the Confederacy. The West was the key to the Confederacy: it was vital to the supply of its manpower and food-stuffs. The two parts of the Confederacy could be severed by the seizure of a few key communication points. First, Federal forces took Cairo at the junction with the Ohio River, then Forts Donelson on the Cumberland and Henry on the Tennessee. After this Vicksburg on the Mississippi was besieged and taken. This chopped the Confederacy in two and cut off a great deal of the food supplies from the front in northern Virginia. The seizure and cutting of the railheads at Chattanooga, Atlanta and Macon further segmented Confederate ter-ritory and isolated the Carolinas and Virginia. In essence, the Federal forces arrived almost by accident at a strategy that broke up their opponents, one far more effective than the crude and costly sallies towards the Confederate capital, Richmond, in the East.

The battlefields in the East were surprisingly modern, although few lessons were drawn from this in Europe. Masses of soldiers were crammed into a relatively small area. Union armies became large con-script forces. Defence was dominant, with the widespread use of entrenchments and field fortifications. Neither side had modern breech-loaders, but both had deadly Minié rifles that could fire perhaps three times a minute out to a practical maximum range of 1,000 metres. Thus at Gettysburg in 1863 Pickett's division of about 12,000 men was destroyed in mass charges against the Union lines. This was the experience of Colonel Lyman:

> I had taken part in two great battles and heard the bullets whistle both days, and yet I had *scarcely seen a rebel save* killed, wounded or prisoners! I remem-ber how even line officers, who were at the battle of Chancellorsville said: 'Why, we never saw any Rebels where we were; only smoke and bushes, and lots of our men tumbling about.'[36]

Deadlock

The advantages of railways ended at the railhead. Then armies returned to their pre-industrial limitations. Men and horses moved no faster in the early twentieth century than the Roman legions could. At best, enemy rail networks could be brought into service; at worst, new lines had to be laid. This took time. The German operations in 1914 were aimed at destroying the offensive power of the French Army quickly. Then the Germans would turn with a large portion of the forces from the West against Russia. It was assumed in German planning that the Russians could not overrun the small local defensive forces in East Prussia inside the six weeks notionally allowed to defeat the French and move east. In fact, Russian mobilization proved more efficient and their railway network was able to concentrate large forces against eastern Germany more quickly than expected. However, what really disrupted the campaign plan was that the German command in East Prussia panicked. This upset the calculations on which the advance of the German right wing through Belgium was based. Supplies were not the real problem in causing the advance into France to fail. Railways in Belgium were brought into service and by and large the troops were adequately fed. More serious were the ambitious timetables for advancing by foot march into France. Despite sustained efforts that left the spearheads exhausted, the German right wing failed to outflank the French Armies in Lorraine and thus to roll up the French Army against its own line of fortresses from the rear. Instead, the encircling movement failed, a gap opened between the two right-wing German Armies, and the German advance was checked by the redeployment of French forces on the Marne.[37]

The result of the failure of this knockout blow was a stalemate that led to an almost static four-year war of attrition. The Western Front in 1914–18 resembled northern Virginia during the American Civil War. Millions of men were fed into a limited space. Vast armies were sustained by industrial mass production and supplied by railways. Firepower and the defence dominated: this fact was not due to machine guns, but had been true in some form or another since the gunpowder revolution of the early sixteenth century. Strongly manned linear entrenchments, reinforced by barbed wire and combined with modern weapons, were all but impregnable. In chapter 10 we shall examine the architectural and spatial aspects of the trench systems in more detail.

Here the point to make is that modernity all but ended once one entered the communications trenches leading to the front. Then one returned to the physical conditions of a seventeenth-century siege, but with the firepower and robust supply systems that made the ordeal both far worse and more sustained. Communication and command reverted to early modern conditions inside the trench system. Railways terminated some miles behind the line. Telegraphs ended at brigade headquarters and field telephones at frontline battalion or company command posts. Once troops attacked across the trench line, or when heavy bombardment cut the telephone wires leading to the rear, armies were beyond control.[38] Frontline troops had then to fight a series of unconnected local battles, and could communicate only by runners with written messages. Sophisticated higher-level control based on up-to-date intelligence was impossible. Armies became disorganized hordes once sent forward from the trench line. Command could only be exercised prior to action. It was inevitably centralized and hierarchical and took the form of detailed planning of operations. To begin with, such operations had to be rigidly orchestrated to ensure coordination between the different attacking units and to synchronize the movements of the infantry with the artillery barrage. Once the attack commenced, senior officers could do little but sit and wait.[39]

This tendency towards disorganization in attack was made worse by the fact that all the mass armies threatened to degenerate into a militia, as the core of experienced junior officers and NCOs was killed or diluted. Tactics had to be adapted to the level of training of raw recruits. The British suffered most from this tendency since their small professional army was all but wiped out by 1915. In its place was a large mass of ill-trained civilian volunteers. The Germans were most successful at avoiding this dilution. They gradually realized the futility of rigid linear attacks on trench lines and of massive prior bombardments. Their high command accepted that control in detail from above was impossible, and indeed that attempting such control prevented troops from achieving and exploiting local breakthroughs. Initiative was devolved to the commanders of specialist assault units. These storm troopers were trained to exploit local success and to penetrate the enemy's front wherever they could, without regard to timetables or to linear cohesion. The very disorder and de-centralization of the German tactics undermined linear defence systems, leading to mass panic and retreat as advanced assault units infiltrated well behind the front.

The spring offensive of 1918 against the British used these tactics with spectacular success. However, the problem was that the defence was still dominant, once it could be reorganized. When the British regrouped and established a defensive front they had the advantage that they were falling back on their supply lines, whereas the Germans had to bring their supplies forward over the broken ground of the old front. Indeed, the underfed German troops slackened their pace because they found large British supply depots and stopped to eat their fill. By 1918 the British were capable of sophisticated tactics and the integration of infantry and artillery too.[40] The Allied counter-attack was extremely successful and drove the Germans back to and beyond their original start lines. Even so, the Germans had the option of retreating to strong prepared positions in the rear, the so-called

Hindenburg Line. This line was organized around a network of mutually supporting strongpoints rather than a rigid linear system. It might have been held, forcing the Allies to mount a new offensive in 1919, were not the German Armies in a state of advanced decay.

An economic and political crisis behind the German front produced a change of government, and the interim regime accepted Hindenburg's request to seek an armistice. The war had been won on the basis of attrition: mass slaughter on the battlefields, the competition to mobilize society and production behind the front for total war, and rival strategies of weakening the enemy through blockade (on the Allied side by conventional search and seizure, on the German by submarine warfare). In the last instance, it was attrition, hunger and the collapse of civilian morale that ended the war. The central powers were exhausted; they also had to face the prospect of the arrival of vast fresh American Armies supplied by a fully mobilized US industry. By 1918 the Germans had knocked out the Russians and driven the French Army to semi-collapse in a series of debilitating mutinies in 1917. The central powers had done this at huge cost, and they had no reserves. An exhausted German Army would have to face a massive offensive alone in 1919, and behind the front was a hungry and rebellious people tired of the war.[41]

The Limitations of Motorized War

If the First World War showed the limitations of mass armies based on railway mobilization and supply, vehicles incorporating the internal combustion engine appeared to provide liberation from both the tyranny of fixed lines and the gap between the railhead and the front. In 1914 motor vehicles were about twenty years old and aircraft just ten years old. The war played a major part in the rapid development and maturing of both technologies. Motor vehicles were used extensively in mostly subsidiary roles in the First World War. In 1914 French reinforcements were rushed to the Marne in Paris taxicabs. London omnibuses and motor trucks moved British troops from the railhead to the front. Tanks were extensively, if indecisively, used in combat by the British and French. In the aftermath of the war, the British theorist J. F. C. Fuller speculated on the formation of an all-mechanized army based on tank spearheads.[42] Fuller envisaged such forces cutting through the frontal defences and then fanning out in the rear to capture command centres and supply bases, decapitating the enemy. Mechanized forces would be free of the limitations of both railways and roads: they would act like a land navy, able to roam at will across the enemy's territory.

Aircraft had also been extensively used during 1914–18, both as an adjunct to the land fighting and to a limited extent for bombing civilian targets. The post-war theorists of air power likewise modelled their tactics on the analogy with the ocean as a great common. Giulio Douhet and Billy Mitchell saw aircraft flying over the deadlocked battlefronts to bombard the enemy rear.[43] Aircraft would achieve quickly what attrition and blockade had done slowly and with mass suffering: destroy industrial output and civilian morale and thus the enemy's capacity to fight. Bombing could disrupt production, but more importantly, as Douhet saw it, it would provoke mass panic and drive civilians to force their rulers to make peace. Douhet's book was called *Command of the Air*, a deliberate reference to Mahan.[44] Air power was more effective than sea power. It could exploit the less dense ocean of the air to act directly by raining bombs on the whole of the enemy's territory. It was not forced to stop at the coast as sea power was, confined in its action against enemy territory to blockade and to landing invasion forces.

Such new ideas were rapidly exploited. Britain created an experimental independent mechanized force in the late 1920s. This early advantage was subsequently wasted. This is usually seen as the result of a reactionary General Staff. However, the army came bottom for funds, after the air force and the navy, at a time of economic depression and financial constraint. What limited money there was tended to be eaten up by policing the empire. In the short term, this was a rational allocation of resources, particularly as Britain had no intention of becoming involved in offensive operations in Europe. Technological backwardness was by no means intrinsic to British defence policy. The RAF as created by Trenchard was conceived as an independent service committed to strategic bombing. Hitler's rise to power enabled the extensive clandestine experiments by the *Wehrmacht* with tanks and bombers in the 1920s to become the offensive core of the Nazi war machine. Mussolini created a large bomber force in an attempt to realize Douhet's ideas. The US Army Air Force sought to defend the continental USA by long-range bombers – the first practical example of which in the 1930s was the famous Flying Fortress.

In practice all these ideas were vastly in advance of both economic and technological realities. No air force was capable of true strategic bombing when the war began in 1939.[45] No major army was fully motorized in 1939, only the very small British and US Armies. In 1940 the American Army was smaller than that of Romania. However, only the US civilian motor industry was large enough that, once mobilized for war, it could create a genuine mass mechanized army. The German industry was much smaller and split into many firms, most of which produced specialist vehicles in low volumes. Thus the German Army in 1939 had a mechanized spearhead, but it was still mainly a 1918-style infantry force. The Nazi forces that invaded Russia in 1941 relied on railways for strategic mobility and on horse transport for the infantry divisions that made up some 75 per cent of its order of battle. In fact, mechanized forces were not like land navies. Trucks needed proper roads. Even tanks could not operate in deep mud or in extreme cold. Hence the German attack in 1941 was slowed by a late thaw, then heavy autumn rains, and stalled by the very severe winter of 1941–2. The old pre-modern problems of mud and fodder supplies remained. Railways and motor trucks mitigated them but could not solve them. Russia was still a backward country, and the German Army had mostly not left the nineteenth century.[46]

The Soviet forces did not just benefit from the weather and the vast spaces of Russia that absorbed the German attacks. The Russians had the advantage of plentiful oil supplies from the Caspian. In contrast, the Nazis had only the small Romanian fields and also their limited-capacity synthetic oil plants. Moreover, the Soviets received vast amounts of American aid, and in particular some tens of thousands of modern trucks. The army that advanced so rapidly to Berlin was if anything more motorized than their opponents. Even in 1944 the retreating Nazi Army was still heavily dependent on horses and on a ramshackle fleet of old and ill-assorted vehicles looted from all over Europe.

Even the most advanced mechanized armies faced a modern version of the fodder crisis. Trucks were not as fuel-efficient in moving large volumes of goods as railways. At a certain point of distance from base, diminishing returns set in as the fleet of trucks had to carry a higher and higher proportion of fuel to a dwindling payload. In the rapid advance beyond Paris in 1944, the US Armies repeatedly ground to a halt for want of fuel. To supply Patton's advance into Germany, thousands of trucks were diverted to rushing supplies to the front via two dedicated routes, one up and one down. Even then supplies were exiguous and only part of the Allied Armies could advance quickly at any one time.[47] Allied operations were in large part dictated by logistics, in particular the need to capture and open the port of Antwerp. Industrialization thus imposed its own distinctive constraints on supply. Allied mechanized divisions used thousands of tons of supplies a day. German divisions consumed far less, but they were smaller and less able to sustain intensive operations from their own resources.

Only in 1944 did British and American strategic bombing become fully effective, that is, able to destroy cities and to disrupt communications. It was very costly, both in the proportion of national output diverted to it and in losses of highly skilled manpower: nearly 50,000 British airmen died in the bomber offensive against Germany.[48] Allied air power became more effective as the war went on, whereas Nazi conventional bombing forces withered. The Luftwaffe's bombers were replaced in conventional aircraft output by fighters for the defence of the *Reich*. They were also displaced by a vast investment in building 'revenge weapons', the V1 and V2. The V2 was the first real ballistic missile.[49] It escaped all the spatial constraints on aircraft and all possibility of defence in following a ballistic trajectory to its target. It was, however, an expensive and inaccurate way of delivering a ton of explosive, carrying a fraction of a heavy bomber's payload on a single mission, whereas the latter might manage up to twenty-five missions. It could not thus alter the outcome of the war. Even saturation attacks on London could not seriously damage the Allies' capacity to wage war. At worst, London could be evacuated. The V2 could not hit small targets like industrial plants or loading docks. The Nazis did have two weapons that, if developed quickly enough and used appropriately, could have prolonged the war. Both could have been available in large numbers in 1944 for the cost of the V2 programme. The Me262 jet fighter could have cleared the skies of Allied bombers by day. The Type XXI submarine could have seriously threatened the transatlantic shipping on which the Western Allies' military power depended. Both were wasted by a regime mired in irrationality and conflicting purposes.

The Americans were the first real beneficiaries of the V2's huge R & D effort. They captured the key production facility, *Mittelwerke*, and looted it. They also acquired Werner von Braun and his design team. At the time when the Nazis squandered huge resources on a plethora of 'wonder weapons' that were either useless or too late, the US spent $2 billion in contemporary values on developing the atomic bomb. By 1945 the bomb was not essential to Allied victory. It had been developed to forestall and deter a Nazi bomb that had come to nothing. Atomic bombs cut the cost of destruction, by greatly reducing the number of planes needed to destroy a city. The conventional Tokyo raid of 9 March 1945 killed more victims than either of the two atomic bombs which were dropped. The difference was that three planes raided Hiroshima, only one of which carried the bomb, whereas 279 attacked Tokyo.[50] Strategic bombers and atomic bombs seemed to offer the prospect of world power on the cheap for the USA, that is, until the Soviets developed the atomic bomb in 1949. It was quickly found that the deterrence of a rival atomic power required the credible threat of wholesale retaliatory destruction in the face of an attack. This meant effective rapid-response attacks against hundreds of Soviet targets: the necessity for hundreds of strategic bombers had resurfaced, and with it a huge defence budget. The answer to this escalating cost was thermonuclear warheads and vastly improved versions of the V2. The ballistic missile combined with atomic weapons was a worthwhile weapons system. It could not be stopped, it was cheaper to maintain than a huge bomber fleet, and it was also harder to destroy on the ground, ensuring the threat to the enemy of destruction in return should they strike first. Ballistic missiles had removed the old physical and spatial constraints on the projection of force. The problem was that they had rendered war pursued with these means impossible to fight. The use of these weapons could achieve no possible objective that a peacetime state might choose to pursue. Such weapons served only one purpose: to deter the enemy from using them. Thus their non-use was the sole rational measure of their utility.[51]

The City as a Battleground

In 1945 cities were the main targets for the most destructive weapons of modern war. In the 1950s and 1960s there were sustained but ultimately futile attempts to respond to this with civil defence and shelter-building, and with strategies of suburbanization and industrial dispersal to minimize concentrated targets. As the key hubs of an industrial society, large urban centres were, along with certain major raw materials, the foundations of military power. The H bomb rendered the protection of civilian urban assets all but impossible. As we shall see in chapters 9 and 10, cities were being extensively fortified until the late nineteenth centuries. Antwerp and Copenhagen offer excellent late examples of this attempt to carry the classic fortified 'defence of places' into the industrial age.[52] The First World War revealed the impossibility of formal external defensive fortifications for cities.

However, the decline in city fortification which began in the nineteenth century did not stop cities from becoming battlegrounds. Dense built environments offered a form of defence in themselves. Streets became killing grounds when troops were stopped by barricades and cut down by enfilading fire from surrounding buildings. Extensive areas of ruined buildings became labyrinths in which the defenders could take cover in cellars. The larger the city, the bigger the obstacle it became when it was ruined, and the less effective mechanized vehicles could be within it. Bombing and shelling a city in order to take it merely increases the chaos, gives the defenders plenty of shelter, and provides plenty of cover from which to use simple weapons like

Molotov cocktails against armoured vehicles. Ruins are great equalizers, and the more sophisticated the army, the harder it would be to maintain the advantage in street fighting in a large city.[53]

The first example of the deliberate choice of the city as a battleground, rather than as the object of a formal siege, is revolutionary warfare. Insurrectionaries aim to seize the capital and other key urban centres. Either they succeed with an armed *coup d'état*, or they build barricades to impede the advance of the armed forces of the regime and turn their resistance into propaganda by deed.[54] In pre-industrial or semi-developed countries, this strategy of seizing power in the capital could be effective. Paris was the key to France in the late eighteenth century, and St Petersburg and Moscow to Russia in 1917. In an absolutist state, the key administrative and social resources were concentrated in the capital. In general, however, insurrection at the centre could only work as a political strategy in the context of deep divisions within the ruling elite and in the armed forces.[55] Where this happened, in France in 1789 and in Russia in 1917, then a radical change of regime was possible as a consequence of the initial seizure of power. Many nobles and *haut bourgeois* in France supported political change, and saw the storming of the Bastille and the march to Versailles as opportunities to further their own agendas. In Russia the army, the bulwark of the old regime, was decomposing as a result of the war and the peasantry were largely unwilling to rally to the Tsar or the Provisional Government. Where this process of elite fracture and military disorder did not occur, then army and society beyond the capital generally rallied to the established order. In 1848 came the 'year of the barricades', with revolutions in Austria, France, Germany, Italy and Hungary. In each case the revolutions failed and troops reoccupied capitals like Paris and Vienna to suppress the revolts.

The barricade as a tactic only makes sense in a political context. Revolutions mostly failed in the nineteenth century. In an age of romantic radical politics and conservative reaction, the reactionaries usually won, with the spectacular exception to this rule being Garibaldi's landing in Sicily in 1860. The Commune of Paris in 1871 failed, and not because of Baron Haussmann.[56] His rebuilding of Paris was primarily an exercise in property development rather than opening up the streets to artillery fire. The Communards easily took the city. The Commune failed because of political isolation of the city.

What classic insurrectionary politics did was to keep the myth of the efficacy of streetfighting alive until such tactics really did become militarily consequential. Urban guerrilla tactics became part of mainstream warfare in 1936 with the siege of Madrid by the Nationalists. Sieges did not end because cities had ceased to be formally fortified.

The resistance of cities to besieging forces became at once a way of slowing down and damaging enemy armies, and a source of potent political myths. Stalingrad really did consume a large part of the German forces in southern Russia.[57] Tanks and Panzergrenadiers were misused in streetfighting, where the battle degenerated into house-to-house fighting. It also allowed the construction of a (mostly true) story of heroic resistance by workers' militias in defence of their factories. Likewise, the Warsaw Uprising and the defence of the Warsaw Ghetto, while both defeated, created myths to sustain Polish and Jewish nationalism.

Hitler in turn became so enamoured of this strategy of resistance in cities that he nominated city after city as 'fortresses'. The first major example of this tactic was the Channel Ports, with the aim being to prevent an Allied advance from the beachhead by denying them supplies while the Germans either held on to or wrecked every major port from Bordeaux to Antwerp.[58] The Allies countered this strategy by building a mobile 'Mulberry' harbour and an undersea oil pipeline 'Pluto', and bypassing most of the ports. Berlin became a 'fortress' in 1945, a key site of national resistance. Indeed, it had to be taken by the Soviet Armies with street-to-street fighting as tough as it had been in Stalingrad.[59]

The year 1945 did not see the end of the use of the city as a battlegound. Streetfighting resurfaced in many different places and under varying political conditions, from the FLN in Algiers to the rival confessional militias in Beirut. Revolutionary forces seized cities to force the militarily superior enemy to fight for them street by street. This evened up the odds, inflicted casualties on the superior force, alienated civilians and upset world opinion. The NLF and the North Vietnamese Army occupied Saigon and the old city of Hué during the Tet Offensive in 1968. The US troops were forced to retake the Citadel in Hué, driving the enemy from the Vauban-style fortifications built for the Vietnamese emperor in the eighteenth century. Tet was a military failure for the Vietnamese, but its effects on American political morale were devastating. The strategy always used military means to political ends, and the US military were nonplussed that they won battles and at the same time lost the propaganda and the political wars.[60]

Such conflicts continue. The Chechens seized Grozny in the first phase of their struggle for independence. They succeeded in ambushing the inexperienced Russian conscripts sent in mechanized columns to occupy the city. Raw troops were cut to pieces by classic streetfighting tactics. The Russians were forced to reduce Grozny to rubble to reoccupy it, losing local support and outraging world opinion. In 2001 Palestinian fighters inflicted heavy casualties on Israeli troops attempting to occupy the refugee camp in Jenin. This forced the Israelis to destroy a large part of the urban fabric and again suffer a major propaganda defeat. It is highly likely that the sprawling cities of the developing world we discussed in chapter 2 will become one of the key battlegrounds of the twenty-first century. They are all but ungovernable and almost impenetrable. This bodes ill for attempts by the major powers to impose order. Anyone who doubts this should watch *Blackhawk Down*, an honest if brutal account of the American role in the 'humanitarian assistance' mission in Somalia.

7

Information, Space and War

The transformation of war by information is a mere 150 years old. Before then, intelligence and communications remained either in the stone age, the MK1 eyeball, or the bronze age, the horse and writing. The irruption of the telegraph into this pre-industrial world was revolutionary, as we have seen in chapter 6. But the telegraph, although it transformed the economy, had real limitations in war. As a rigid landline-based technology, it could not cope well with mobile operations and it could not be used at sea. The invention of radio and its widespread application in the early twentieth century transformed war. It made the coordination of mobile operations possible. It also created a series of other related and follow-on technologies: radar, electronic computers, satellites and the Internet, all of which have transformed the flows of information and the means of control available to the military. The conquest of the ether did not merely create new technologies ancillary to war: it has constantly transformed the character and pace of operations, and also created a new theatre of war as rival users sought to jam opponents' transmissions, eavesdrop on communications and practise deception.

In the two parts of this chapter we shall consider four themes. In the first part we shall concentrate on radar. This, rather than radio itself, is the driving technology of the radio-wave era of transformation in military practice. Radar changed the nature of air and naval operations, which became decisive in the Second World War. Command of the air was central to combat on both land and sea; without it land and naval surface forces became highly vulnerable. Radar also became the crucial source of technical advance in electronics in the 1930s through to the 1950s. Radar interacted with and integrated all the other dimensions of electronic warfare – radio, signals intelligence, code-breaking and electronic disruption – in an operational context. Thus we shall use it as the theme to tie these different dimensions of information and war together with examples of particular operations. Radar also led directly to the key innovations that made modern information and communications technology possible: the cavity magnetron and the semi-conductor. In the second part of the chapter we shall consider the notion that cyberspace is a new virtual dimension to war that abolishes spatial limits. Here, we shall criticize the fashionable ideas that see war as being either de-materialized and/or as being usurped by intelligent machines. In this context we will consider the concept of the Revolution in Military Affairs (RMA) and the widespread belief among its advocates that it has abolished the constraint that limited information imposes on operations, for example, that it has lifted 'the fog of war'. Lastly, space is the principal new environment both for information acquisition and potentially for war. Space war involves both weapons directed at earth and battle between platforms in space. We shall see that this near-planetary environment has distinct spatial peculiarities and constraints.

1 Radar: The Key Technology of the Radio-Wave Era

Radar and air defence

Radio makes possible command at a distance. Radar enables the detection of distant objects and works at night and in poor visibility. However, both technologies are limited by the properties of radio waves which, depending on the height and power of the transmitter, are either limited in range by the curvature of the Earth, or have to be bounced off the ionosphere. Satellites have greatly relaxed these spatial limitations, but they too have spatial limitations in terms of possible orbits. Radio-wave based technologies are highly sensitive to disruption: weather, land configurations and electromagnetic disturbance all distort or disrupt signals and can give rise to false information. This is in addition to the problems created within the technologies themselves and their ancillary processing: radar needs careful calibration; radar networks are often made up of equipment of different ages with poor interfaces; and computers, while vital to assessing radar information, also create processing problems.[1] Heavy rain, sunspots and technical problems can all create havoc with radar. Very low-flying aircraft are very difficult to detect, except by downwards looking airborne radar or at quite close ranges. Stealth aircraft rely on the fact that flat planes do not propagate radar signals well. Radar is always generating false echoes, 'sprites', and thus UFOs.

Radar is thus a highly problematic technology, something those who believe in automatic and information war often forget. Without an endless process of calibration, tinkering, maintenance and interpretation, all of which require constant human intervention and judgement, the core military technology of the information age would work so badly that it could not be trusted.[2]

Radio-based technologies have always put a premium on the skill of their operators and on the integration of the technology with military operations as a whole. Thus, for example, the Germans in the 1930s created a radio command system that would enable rapid-paced operations by their mobile spearheads. This was decisive in the German breakthrough in 1940 in northern France. The French were operating on an entirely different system of command, one that was incapable of adapting and responding to fast-paced operations. In 1914 the two armies had roughly the same system of communication, control and movement: thus the French were able to re-form their line on the Marne and halt the Germans. In 1940 the Allied and German Armies were generally comparable in size and in the number of tanks: the French had the advantage in artillery and in permanent fortifications. But the French high command remained stuck in 1918 as far as the ability to control mobile operations was concerned.

In the early 1930s aircraft were transformed by new construction techniques and more powerful engines. This meant bomber speeds more than doubled from around 100 kts to 200–220 kts. In 1918 the British had created an effective system of air defence for London, one that relied on an outer AA and detection zone, an inner air-fighting zone, and finally a close-in defence with AA guns and searchlights.[3] It was something of a deterrent against the slow Gotha bombers. Heavy bombers remained ponderous in the immediate post-war period when the UK faced no credible airborne threat. Germany was forbidden combat planes by the Treaty of Versailles, and France had the largest and most powerful air force in the world but was hardly an enemy.[4] The 1918 system was dismantled. In the mid-1930s the Nazis re-armed and created a powerful bomber force. The prevailing British doctrine was deterrence – the threat of effective retaliation by an equally strong bomber fleet. With the speed advantage of fighters relative to bombers falling from around 100 per cent to less than 50 per cent, interception was becoming more difficult, and this was even with the approaching introduction of modern fighter aircraft like the Spitfire. The available systems of visual warning and reporting were wholly inadequate and would not provide enough time for fighters to scramble and gain enough height to be directed on to incoming bombers. Standing patrols of fighters required huge numbers of aircraft and were unlikely to be effective against large raids. Increases in bomber speeds also greatly reduced the time that aircraft were exposed to a given AA gun, and vastly increased the problems of fire control and prediction. Thus AA barrages were unlikely to provide an effective deterrent to mass bomber raids. London was the largest city in the world and an easily identifiable sitting target. Thus the British Prime Minister, Stanley Baldwin, was both well-informed and truthful in 1934 when he asserted that 'the bomber will always get through'.[5]

Faced with this challenge, the Committee of Imperial Defence and the Air Ministry searched for technologies that would even up the odds against the bomber. These varied from the absurd, like death rays, to the ineffective, like aerial mine barrages, to the only marginally useful, like sound location. Eventually, the British hit upon the fact that aircraft caused disturbance to radio-transmitting stations and reflected back radio waves. They utilized this to create radar. Several countries 'invented' radar in the 1930s: the German Navy was first and the USA close behind. Others such as Japan and the USSR had come close to inventing it, but failed to develop it either because of political purges or official indifference. Germany and the USA had equipment that was probably better engineered and of higher quality than that of the UK in 1940, from a purely technical point of view. Radar had become possible – indeed, its discovery was almost inevitable – because of the growth of civilian radio industries in the 1920s and 1930s. The rapid evolution of radio components and in particular those for the nascent TV industries, like the cathode ray tube, were vital for building radar transmitters and receivers.[6]

Radar was not, therefore, a great scientific achievement, nor did it initially involve breakthrough technologies. The basic concepts were derived from the work of Heinrich Hertz in the 1880s, and the new sets were reapplications of existing well-known radio technologies. Britain did not 'invent' radar: what it did invent and develop was an effective air defence system. The UK's Chain Home radar was a 'lash-up' by prevailing standards of German radar and was below the engineering standards of the UK electronics industry. Indeed, it was of such an unlikely nature, with a long wavelength and a continuous beam, that German signals intelligence failed fully to appreciate it. This was even though the head of *Luftwaffe* signals intelligence sent the electronic surveillance airship, the *Graf Zeppelin*, along the English coast in August 1939 in order to see if there were radar transmissions. The ship failed to find any.[7]

The British early warning system was built by scientists working on a dedicated programme, not by military technical establishments or by civilian industry.[8] The advantage was that radar was designed as the core component of a complete air defence system, initiated by a scientific committee enjoying high-level political support and funding, and fully integrated with the RAF. As an example of a major scientific and technical innovation developed and integrated into an operational system in less than five years, it stands as a model for public policy in the management of complex technologies.[9] The scientists directing the programme concentrated on technologies that could be successfully developed reliably and quickly, and focused on continuity of purpose. The civilian electronics industry was excluded from core R & D or manufacture above the level of components and sub-assemblies for reasons of secrecy. Radar was the UK's one real advantage and it had to be safeguarded, even at the cost of engineering quality. Far from encountering the resistance of entrenched military conservatives, the scientists were fully backed up by the relevant sections of the RAF. Air Marshal Hugh Dowding was first head of RAF R & D and then head of the key user of radar, Fighter Command.

Without strong service support and involvement, radar would have been of little use in the Battle of Britain. Germany had radar sets but no coherent air defence system. The *Luftwaffe* was conceived as an offensive arm, and became concentrated by 1940 on the support of ground operations. The high command did not fully appreciate radar: they saw it as another piece of technology, rather than as a core component of a system. Thus the *Luftwaffe* failed to press home attacks against British radar stations in 1940 and it was hurriedly forced to improvise a defence against British night raids in 1941–2. Similarly, the USA had several very good radar sets on Oahu in December 1941, and one set did identify the incoming attack on Pearl Harbor in ample time to mount a defence. The reports were ignored. But even if they had not been discounted, there was no real system to direct fighters against the attackers and no waiting squadrons ready to be scrambled.

Britain enjoyed a huge advantage in developing radar: it was an archipelago. Radar worked well over water but faced serious interference over land, given the technical standards of the 1930s. Britain's radar screen was arranged as a linear chain of stations along the coast, forming a forward-looking linear system and, indeed, it had to be blinded behind to avoid confusing echoes. Radar represented a moving frontier in the ether, pushing the defence forward 150 km and allowing fighters to get in position on land behind this virtual frontier over the sea. Faced with a reciprocal British threat, Germany created a remarkably similar linear system, the Kammhuber Line. Until recently superseded by AWACS, satellites and very powerful phased-array radars like those now installed at Thule and Fylingdales, land-based radar defence had taken the form of a frontier-hugging linear chain. Thus the early US post-war system relied on radar picket ships and offshore platforms to push forward the frontier and on the Pinetree Line in southern Canada. Later, the USA created the sophisticated Distant Early Warning (DEW) line in the Arctic, linked to early electronic digital computers.[10]

Radar is a 360° technology, but major land-based air defence systems have tended to take a linear form, concentrating on looking 'forwards', precisely because they have been part of a system of territorial exclusion. The object of radar, even when it does not have technical limitations like Chain Home, is to enable fighters or missiles to stop bombers or missiles as far forward as possible from the territory of the nation-state. With the advent of the A-bomb threat in the 1950s this became even more important, not just to protect cities but rather to give time for the bombers on which the deterrent rested to scramble. Hence the DEW line lengthened warning times enough to get the Strategic Air Command bombers off the ground. Cities were written off. The USA and USSR relied on dispersal for the survival of civilian and military infrastructure in an atomic exchange. Other densely settled countries like the UK had no option but to rely on pure deterrence: radar warning was for the V Bomber force.

Radar is thus an electronic frontier that mirrors the exclusive territoriality of the modern state – a homogeneous space defined by external borders. Aircraft change the role and status of the frontier. Only states of a certain size can hope to defend themselves against air attack. This depends both on aircraft speeds and geography. By 1940 the Netherlands was already too small to mount an air defence based on warning. In contrast, Sweden, with a modest population, has the Baltic and Arctic to serve as radar warning zones, and during the Cold War it maintained one of the largest air forces in Europe and a domestic aircraft industry untypical for countries of its size.

From the beginning, radar defence took a linear form, but it possessed neither of those features we associate culturally with radar: the Plan Position Indicator (PPI) screen or the rotating antenna. Chain Home had neither, and the German Freya set only the latter. PPI presents information on a circular screen with the station at the centre, and thus shows the movement of targets relative to the station graphically. This is easy to interpret and useful for information-processing at air defence centres. But the initial A scopes presented the information in a linear form as moving towards the station down the screen. This did not matter with skilled operators or with the layout of control rooms, with manual presentation of information on tables or situation boards. Chain Home antennas were fixed lattice masts. They did not 'sweep' with a focused beam; they broadcast continuous waves rather than sending a narrow beam like a searchlight. The PPI and the rotating antenna were therefore specific technical choices, and thus not bundled in as inevitable concomitants of the technology, even though they signify 'radar' in every movie. Once computer-processing became inevitable as aircraft and missile speeds increased, the PPI became a convenience for humans and not a core piece of information-processing. Similarly, large phased-array antennae like Thule do not rotate: they 'sweep' by switching between numerous transmitters gathered in a billboard-like aerial.

The British air defence system in 1940 did not have digital computers, but it was based around a system of information management adequate for aircraft speeds at the time. The crucial elements of this system were as follows:

1   Radars were not isolated instruments but part of a complete interlocking network from the north of Scotland to Portland in southwest England.
2   The radars reported to filtering centres. Filtering was crucial because it assessed and correlated information and indicated how reliable and timely it was; all information more than ten minutes old was removed.
3   Filtered information was passed to fighter controllers who directed the most available aircraft towards the incoming formations. Central to this process was the newly introduced VHF radio link that enabled controllers to communicate with planes, an Identification Friend or Foe (IFF) system to establish where friendly aircraft were, and a Radio Direction Finding (RDF) system to enable aircraft to navigate easily back to base via homing beacons.
4   Height, bearing and range of incoming formations were crucial. Warning was not enough for interception, and all those parameters required operator skill at the stations and judgement by controllers.
5   The radar stations required an elaborate process of calibration to set them up which had to be periodically repeated, requiring aircraft being made available for the task in some numbers.[11]

The control system only worked by elaborate learning-by-doing and subsequent training of new operators, filter-room personnel and controllers: these elements were crucial to a working system and required detailed innovation and attention in the period 1938–40 as the system came into being. Without this vital 'software' the whole system would have broken down. The British identified early the essential role played by filtering, as well as the need for highly intelligent and specially selected personnel to perform it.

The UK's air defence resources were very limited in July 1940: about 600 modern fighters and around 1,000 aircrew were pitted against four times that number of enemy machines. There were no reserves of pilots, and replacement aircraft had to be sourced from current production. The RAF had high-speed fighters in service equal to those of the Germans, unlike the French in 1940 or the Russians in 1941. But they would have been unable to maintain command of the space over southern England without the air defence system. Radar warning maximized the fighter's effectiveness and reduced to a minimum the time spent in the air, thus also decreasing wear and tear on crews and machines. Patrols were ineffective and costly, as the British defence of the Dunkirk beachhead had just proved. In the absence of radar, the only possible strategy would have been to cede control of the air over Kent, to retreat outside single-engine fighter range, and await the attempted invasion, sending fighters forward to meet it. The results hardly bear thinking about.[12]

After the containment of the *Luftwaffe* by day in September 1940, air warfare over the UK switched to the night. Existing radar could not direct fighters to within visual range at night. Airborne Interception (AI) radar had not been developed quickly enough by the British. The result was that cities like Coventry, Glasgow, Liverpool and London suffered from major raids virtually unopposed during the winter of 1940–41. Thereafter the bulk of the *Luftwaffe* was transferred to Russia. The air war then turned into a struggle between British night bombers and the German defences. This involved a complex scientific war to devise electronic bombing aids, to jam and detect the radars of bombers and night fighters, and to blind ground radars; this latter tactic eventually involved dropping huge quantities of aluminium foil strips, 'Window', to confuse defending German radars with a mass of echoes.[13] 'Window' consumed a large part of US aluminium production and had to be used in heavier and heavier doses as the Germans learned to filter it out and read moving raiders through the mass of noise generated by 'Window' reflections. The German defences remained resilient, even if they did absorb an increasing amount of manpower and scarce resources. Civil defence, AA guns, radar and fighters consumed an equal proportion of GDP to that used in the Allied bombing offensive, plus losses due to the damage caused by bombing. The Allies only mastered the German defences when they were able to escort the bombers with day and night fighters, thus destroying the defending airforce in the air and enabling the destruction by daytime precision-bombing of the synthetic oil plants on which it depended. Even so, German FLAK artillery remained effective until the end and took a heavy toll of Allied aircraft up to the surrender.

Radio and radar at sea

We have seen that steam transformed sea transportation. Commercially, this made a huge difference. Ships were able to keep to deadlines and to travel between ports where they would receive new information by telegraph. This made possible the coordination of ship movements and the ability to act on market information. The regular liner sailing a predetermined route could be relied upon, and the tramp steamer could pick up cargoes of opportunity as directed by its home shipping office. But in war the advent of steam was a mixed blessing: it made ships faster, but it also tied them to a limited number of fixed coaling stations. Before radio, ships could not be controlled at sea or receive new information.

Once a ship or fleet had left harbour it was on its own, as until it reached a port with a telegraph it could receive no new orders or external information. Radio made intelligence vital in naval affairs. It became essential for intelligence to be centralized and assessed, pushing navies towards the control of operations by naval staffs. This parallels the effects of the railway and telegraph in promoting control of armies by general staffs and their railway sections. Before radio, a ship could only be ordered in advance to sail between fixed points or cruise in search of enemy vessels. After radio, a ship at sea could be directed anywhere within a circle defined by its steaming radius: assuming an economical speed of 15 knots and twenty-four hours as the limit of useful information, anywhere within a circle with a radius of 360 km. Radio control rapidly created the necessity of naval signals intelligence and code-breaking. During the First World War the British Admiralty's Room 40 was extremely effective at breaking their opponent's naval code, and at using analysis of radio traffic to determine the position of the German fleet. This evolution was very rapid, given that radio at sea was less than ten years old.

Even so, a ship with radio could see no further than one in Nelson's day. The key naval battles of the pre-radio steam era were fought in narrow coastal waters where the objectives and thus the movements of the enemy fleet were predictable and therefore easy to intercept. The principal engagements were Lissa in 1866 in the Adriatic between the Austrians and Italians, and the Japanese annihilation of the Russian fleet at Tsushima in the Straits of Japan in 1905. At Jutland in 1916 the

British enjoyed the advantage of signals intelligence indicating that the German fleet would emerge. Both sides had a limited air-reconnaissance capability in the form of Zeppelins on the German side and shipborne aircraft on the British, but neither made effective use of it. At Jutland, as on the Western Front, weapons had outgrown the capacity to command and control them. The result was hundreds of ships blundering about at night after an inconclusive engagement late in the day. The German Fleet escaped to safety through a series of confused actions and accidental clashes.[14] Radar would certainly have helped, but the principal reasons for the British lack of success in cornering the retreating German fleet were the failure on the part of individual ships to assess and transmit the information available, and excessive caution on the part of the high command. In the absence of a coherent night-fighting doctrine and a less centralized and better developed system of reporting, radar might well have failed at Jutland too, as we shall see in the case of American errors in the Solomons.

Jutland is often seen as the swansong of the battleship dinosaur. Yet until the adoption of radar at sea, the surface combat ship was dominant, and the battleship was the most powerful surface combatant. Night and bad weather limited visibility and, therefore, the ability to use aircraft. In these conditions aircraft carriers were very vulnerable; witness the destruction of HMS *Glorious* during the day and in good weather by German surface ships during the Norwegian campaign in 1940. No pre-radar navy could dispense with battleships: the admirals of all the major navies were not fools in wanting new battleship construction in the 1930s. Radar was only available at the beginning of the Second World War. Thus the ship designs of the post-1918 period were conceived in a pre-radar era and that includes about 90 per cent of the ships built before and during the Second World War. Initially, radar was limited to a range of about 20 km, but that enabled ships to see at night and in bad weather and to evade their enemies.[15]

Here we will consider three examples that illustrate the interaction of radar with other electronic technologies and with aircraft and aircraft carriers. The first is the search for the surface raider, the battleship *Bismarck*, in May 1941.[16] The hunt for a single ship in the whole of the North Atlantic was virtually impossible in the pre-radar era, even with the entire British fleet. A ship as powerful as *Bismarck* was more or less guaranteed to overwhelm any small force it did bump into and then to be able to hide. The success of the search for the ship was heavily dependent on aircraft and electronics and radar was the core technology. First, the ship's mission was identified by signals intelligence and code-breaking.[17] Second, its departure was determined by air reconnaissance of the Norwegian fjords. Third, radar-equipped cruisers, HMS *Norfolk* and *Suffolk*, shadowed the big ship. Fourth, a long-range flying boat with air-to-surface radar found the ship again after she had given her pursuers the slip. Finally, aircraft carriers launched torpedo attacks, which crippled her steering and doomed her, and such aircraft could only operate because their ships had an RDF beacon that enabled the torpedo planes to find the carrier again. Even so, *Bismarck* was found by the narrowest of margins. Without a lucky torpedo hit that made surface action possible just outside the range of supporting German aircraft from Brittany, she would have escaped to France.

The second example is the first decisive carrier battle at Midway in June 1941. Again the battle began with effective code-breaking.[18] The Americans were aware of the objectives of the Japanese plan: to force the Americans to fight in defence of the key island base and thus commit their carriers to destruction by a superior Japanese force. The Americans were thus aware of the relative forces. They were able to even them up considerably by repairing the carrier *Yorktown* in record time and thereby augmenting US naval air power for the battle by a third. This stands in contrast to the failure to utilize the success of American code-breakers in determining the timing of the attack on Pearl Harbor – compounded by local incompetence in not using radar warnings.[19] Code-breaking gave a decisive advantage to the US in that they were able to anticipate and counter the Japanese strategy, thus minimizing the risk to the fragile defensive shield that depended on a small number of carriers. Japanese carriers did not have radar at Midway. The carrier *Junyo* did have radar and was used in the parallel and diversionary Aleutians operation, but she was slow and could not have coordinated with the fast carriers. The Japanese had paid little attention to radar; much like the *Luftwaffe* they saw their forces as inherently offensive and had no need for defensive measures.[20]

The USA could take calculated risks because of code-breaking and the possession of defensive radar sets on their carriers. They calculated that they would not be ambushed.[21] The Japanese took uncalculated risks because they were unaware their plans had been compromised and because they were supremely confident after six months of overwhelming victories. Hence the sloppy prior reconnaissance by both submarines and aircraft, and the failure to use enough scout planes during the battle. This was compounded by rigid adherence to radio silence. Due to intelligence failures and tactical errors, the Japanese carriers were caught re-arming in the face of a major US attack. The few fighters available were directed at the American torpedo bombers. A large formation of American dive-bombers was lucky to find the Japanese fleet and fortunate to find themselves unopposed. They destroyed three of the four Japanese carriers, and in the ensuing later phases of the battle the Americans destroyed the fourth ship and also lost the *Yorktown*. At the end of the battle the Japanese had been reduced from overwhelming superiority to having two fast fleet carriers to the American total of four. Moreover, the building programme in the USA was about to lead to a flood of new construction whereas the Japanese had very few carriers under manufacture or being converted.

We might consider here why the carrier displaces the battleship as the principal naval combatant in the radar era. The answer is simple. Battleships had an effective maximum gun range of 15–25 km in good weather, whereas carrier bombers had a combat radius fully loaded of about 100–150 km. Radar was able to spot surface ships before they closed in on carriers, and carriers could attack surface ships far beyond gunnery range. The powerful Japanese battleships in the Main Body at Midway, the flagship a monster of 68,000 tons, therefore could not alter the course of the action and were forced to retire having achieved nothing. Carriers relied on air reconnaissance to spot other ships and at Midway none of the scouts had ASV (Airborne Surface Vessel). Radar was defensive: it gave warning of surface threats and enabled fighter planes to be directed at raiders. However, the US Navy found that only ships with a proper CIC (Combat Information Centre) could cope with large numbers of attackers. The CIC became the command centre of the ship, not the bridge. In the Second World War it relied on the human evaluation of information. Nowadays, ships have highly developed computer-based systems like Aegis that allow for automatic identification of targets and their destruction by missiles. This technology now relies totally on IFF (Identification, Friend or Foe). This even now is a far from robust technology and it can fail in complicated situations where human judgement is an essential supplement to automated and also fallible systems, as, for example, when the USS *Vincennes* downed an Iranian civilian airliner during the Iran–Iraq war.

Even with a radar picket of destroyers in advance of the fleet and large numbers of carrier fighters, the US fleet suffered heavily from kamikazes in the last year of the Pacific War. Mass kamikaze attacks came close to swamping the information-management capacities of CICs. By 1944 conventional Japanese attacks on the US fleet were suicidal *and* ineffective. Long-range radar (150 km) based on both carriers and pickets, large combat air patrols of fighters directed to targets by the CIC, and radar-controlled AA guns with radar proximity fuses as a last line at defence had created a system of layered defence through which it was almost impossible to break.[22] Kamikaze attacks may seem inhuman, but, faced with almost certain death, for the aircrew anyway, they made sense as they turned planes into ballistic missiles. They had a higher probability of inflicting damage because even if hit at close range, the plane could follow a ballistic trajectory straight to the target. Missiles, such as surface skimmers, are still difficult to counter. Missiles close to the sea are lost in the clutter of the waves, and this is compounded when other ships and coastal features are present. Thus HMS *Coventry* was sunk in the Falklands by attacking Argentinian bomber aircraft exploiting the terrain, despite being escorted by the short-range-missile-armed HMS *Broadsword*.

The third example is the battle of Savo Island on 8/9 August 1942.[23] The Allied cruisers and destroyers were crushed by a Japanese force aiming to prevent a landing on Guadalcanal in the Solomons. Some of the Allied ships had radar systems but were either unable to use them because of the configuration of the coast in confined waters, or because they were incompetently handled tactically. The Japanese, on the other hand, were well-versed in night-fighting tactics based on early visual identification and the use of long-range torpedoes. Four Allied cruisers were sunk. This demonstrates how far radar depends for its effectiveness on being integrated into effective information-management and tactics. In confused battles in coastal waters, superior doctrine, training and coordination were crucial. This is the case today too, despite more powerful radars and high-speed computers. As we shall see in the section on the Revolution in Military Affairs, there are tactics for checking superior information-dependent forces. Although the Japanese were unaware of it, they were practising asymmetrical warfare in the night battles in the Solomons.

In the examples of the Battle of Britain, the hunt for the *Bismarck* and the Battle of Midway, radar was the key equalizer. All these engagements were won by a narrow margin. In the two naval battles, code-breaking and radar changed the balance of forces. The RAF was outnumbered in 1940. Britain had too few ships to hunt down *Bismarck* by conventional means. Random searches would have yielded little. The US fleet prior to Midway was not only outnumbered, but its planes were inferior and its pilots less well-trained than the Japanese. In both Britain and the USA, political elites were receptive to science, and they were prepared to listen to key advisers like Sir Henry Tizard and Vannevar Bush. They were willing to mobilize resources rapidly to exploit new technologies, aware of the need to maximize their ability to blunt Axis attacks.[24] The Axis powers, dominated by militaristic and authoritarian elites, failed to appreciate the value of radar early enough and, in the Japanese case, anti-submarine sonar too. The cult of the offensive and the relegation of science to a purely technical role cost them dear. Had the *Luftwaffe* attacked the Chain Home stations systematically at the outset, aware of the value of radar, it could have won control over southern England. Had the Japanese acted more cautiously at Midway and also concentrated the forces available to them, they could have avoided defeat and delayed the American reconquest of the Pacific. Radar is now just another technology. But in 1940–2 the ability to exploit radar was a defining feature of the difference between the Anglo-Saxon democracies and the authoritarian regimes.

II The Illusion of Virtual War

Postmodernism meets the Pentagon

The 1990s were a decade of hype in which the futurological avant-garde took over the mainstream. Central to the excessive expectations of technological change and social transformation was the belief that information had now become the dominant factor in fields as distinct as culture, economics and war. The notion of an information revolution was first popularized in the 1980s by futurologists such as Alvin Toffler.[25] It became mainstream in the 1990s when the following propositions could seem entirely credible: that information technology in combination with the mass media had created a virtual society and media events now defined the world; that an information-based 'knowledge economy' had suspended the old laws of economics, abolishing scarcity, removing limits to growth and transforming the functioning of capital markets; that a 'Revolution in Military Affairs' (RMA), that is, the shift to information-centric warfare and precision-guided munitions, had changed both the nature of war and the balance of power: America now had an 'information edge'.

In this revolution of expectations, most of the old spatial-physical limits and social constraints were perceived to be absurd. Thus the Gulf War of 1991 was widely seen by cultural commentators as primarily a media event; in Jean Baudrillard's provocative words, it 'never took place'.[26] People had ceased to be citizens in a world of real events; rather, they now responded to 'simulacra', that is, ensembles spun out of information that are indistinguishable from the real. Economists could argue that those societies like the USA that had adopted the forms of social flexibility necessary to the new economy would enjoy prolonged inflation-free and rapid growth. As a result of this, stock markets would rise in value exponentially: the old limits of price earnings ratios and cycles of bull and bear markets were over. It was even possible for commentators to assert and be believed that we were entering a 'weightless world' in which it would be possible to 'live on thin air'.[27] It is in this context that some of the extreme proponents of the RMA could predict that the USA would fight wars with hypersonic cruise missiles at long range, targeting enemies from the homeland and striking them in close to real time.[28] The military mainstream was not far behind the excesses of *Wired* magazine. Analysts from specialist military think tanks like RAND could be found quoting Heidegger, while admirals sounded like Baudrillard.[29] The reason for this unlikely convergence is that both the cultural studies postmodernists and the military techno-modernists believed in the abolition of the old constraints of distance, scarcity of resources and fallible knowledge.

We can see now that computerized information-processing has radically changed the limits imposed by electro-mechanical control systems, but not other limits. Each of the above propositions about information dominance has come to grief on constraints that derive from the lumpy non-digital world of space, time and scarcity, and from the necessities of social interaction. The Gulf War of 2003 was preceded by an upsurge of protest across the world. Far from behaving like the inhabitants of a virtual world, people acted as if they were citizens guided by a moral sense, and they led rather than followed the media.[30] The stock market crash in early 2000 showed that bubbles do still burst, that there are limits to growth and that markets are fallible. New economy companies were over-investing on rising stock prices, often with no possible prospect of return. The immense value destruction of the crash showed that the growth in capital values had outpaced any possible productivity gains, let alone the modest rise in the level of US productivity attributable to the new technology.[31] The Gulf War of 2003 was preceded by a relatively long build-up in which the USA and UK shipped an air power-heavy and armour-light force to the region. Ships were essential to move most of the hardware, not at the speed of light but at a modest 20 kts. Bases for much of the air power were provided by 60–70,000 ton aircraft carriers. The paradox of the reliance on aircraft and missiles is that this was the most infantry-heavy army of modern times. High-tech weapons clear the way for infantry, but, just as in Alexander the Great's day, it is infantry that occupy territory.

It would be foolish to argue that information technology does not matter or that significant aspects of war have not changed. The point, however, is that war has not and will not change in the way that the most enthusiastic prophets of information-centric war have believed. Their view is typically unilinear and technologically determinist, and everything we know from past revolutions in military technology leads us to doubt this approach. To examine this we shall consider how the concept of RMA began, the claims of its strongest proponents, and what are likely to be the actual outcomes of military-technical change.

The RMA debate and its vicissitudes

Major changes in the practice and technology of war – 'military revolutions' – are generally prefigured and defined by intellectuals, both civilian and military. Since the Renaissance, intellectuals have shaped both strategy and tactical doctrine. Think of Machiavelli or Justus Lipsius.[32] Thus philosophers thinking about war and officers in military academies quoting philosophers are not unusual.

Postmodernist thinkers caught on to information war early on. Manuel De Landa's *War in the Age of Intelligent Machines* adapted Deleuze and Guattari's notion of the 'war machine' to modern information-based weapons and the shift towards artificial intelligence in information-processing.[33] Using the concepts of non-linear causality and the 'machinic phylum', he envisaged a future in which intelligent robots have displaced humans and write the history of intelligent life on the planet as the evolution of self-governing machines. Paul Virilio sees modern society as dominated by speed and in which space is annihilated. Commenting on the Gulf War of 1991, he observed that: 'the military environment is no longer so much a *geophysical* one of the real space of battles (terrestrial, maritime, aerial, etc.) as a *microphysical* one of the real-time electromagnetic environment of real-time engagement'.[34]

These authors are not just cultural theorists: they know a good deal about war. However, they express neatly the three ideas central to the postmodernist intellectual reprise of the RMA: autonomization, virtualization and de-spatialization. War at the speed of light takes place in a new dimension – cyberspace – that abolishes conventional spatial limits and displaces time. The intelligent 'war machine' becomes the new manager of war and displaces humans, and thus removes both 'friction' (chance and uncertainty) and the morally exacting dimension from combat. Although cleverly expressed, both these propositions are absurd. Cyberspace is no place: information must work in war primarily by interacting with real systems that move objects in a world constrained by limits of speed and distance. Information technologies also have limitations that are inherent to them, as we have seen in the case of radar. 'Information war' is likely to take the form of the blinding and deception of complex systems, leading to chaos on the battlefield for information-dependent forces. Computers and accurate weapons make war harder for humans, that is, more physically and morally demanding, but they do not eliminate the central role of humans. Attempts to remove humans from the loop of strategic decision and replace them with AI or to subordinate operations to the imperatives of a given technology will lead to military disaster, and thus to wars that are lost because the strategic objectives were unrealistic, and to battles that are lost because men depend too much on machines that fail them.[35]

The RMA concept did not originate in the University of Paris-Vincennes or in Californian think tanks into complexity and chaos theory. It began with the Soviet military in the 1980s.[36] Russian analysts recognized that the USSR was being left behind by the new American military and civilian technologies. They knew the USA had a huge superiority in IT. Hence they created the concept of military-technical revolution. The USA in turn had adopted the new conventional weapons systems and operational doctrines to counter the vast Soviet superiority in tanks and fighter planes. The Americans evolved the doctrine of the air–land battle, seeing the European theatre as a deep three-dimensional battle space. Rather than responding to Soviet tank thrusts should war break out, the aim was to disrupt the attack deep in Poland and Russia. For this the USA needed both new weapons and also new techniques of battlefield management. An integrated ground–air battle stretching over thousands of square miles had to be fought differently. This initiated a new concept of military topography to replace that of 'front', with its implications of linear ground combat. Combat no longer took place throughout a three-dimensional 'battle space' of hundreds of cubic kilometres volume.

The elements of the new American system were as follows: new precision-guided munitions to destroy tanks delivered by helicopters, artillery and fighter planes; guided bombs and cruise missiles to improve the accuracy of attack on targets like airfields and bridges; systems like AWACS (Airborne Warning and Control System) to manage the fluid air combat situation; and, finally, the greater use of satellites for purposes of conventional intelligence and communications. The end of the Cold War enabled the USA to convert the elements of this system designed for meeting Soviet mass attacks in Europe into the basis of a new form of global power. What had held back the creation of new forces and strategies was the armlock that the nuclear stalemate with the USSR had on access to satellite intelligence and communication for conventional forces. Satellite intelligence was originally fenced off from direct access by conventional forces. It was feared that the Soviets would discover capabilities that should be reserved for the ultimate nuclear showdown. The US forces also benefited in the 1980s from a revolution in civilian computing. Up until then the military had both sponsored civilian R & D and procured computer systems to their own specifications. Computer development had soon become driven by rapidly expanding civilian markets and was experiencing massive cost reductions and exponential increases in processing power and memory. Staying with military systems would have meant that the services were rapidly left behind and so the military chose to buy off the shelf.

Thus, by the early 1990s the armed forces could use satellites to the full and exploit the IT revolution. Of further great benefit were the two programmes coming into widespread service that the military had developed: the Internet and the GPS (Global Positioning System). The Internet provided a basis for secure networked communications and the GPS made really accurate targeting possible for the first time. GPS data were transmitted directly to users by satellites. Thus were assembled the elements of a new integrated system of information-gathering, battlefield management and low-cost precision guidance out of a series of separately developing programmes. What was new was the synthesis, and it was first achieved during the Gulf War of 1991. The gains were immediate and rapid: frontline commanders could directly download intelligence data from satellites in close to real time; by using the GPS system, cruise missiles could be quickly reprogrammed (instead of using heavy target-specific guidance disks), and this made every large surface ship in the US fleet an offensive combatant rather than just part of a defensive screen for the big carriers; and aircraft could bomb accurately because positions were known from GPS and they used munitions that relied on such data themselves, rather than having to be actively steered on to the target.

This system had evolved: it was not planned *ab initio* and some of its elements were highly contingent. The system managed and guided hardware, which mostly stayed the same. Ships and planes had much the same performance as they did in the 1970s, and many were already close to feasible engineering limits. The design of the oldest US carriers dates from the 1950s. Most current combat aircraft, the F14, 15, 16 and 18, were either designed in or entered service in the 1970s. The new systems enabled this hardware to be used more effectively: they became 'platforms', means to access information systems and carry smart weapons.[37]

So far, so good; information technology really has changed war. But so, as we have seen, did radar. This is a long way from the postmodernists' and the RMA visionaries' claims. The RMA has just begun and it is a mistake to extract the current transformative element of IT and communications and project it forward as the decisive factor. Similarly, it is an error to concentrate on technology to the neglect of the whole environment of war in making predictions. Currently US military dominance relies on two quite distinct elements. First, its unmatched worldwide capacity in intelligence-gathering and communications, based on its satellite network. Satellites handle information but the constraints of their launching and their orbits put them firmly in the world of geometry and old-fashioned mechanics. Second, its huge airlift and sealift capacity. This rests on large numbers of relatively slow (20 kt) amphibious assault ships and big freighters, and on big but entirely conventional transport planes like the C130, 141 and 17. Both elements matter equally: without the latter the fighting forces cannot get to the theatre of war or be sustained there.[38] Even a B2 bomber flying from Montana to bomb Serbia in 1999 would have been useless without large numbers of refuelling tankers based on airliner designs (up to seven top-ups and several tankers per bomber per mission). The reason that the USA can invest in this vastly expensive network of satellites, transports and bases to support its worldwide operations is that it is the world's richest state with a $9 trillion economy. Economic dominance is thus as vital to military power as is an information edge.

The USA has had two other huge advantages in its recent wars that help to explain why it has such an enormous military advantage over other powers, and why it has prevailed so apparently effortlessly and at low cost in American lives. First, most other military powers have built up their conventional forces either in order to match – or as copies of – Cold War Soviet forces. The new American systems were designed precisely to counter and destroy such forces: conventional air defence systems and armies based on mobile armoured warfare. Such forces rely on electronic signatures and movement to function. US air power was designed to identify, deceive, jam and destroy enemy radar, and to destroy enemy planes on the ground. US precision-guided weapons are designed to hit moving tanks. Thus, in the 1991 Gulf War, Iraq had an air defence system based around French radars and Soviet fighters and an army equipped and trained on Soviet lines. Both the air and ground forces of its enemies have played to US strengths: victory at low cost is therefore hardly surprising. What will happen if rival powers with some military competence configure their forces precisely to avoid and to blunt these strengths? Second, the USA has recently faced regimes that were politically and thus militarily weak because they were illegitimate: Iraq in 1991 and 2003, Milosevic in Kosovo in 1999, and the Taliban in 2001–2. Dictatorships that do not include the people, like the oil-based autocracy of Saddam Hussein, or that seek to include them by subordinating them, like the totalitarian tyranny of the Taliban, are fragile. Authoritarian regimes are usually even weaker militarily than they appear to be: not only do their armies have low morale and low public support, but the consequences of playing a role in tyrannizing the people corrupt the army and erode its competence. Tyrants who can rely on competent military forces that fight with a will are rare. Hitler is an example, but he threw away the skills of an army, the competence of which derived from sources long before 1933, beginning with the reforms of Scharnhorst and going forward to those under the Weimar Republic. Can the USA rely on facing only such politically weak and brittle regimes in the future?

RMA doctrine and strategic constraints

By the early 1990s the concept of the RMA had transferred to the USA and had received a huge fillip from the Gulf War. Its proponents quickly established influential positions in the think tanks, the military technical schools and the Pentagon. Leaving aside extreme hypotheses, the following positions quickly became the central components of the new doctrine.[39]

1. New information technologies would all but eliminate the 'fog of war' and thus reduce 'friction' to an insignificant factor in deciding outcomes. The USA already enjoys an 'information edge'; soon it would have complete high-level strategic and battlefield intelligence available in real time.[40] Systems from spy satellites to frontline motion sensors will enable US forces to find their enemies first and to fight them at night and in all weathers. The ability to conduct twenty-four-hour operations and superior knowledge of the enemy's movements will permit rapid and sustained operations that will keep the initiative and deny the enemy the capacity for effective response. In effect, combat will become one-sided rather than reciprocal in the Clausewitzian sense.

2. Organizing the armed forces, especially the army, around real-time intelligence and communications will lead to two opposed but complementary tendencies: the elimination of hierarchy and the ability of senior commanders to enjoy total control of the whole battle space. Elaborate command and control hierarchies in which orders are passed down and information filtered up are obsolete: frontline soldiers down to squad sergeants will be able to call on vast firepower from across the whole theatre of war. A direct dialogue between frontline and senior commanders will be possible through a military version of the Internet. Senior commanders will be able to integrate all

sources of information and synthesize them through informatics, and to eavesdrop directly on lower levels without filtering through intermediate commanders.

3. The domination of war by information and highly accurate weapons will do away with the need for huge expenditures of munitions and heavy armour. This will shift the armed forces toward lighter and air-portable systems. Mechanized forces will give way to infantry with high intrinsic firepower and also able to pinpoint targets for aircraft. Expensive manned fighters will be supplemented and increasingly replaced by lighter, remotely piloted vehicles.

4. Information-based war will create new opportunities for deception, disabling the enemy by destroying or jamming his sensors and communications. Equally, this will place a premium on guarding one's own systems from a variety of threats, including hackers. Information-rich societies will become vulnerable to disruption by information war. Hackers will try to interrupt the operation of systems and corrupt data. This may have devastating consequences for vital civilian installations like nuclear power stations, or for services such as social security payment systems. This may lead to a distinctive form of cyber terrorism against information-rich societies that will be difficult and expensive to deal with, and that will require highly skilled specialists to counter.[41]

5. Highly accurate weapons change the ratio between munitions expended and hits scored.[42] This shift away from crude statistical probability of hitting changes the relationship between inputs and outputs and means that relatively small forces can quickly prevail over larger but less effective forces. This means that an RMA-equipped army can be smaller than conventional forces hitherto, and it will need fewer overseas garrisons and pre-positioned depots of weapons. This will enable rapid airborne deployment and less time to build up a viable striking force.

6. These changes make possible 'post-heroic' war. The USA will be able to substitute smart weapons for troop numbers, thus removing the fear of losing troops in conflicts where the government wishes to intervene but which are not so vital as to risk heavy military casualties.[43]

7. The RMA provides the technical basis for a variety of strategies, from isolationism to active interventionism in defence of human rights. The new post-September 11 US strategic doctrine is the first to fully build in the RMA. It is made possible by the RMA, but it is not a direct or inevitable consequence of it.[44] The new doctrine is based on three principles: the unchallengeable dominance of US forces, which means that America must configure its armed services so that

they are not merely superior but without any possible rival; unilateralism – the USA will rely principally on its own power, and where necessary on building ad hoc 'coalitions of the willing', and only secondarily on international institutions like the UN or formal alliances like NATO; pre-emptive and preclusive defence – the USA will act to destroy powers that challenge it before they can threaten the homeland or vital interests abroad either by acquiring weapons of mass destruction or sponsoring terrorism, and it will do so by all means including nuclear weapons. Without the RMA it is difficult to imagine this politically inspired move to unilateralism and pre-emption. In a world of crude probability, numbers matter: until the 1990s the USA needed the tanks and planes of its allies. Technological change, increasing capacity of the armed forces and the definition of strategy have all evolved together. Technical change has played a role in creating the strategic opportunity and the temptation for the USA to become a hyper-power and this change has been recent and rapid, occurring since the early 1990s. Whether this change in strategy and the apparent reliance on the RMA is wise we shall see below. The point is, one does not have to visit the wilder shores of the RMA to see a convincing case for a radical discontinuity in the whole power position of the USA, based on a military-technical revolution derived from new possibilities of information-processing.

The limits of RMA doctrine

The current RMA is not the only one to use information to radically improve the performance of existing platforms; nor is it the only one to use technology to promise a revolution in command in armies. Thus in 1917–18 the British and German Armies began to use artillery as a flexible system both for attack and for the support of frontline troops.[45] Using a variety of information techniques including surveying, prediction, radio and forward observers, sophisticated targeted fire on enemy positions and guns and moving barrages were possible. This contrasted with the cumbersome prior saturation bombardments and rigidly timed barrages still in use in 1916. In the 1920s and 1930s armoured forces were converted into mobile spearheads by combining tanks with radio command, first in Britain and then in Germany. In 1931 an entire brigade of British tanks manoeuvred en masse on Salisbury Plain, turning as one on Colonel Charles Broad's commands.[46] We now take these things for granted, but at the time they were step changes of an almost equivalent scale to the improvement in the capacities of conventional attack aircraft made possible by the new munitions. Both of these earlier systems of information-centric offence were capable, as it turned out, of being countered by defence in depth.

Some RMA theorists believe that the changes of the 1990s have produced a dramatic shift to the dominance of the attack. This reduces the capacity of lesser powers to resist locally and also to pursue policies at variance with the military hegemon. Shifts in the balance of power between offence and defence are a normal part of the evolution of war. Usually the long-run tendency for the defence to be the stronger form of war reasserts itself after a brief period in which other powers learn more or less painfully how to adapt to and to adopt versions of the new technologies. Is the current RMA unusual? Will it change the balance of power in favour of the attack and the greatest power for a long period?[47]

If the current RMA did so, it would be a radical change from our experience since the use of really effective gunpowder weapons in the late 1400s. The defence returned to primacy and checked the imperial pretensions of the then dominant powers like Hapsburg Spain and the Ottomans. The USA has become the principal power because it is both relatively big and very rich, secured from attack by two oceans, and possessed of huge air and naval power. If it were to be without effective defensive challenge, then its hegemony would acquire a new dimension, but its leaders would be presented with new political temptations.

In fact the propositions of the new military-strategic doctrine based on the RMA are capable of challenge. Here are six counterclaims for those seven propositions.[48] It is not that these claims for the RMA are wholly wrong but that, once qualified, they may point to very different outcomes.

1. The notion that information-gathering and processing will remove the 'fog of war' ignores the fact that information-centric systems will create their own forms of fog.[49] We have seen in our case study of radar not only how the new systems gave rise to problems of information-processing and interpretation, but also how they prompted both deception and counter-measures such as 'Window'. Information-based technologies are far from foolproof. For example, India was able to hide its preparations for nuclear testing by carrying out work at night when the satellites were not overhead. Again, in 1999, an obsolete street directory of Belgrade was fed into a computerized targeting database and led to the politically embarrassing bombing of the Chinese embassy. These are not extrinsic failures that can be eliminated by better computer systems or more rigorous procedures: they are intrinsic both to war and to complex information

systems. It is only sensible to suppose that, faced with a competent opponent, such failures can prove deadly. Highly successful code-breaking and radar did not prevent Pearl Harbor, and the outcome of Midway, where signals intelligence was properly used, still involved a huge amount of luck. The answer is to devise robust, not rigid, military responses that can cope with everyday failures and avoid catastrophic ones. These intrinsic problems with information are not solved by introducing automatic battlefield-management systems. The best systems allow humans to see the situation and to make decisions more effectively, like AWACS. However, the effectiveness of AWACS depends on two factors: one technical, fragile IFF systems; the other operational, in effect drawing a line in the air and assuming all unidentified aircraft crossing it to be hostile. Creating fully automatic AI decision systems above the level of targeting will lead to disaster. Such systems will programme war, reducing it to given decision procedures and a certain menu of moves, and thus tailoring operations to the capacities of information-management software. This is the high-tech version of bureaucratic rigidity. It is like the rigid pre-planned offensives of 1915–17 or the process-oriented decision-making of the Vietnam War.[50] Only assume an intelligent opponent of some military capacity who does the unexpected, and this rigid management of information will be a road to defeat.

2. The best way to cope with information overload is not through automation of decision-making, but a shift in command to the front. If overall control is impossible beyond the initial phase of operations, then armies not fixated on technology will devolve command to the lowest appropriate level and encourage initiative by junior officers. This is not something created by the RMA: it was the operational doctrine of Moltke the Elder in the nineteenth century.[51] The problem for senior commanders practising such devolution is how to manage support for frontline commanders. This means reserves. Everything cannot be in action at once, and information-centric war therefore cannot reduce force sizes quite as much as its most ardent advocates believe. A shift to lighter forces and more infantry rather than heavy armour means that soldiers are vulnerable; they need redundancy not only for reinforcements, but also as insurance in case air support fails and in order to replace exhausted troops. Hence the conventional military skills of tactical leadership and operational art are not irrelevant on the information-centric battlefield. Machines cannot make these decisions, which are complex matters of judgement that cannot be written into the decision protocols of AI software.

3. 'Post-heroic' warfare is an illusion. It will only be possible if the enemy is so weak or outclassed that war becomes one-sided. Thus

Omdurman in 1898 was a one-sided battle, or rather a massacre – 48 Anglo-Egyptian dead as against 11,000 Sudanese. This did not prevent battles immediately afterwards against a capable foe with the right weapons and tactics being heavy defeats for the British, like Magersfontein in 1899 and Spion Kop in 1900 in the Boer War. Thus, assuming both a real enemy and the pressures specific to information-centric war, then combat will become more exacting, not less. Armies both using highly accurate weapons and fighting in a complex and fast-changing battle space will impose immense challenges on front-line troops and senior commanders alike. It will require those moral qualities that Clausewitz argued were intrinsic to war, not just technical skills. Such qualities are ultimately founded on soldiers' belief in the legitimacy of their cause. High-tech warriors fighting a war they don't believe in are likely to lose if matched by well-motivated and capable opponents. To assume that one will never meet such forces is pure hubris.[52]

4. One also should not assume that opponents will be so compliant as to act to match the expectations built into one's weapons and tactics, let alone strategy. War is a contest based on reciprocal interaction between the two sides. The successful army is the one that finds and best exploits its opponents' weaknesses. Armies facing a high-tech opponent may choose to go in the other direction, avoiding both complex electronic communication and mass motorized movements. Thus in Kosovo the Serbian Army dug in and hid. Extensive air strikes and large-scale use of precision-guided munitions failed to destroy or dislodge the forces: only the prospect of ground action and heavy bombing of the Serbian homeland did that. Opponents may combine local defence with offence elsewhere, such as terrorism or information war. Information-rich armies and their homelands are highly vulnerable to disruption and deception. Rival armies may avoid using active sensors and rely on passive systems that home in on the enemy's transmissions. They may use weapons that are hard to detect like anti-aircraft guns or mines or chemical and biological traps. They may also choose to produce low-tech copies of or rivals to the most sophisticated systems, using weapons like micro remotely piloted aircraft or guidance systems like optronics. Some countries will be able to manufacture medium- to low-tech weapons that threaten heavy casualties that could impose on American troops if they attack. China is the obvious example, but countries like Iran may soon be able to do this.[53] It would be prudent to envisage a politically strong and well-motivated enemy that has made appropriate choices to counter US military methods at both the strategic and technical levels. That will require troops capable of hard fighting against prepared defences, not a post-heroic force of joystick

jockeys. It will also require politicians and generals who understand the basics of strategy.

5. We are still at the beginning of the RMA and this may work against the current prescriptions of its enthusiasts.[54] The mix of weapons, information systems and forms of organization advocated as cutting edge now may look odd thirty years from now. Five technical revolutions with a profound potential effect on military affairs are ongoing: the continuing miniaturization of computing, robotics, biotechnology, new materials and nanotechnology (that is, machines of molecular scale, measured in microns). These may produce changes that do not lie principally in the field of information-processing and may reduce the information-centric emphasis of war. One can expect whole new families of weapons as an outcome of these technologies and their interaction.[55] Most of these new technologies will quickly become generic and civilian: they are already substantially driven by civilian corporate research. As the new materials and components become widespread they will become relatively cheap and will be widely manufactured outside the USA, mainly in Asia. Imagination alone limits our ability to anticipate whole families of new weapons: micro aircraft the size of a dinner plate that fly by their own sensors and deliver deadly miniature sub-munitions; jumping mines that explode when they sense English being spoken and which combine shrapnel with chemical or biological agents. Against such weapons chemical and biological warfare suits would be useless. A lot further off are nanomachines that can act like bacteria and eat flesh or consume cables, rubber and plastics. They would be impervious to antibiotics and antiseptics. Such weapons, because they have a short life and can be programmed not to reproduce, can be used without the fear of epidemics breaking out among one's own troops (this is one reason why armies, unlike terrorists, have generally been unwilling to use bio agents); intelligent bio agents that act in the same way against materials, selecting specific targets like fibre-optic cables; electromagnetic pulse generators that interrupt radio waves and small air-burst nuclear weapons that do the same (crippling GPS signals, for example); chemical energy-stored lasers and new high-energy beams that come close to being real 'death rays'. Some of this will not happen (nanotechnology may be just too difficult and expensive to mass produce), but some will – and a lot else besides.

6. Such new weapons are likely to be networked. They will each use one or more of a variety of different sensors, mostly passive, and they will intercommunicate. The division between sensors (radar, sonar, etc.) and weapons will break down as computing power increases on the micro and nano scale. Thus weapons/sensors will form a dense

web, each part of which will be relatively simple, but which by local communication will form a de-centralized intelligent system. It will offer a coordinated response to attacks and will transmit information higher up the chain of command. Such net-centric warfare will be a revolution in the RMA.[56] Net-centric systems will be quite unlike the highly centralized forms of warfare based on active information systems on which the current American style of warfare depends. Such weapons and such networks can be the arsenal of the weak as well as the strong. They will be most effective in defence and thus blunt the current dominance of the attack. Such webs will be able to absorb and disable attacks by high-end information-centric armed forces. This type of warfare poses fewer problems of information-management and control because it is de-centralized and locally self-organizing.[57] The future may thus not unambiguously belong to the USA as a military power able to exercise unchallenged global hegemony.

Like Hapsburg Spain, the USA may be faced with defences it cannot overcome, determined warriors and deadly webs of weapons. The more it seeks exclusive and preclusive dominance, the more likely it is to produce resistance. This century beyond the first couple of decades may not be an 'American century' in the way the last one was. This may be due in substantial measure to the consequences of a military-technical revolution that the USA has initiated, but over the evolution of which it has no monopoly. The USA, of course, also has the option to adapt strategically. The Bush strategy is imperial in its scope and aims. A future government may rediscover the virtues of multilateralism. It may see the value of formal alliances and appeasing potential enemies where possible. It might thus return to the long-run US practice of reserving unilateral action for last-instance emergencies rather than using it as everyday policy.

Space

It is unlikely, however, that any future electable government will make the security of the USA dependent on the goodwill of others. If the change in military technology in the next thirty years is capable of dwarfing that since the 1980s and of changing the balance of power against the USA as much as it has turned in its favour in the last twenty years, then how might America respond?

Space is vital to the contemporary capacities of the US military: satellites are now essential for intelligence, communication, navigation and weapons guidance.[58] The GPS system is vital for the majority of the current high-precision weapons and for all the ones that make high-tech bombing cheap (the JDAM is a 454 kg bomb with a $20,000 kit to steer it by GPS signals on a designated target, and this is much less than the $500,000 of a cruise missile). Thus the US needs space for conventional war. It also still needs it for the nuclear deterrent forces. It will need it for the warning and guidance systems for any effective ballistic missile defence system. Satellites will be the first line of identification of ballistic missile launches. Faced with an environment in which the defence was far stronger and able to contain US air power locally, then the American military would have no option but to rely even more on space.

This necessity would push the USA towards the active militarization of space.[59] Space is currently conceived as a de-militarized common, where weapons are forbidden by treaty. This is quite unlikely to last long in the face of military necessity. Space weapons could provide one effective counter to net-centric defences. Space platforms could overfly such local defences with impunity and attack key targets with missiles, free-fall guided bombs and powerful new lasers. Space-battle satellites may defend intelligence and communication satellites from attack by enemy missiles or killer satellites, and destroy the enemy's own information platforms in space. Orbiting battle stations may use chemical-energy lasers and laser-particle beam hybrids to defeat ballistic missiles. This time against modest numbers of missiles such systems may work, unlike SDI and more effectively than the current ground-launched ABM missiles. The creation of Space Command showed that the USA understood the stakes. It will undoubtedly seek to maintain its dominance by building new automated space stations and replacing the Shuttle fleet with a more militarily effective and safer system.

Space is a distinct environment. It has its own constraints, both physical and spatial. Because there is no air, and low to zero gravity, space stations are expensive and difficult for humans to inhabit. Space war will thus be far more automatic and inhuman than terrestrial war, no great consolation to RMA advocates. Even lasers, although they are speed-of-light weapons, are very dependent on old-fashioned geometry and mechanics. Satellites face severe constraints on their orbits. First they face a trade-off between closeness to Earth, and thus the effectiveness of sensors or weapons, and the pull of gravity, and thus length of time in orbit. Second, orbits are complex in their geometry because the Earth is basically a sphere and the problems of orbits become more pronounced as one moves away from a geo-stationary orbit above the Equator to the Poles. Most satellites have eccentric elliptical orbits, which means they are close to Earth for a relatively short period of time and then spin further out into space. This is how proximity to Earth and a long life in orbit are effectively traded off. However, this means that several satellites are needed to ensure twenty-four-hour coverage of most of the Earth. Enough satellites for all functions (photo-reconnaissance, electronic surveillance, communications and navigation) and with global reach are hugely expensive. Space war is thus one area where the USA could convert its vast wealth into military advantage over lesser powers even if they did adopt versions of the RMA for defence. Even Europe, with a GDP comparable to the USA, lacks anything like the same range of satellites. Thus neither the EU nor any of its member states has a system to rival GPS. It is therefore wholly dependent on the USA for the foreseeable future.

The upshot of this account from radar to space stations is twofold. First, electronic systems are complex and vulnerable to failure. They face physical constraints and they function badly when divorced from human skill and judgement. Second, war is never virtual: it involves morale and strategy. Even space weapons will not allow the USA to occupy another country unassisted by fighting troops. Nuclear weapons appeared to offer absolute power, but they frustrated their own use. They could only play a part in war by proxy. War can never be virtual and it can never be de-spatialized, even in space.

Part III

8

Foucault and Architecture

The French philosopher and historian of ideas, Michel Foucault, is
now an established intellectual resource for architectural theorists and
historians.[1] The object of this chapter is to indicate the points where
the concepts and analyses in his major works bear directly on architecture and the built environment, or have an immediate application
to the analysis of architecture. It is usually the case in criticism and
commentary that his later works are emphasized and seen to be different from his earlier studies.[2] The point here is not merely to stress
the continuity of his work, but to argue that separating the two parts
is often accompanied by a shallow understanding of his treatment of
power in the later works. The analysis of power/knowledge is present
from the start. Nevertheless, there are distinct emphases as his work
developed and so this chapter is divided into two parts. The first draws
on Foucault's books, *The Order of Things* and *The Archaeology of
Knowledge*, in order to show how his analysis of discursive formations enables us to re-pose the roles of ideas and theory in architecture, and to examine in a new way the relationship between discourse
and buildings.[3] The second draws on two later works, *Discipline and
Punish* and *The History of Sexuality*, vol. 1, and considers the prison
as the exemplar of a new relation between power and knowledge.[4]

I Architecture and the Statement

The Archaeology of Knowledge is of interest to architectural theorists
because it broadens and transforms the concept of discourse.
Discursive formations are patterns of order in statements quite distinct
from the familiar unities of the history of ideas – authors, books,
schools and so on. Foucault's vocabulary and method displaces or

transforms much of the intellectual apparatus of the conventional history of ideas. First and foremost it challenges the concept of 'idea' itself and its location 'in' the mind of a subject.[5] Further, it challenges the notion of influences whereby ideas pass from subject to subject and undergo subtle transformations in new minds. Discursive formations extend beyond that product of the age of humanism, the author, and beyond the provinces of humane learning.

Central to Foucault's category of discourse is the concept of the statement. Discourse is conceived as forms of order and inclusion/exclusion of statements. He defines the statement in a way that separates it very clearly from either a sentence or a proposition. Statements are not discursive in the narrow sense of being linguistic or found merely in books. To give an example, consider the tabular form of presentation. A table as a statement can be far more than just a convenient visual device illustrating an otherwise discursive text. Indeed, the table can be the crucial and constitutive form of order in a discursive formation. Consider, for example, physiocratic economics. Quesnay's *Le Tableau Economique* constructs the economy as a totality of interrelated transactions between agriculture and the other non-productive sectors: a totality that is conceived and presented spatially.[6] Such forms are no relic of the eighteenth century, but can be encountered in a transformed and highly mathematicized type of analysis in modern economics in Vassily Leontiev's input–output matrix.[7] Again, we encounter in the eighteenth century other distinctly tabular discourses, such as the classificatory natural history of Buffon and Linnaeus. Here, the whole of living nature is regarded as a series of places, an order – conventional or natural – into which all living beings can be situated as part of one exhaustive description/classification. This discursive order also exists beyond books, in the systematic layout of museums and collections, and in the practices of observing and classifying living beings themselves. In like manner, buildings or groups of structures can be regarded as 'statements' and their relations to discourses specified. Foucault is concerned to remove the concepts of statement and discourse from the ghetto of ideas, to demonstrate that discursive formations may be regarded as complex structures of discourse-practice in which objects, entities and activities are defined and constructed within the domain of a discursive formation. Thus we can regard practices of observing and recording observations as part of the order of statements: observing, drawing and presenting become discursive activities.

In *The Birth of the Clinic*, Foucault is concerned with the development of an observational-clinical medicine at the end of the eighteenth century.[8] Foucault's crucial categories here are the body and the clinical gaze. The body is a *discursive* object for Foucault, not a natural object but the abstraction of the structures and processes enclosed by the skin as a distinct domain, separated from climate, diet, regimen and mode of social life. Previous medical systems had considered man in a space of humours and harmonies; they located and dispersed disease and the body in the environment and mode of life. Clinical medicine isolates and observes bodily states and processes. Its observational 'gaze' is the product of discursive and institutional conditions. It is part of an order of statements which works from observations in a clinical context to establish disease entities and aetiologies. But it is a gaze nonetheless: observation produces results which are irreducible to their discursive conditions and which lead on to new statements, systematic classifications of what is seen.

It should be clear that in Foucault's analysis, statements are not regarded as the free products of the mind; rather, statements have what he calls 'surfaces of emergence', that is, particular institutional-organizational conditions of knowledge under which it is possible for statements to appear. Statements are not the products of human subjects in general: the statements which are part of definite discursive formations emerge from what he calls 'enunciative modalities', that is, definitely constructed subjects specific to the discursive formation, and qualified/constrained to speak in definite ways. Again, we see Foucault move from author-as-subject towards a view of the subject as agent/effect of a discursive formation. Enunciative modalities mean that only certain subjects are qualified and able to speak in particular ways: that certain statements cannot be made by everybody and anybody. Thus judgements of insanity or clinical observations become the functions of particular statuses, those of psychiatrist and doctor. The clinical observation of the body develops within and requires the institutional construction of the teaching hospital. Likewise, the determination of insanity becomes the function of the asylum. So knowledges and the subjects who produce them are connected with particular institutional conditions and forms of power. Foucault's earlier works thus anticipate in important ways the conception of power-knowledge developed in his later works. Foucault differs most dramatically from the history of ideas as conventionally conceived, not merely in his attention to fields beyond the province of 'humane' learning, for of course there are histories of medicine, of natural history and of economics. Where he differs most is in the way he links discourse to what must otherwise be regarded as the 'extra-discursive', the domain of the object. For what he does is to integrate investigative practices, observation and the products of observation within the discursive field. When things stop being words, then conventionally they stop being treated as statements and become objects rather than a part of discourse. Foucault, on the contrary, links in his concept of statement investigative practices or transformational activities and their constructed objects.

In this we can see his importance for the analysis of architecture. Because, following Foucault, we can treat the statement as something that is not merely written down in words but which nevertheless can be part of a discourse. We can consider constructed objects as components of a discursive formation, and relate the practices of the construction, inclusion and exclusion of objects to the rules and patterns of such formations. In this way we can bridge the gap between theory in architecture and spatial constructs, not merely by treating constructs as examples of a theory, but examining how discourses enter into construction and how in consequence buildings or planned environments become *statements*. Hence we are offered the possibility of a link between a discursive formation, the institutional conditions in which it becomes a practice, and the products of that practice – on the model of *The Birth of the Clinic*. If we do this properly, we find a way of superseding the problem of the 'gap' between intellectual 'influences' on architects and the practice of construction – that is, a way which avoids the problem of declared 'intentions', and their absence, and sidesteps the cul-de-sac of trying to enter the mind of the architect-author.

In order to exemplify this, I will consider the question of the 'influence' of Neoplatonic theories on Renaissance architecture, using Rudolf Wittkower's *Architectural Principles of Humanism in the Renaissance*.[9] Wittkower's book was originally well received, though with an undercurrent of controversy, precisely because critics challenged the extent and specificity of the influences he perceives. It can be claimed that his account of Palladio is over-stretched because it philosophizes an eminently practical architect, whose constructions are undogmatic and a-conceptual and whose 'intentions' in relation to key buildings are unknown. If Foucault is of use it is because he supersedes these issues of author-intentions and influences-structures. This enables us to pose questions not merely about discourses *on* architecture, but discourses *in* architecture.

Neoplatonism, resemblance and the subject of the temple

In *The Order of Things*, Foucault contrasts the *episteme* that governs key Renaissance discourses, and in which the organizing forms of knowledge are a set of categories constituting forms of resemblance, with the subsequent and very different *episteme* which replaces it in the seventeenth century, and in which the dominant organizing forms of knowledge are based on the concept of representation. What Foucault is concerned to examine are successive *epistemes* which provide a matrix in which configurations of distinct knowledges share common methods and conceptions of objects. He is concerned with the dominant overall organization of discourse which makes certain forms of existence of objects and ways of speaking about them possible. He prefaces the text with a quotation from the Argentinian writer, Jorge Luis Borges, in which the latter refers to a classification of animals in an imaginary Chinese encyclopedia. In this work animals are classified in diverse and bizarre ways, for example, as being innumerable, as being stuffed, as appearing as small as flies, and finally as being included in the present classification. Now, to us, such a form of putting animals together is incomprehensible because the categories appear to belong to wholly distinct and incompatible orders: there is no single frame for us in which these categories can be placed on the same plane of existence. The reason for this is because such a classificatory scheme has quite different presuppositions from our own about what objects can exist and in what relations. Foucault goes on to cap this by citing the Renaissance naturalist Ulisse Aldrovandi's *Treatise on the Serpent*, which does something analogous to the encyclopedia, treating snakes along with griffins, dragons and all sorts of mythological beasts, as if they were in the same register. Foucault's point is that it is not because Aldrovandi is ignorant or stupid or fails to observe that he does this, but because he has a quite different conception from our own of the order of knowledge, of the beings which are possible, and of the status as knowledge of ancient and medieval texts in which such mythical creatures are referred to and described. It is in this spirit that Foucault goes on to reconstruct the dominant Renaissance *episteme*.

Foucault's concept of *episteme* is crucial for an understanding of the intellectual role of Neoplatonism and its relation to architecture. Central to Neoplatonic thought is the absence of a modern concept of the sign, in which words denote things by representing or standing for them, and in which the sign and its referent are distinct registers. This enables us to comprehend the importance and intellectual seriousness of the key Neoplatonic doctrine of the interpenetration and respective mirroring of microcosm and macrocosm, a doctrine influential beyond identifiably Neoplatonic thinkers. In this *episteme*, the entire world, from its smallest to its greatest parts, from the humblest animal to God, consists of a series of resemblances, similarities and sympathies. Here there is no concept of an arbitrary relation in which one thing, a sign, stands for and represents another. Rather, all relations are real relations and connections between aspects of existence reflect their respective natures and their universal interpenetration. Hence symbolic relations both have significance and are real relations, that is, connections in nature. The entire universe is a set of resemblances and sympathies, with no space for the 'classical' gap between signs and existence. Renaissance thought is hyper-realist and makes symbolic or significatory connections/affirmations of common relations of form or nature. Hence we have a world presented to knowledge which consists of a series of emblems, traces, signatures and resemblances, which are the marks of that network of spiritual–real interconnections whereby the whole tissue of existence is held together. From this follows the Neoplatonic linking of ideas and experience and the doctrine of the Book of the World, whereby the world itself is conceived as a language. Nature is intelligible in itself. Such views are not confined to those who can be dismissed as devotees of magic and Cabbalism, such as Henry Cornelius Agrippa, or as misguided mystics, like Paracelsus; rather, they are subscribed to by the leading conventional intellectuals of the Italian Renaissance, philosophers such as Marsilio Ficino or Giovanni Pico della Mirandola, and, in architecture, major figures like Leon Battista Alberti.

There are in this *episteme* no gaps between thought and signs and signs and objects, as there are in Descartes and Locke.[10] With these latter thinkers there develops a notion of representation that is still identifiable in the modern concept of the sign and that still has traces in Saussure. For Locke, for example, a sensation is the 'idea' – the mental register – of a thing observed. The sign stands for an idea: it is a concept in the mind which represents by convention other concepts in the mind which are perceptions or sensations. Signs thus have a doubly complex relation to things: they 'represent' ideas, which in turn are the mental registers of sensations of things. Hence knowledge consists in what is perceived of the world of things by human sensations – themselves sensory-mental events – and signs order and stand for such sensations. Knowledge is thereby conditional on what is perceived, and signs are referential but arbitrary in the selection of the signifiers which are to stand for things. In this double gap arises the 'problem' of knowledge, that is the problem of the adequacy of the relation between ideas/sensations and the things thus perceived, and, secondly, the adequacy of the relation between word and idea.

But this problem does not exist in the Renaissance *episteme*, or more specifically in Neoplatonic theory. All relations are real relations: there is a world of visible or intelligible traces of harmony, which gives access to the cosmic order. In Neoplatonism there can be no general problem of knowledge, only a problem of the proper *use* of the faculty of intellect and the sensitivity to experience. This use may require spiritual preparation which makes the Knower fit to uncover and understand the harmonies and relations of the world-order. Instead of a problem of the adequacy of knowledge, we have a need to sensitize the subject to knowledge, to create paths for the connection between spirit, intellect and experience.

A central question, therefore, in Renaissance thought is how to present those traces of harmony and cosmic order: not how to represent them, but to make them immediately present to human subjects. Geometry has a privileged position in such presentation. Geometry is the fundamental mirroring of the natural order, since it is both an elaborated science of ordered forms and also the manifest and present form of the order of the world. The figures of geometry correspond to the constitutive proportions of the world, and the two fundamental proportional relations accessible to experience are those of the human body and those of the harmonic scale. Such 'devices' provide traces and resemblances whereby man can be put into immediate contact with the divine. Hence the familiar Vitruvian figure has a philosophical significance which belies the fact that it is a commonplace. Such figures and proportions are, moreover, supra-intentional: they present the cosmic order even if those who draw them do so from mere convention or for different purposes.

But, of course, for the Neoplatonic architectural theorist, the order of the world could best be revealed through conscious purpose, through the rationally planned design of the architect-adept which systematizes experience and puts it at the service of intellect and the superior perception of cosmic order. Hence the philosophical and practical significance of an architecture which links science, art and spiritual concerns. Proportions in structures are therefore the visible and present resemblances of the order of man and the universe. Geometrically planned and appropriately proportioned buildings, in particular centrally planned churches, have an expressive significance and practical consequence which transcend those of mere form. They are not to be conceived as a stylistic device; they are not merely the execution of an aesthetic idea in brick and stone, but are the manifest presence and physical existence of cosmic order. This cosmic order divined and devised through intellect is, in the physical presence of a building, accessible to experience, and this experience in turn produces knowledge. In the Neoplatonic theory, a definite connection is established between intellect and experience. Thus forms are perceived in the intellect, although hinted at in experience. By making the intellect's grasp of form present and intelligible to experience through rationalized structures, so another route is provided whereby the mass of common men may directly experience the immanent order of the world, which is God. The true architect should therefore be a theorist and adept in order to construct buildings, specifically churches, which produce certain direct effects on the human subjects who approach and enter into them.

Philosophy is integral to this conception of architectural practice. The value of the philosophically adept and geometrically knowledgeable architect, intellectually and spiritually prepared for his task, is thus quite distinct from the craftsman-builder or the follower of formulas. The object of theoretical training is thus no simple claim to social status and professional superiority: it is the spiritual-intellectual preparation for an eminently practical function. The task of the architect is not merely constructing spaces, but spaces which have specific expressive-experiential effects on the subject.

To turn to Wittkower, we can see that he identifies the ways in which the theoretical concepts of resemblance or sympathy are active in the architectural treatises of the period. Palladio, in his *Quattro libri*, says: 'We cannot doubt that the little temple we make ought to resemble this very great one, which by His immense goodness, was perfectly completed with one word of His.'[11] The temple mirrors the world. Again, in summing up the central role of geometry and proportion in these discourses, Wittkower remarks that: 'Renaissance artists firmly adhered to the Pythagorean concept "All is number" and, guided by Plato and the Neoplatonists and supported by a long chain of theologians from Augustine onwards, they were convinced of the mathematical and harmonic structure of the universe and all creation.'[12] Now Wittkower continues to use, although subtly and in a subversive way, the conventional theories and practices of the history of ideas. Neoplatonism is identified as a series of 'themes' to be traced as 'influences' in the architectural treatises of the period, and these 'ideas' correspond to aspects of structures. Hence the apparent possibility of criticizing him, locating these 'themes' earlier in the Middle Ages and in discourses other than Neoplatonic ones, and raising the problems of 'intentions', whether or not architect-authors like Palladio had such 'ideas' in mind when they solved practical problems of constructing villas. Foucault offers the intellectual means of sidestepping such methodological impasses.

Foucault links certain forms to a dominant *episteme*, but this concept is not an equivalent of the 'spirit of the age'. Such 'spirits' are always ambiguous. Precursors and different doctrines current at the time can always be found to locate ideas earlier than proposed by a particular concept of a Zeitgeist, or to disrupt their contemporary predominance. An *episteme* is not equivalent to a school: it underlines and governs a disparate complex of discourses, and it is in no sense unitary. Rather, it operates through a complex network of rules of inclusion and exclusion that do not prohibit the coexistence of statements which may appear thematically diverse or which have (in the vocabulary of influences) precedents and anticipations. The questions to be asked, therefore, within a Foucauldian conception of divergent forms or precedents, are the following. First, within the *episteme*, what are the limits to discursive diversity? How do statements apparently diverse when considered as 'themes' coexist, and in what relations of parallelism, contrariety or combination? Second, do statements which appear thematically similar occupy the same discursive positions? If not, in relation to what discursive formations are we to identify their significance?

Foucault thus defines a 'discursive formation' in such a way that it is necessarily complex: 'Wherever one can describe, between a number of statements, such a system of dispersion, wherever, between objects, types of statement, concepts, or thematic choices, one can define a regularity (an order, correlations, positions and functionings, transformations), we will say, for the sake of convenience, that we are dealing with a *discursive formation*.'[13] Thus apparently similar 'statements', considered as linguistic propositions, may occupy radically different places in different discursive formations. Hence it is not enough to say that the Middle Ages approached the 'problem' of proportion. The questions to be asked are in what ways, in relation to what unities of discourse, and what practices?[14] The Middle Ages clearly had a certain access to the knowledges of Antiquity and hence to geometry and proportion. As Panofsky showed, there can be multiple and diverse relations to and rediscoveries of Antiquity, and this fact also in no sense undercuts the notion of a distinctive Italian 'Renaissance'.[15]

Neoplatonism cannot be treated exclusively as a School. If it is so treated it either becomes expanded to be all-influential, or it is restricted to certain limited circles of highly explicit, philosophically influenced thinkers. The search for Neoplatonic themes and influences in Renaissance art and architecture can be narrowed or widened. It is narrowed, for example, by raising the question of 'intentions' and evidence for them or by converting themes into non-distinctive and non-controversial commonplaces. It is widened by finding Neoplatonic themes and symbolism underlying every image and every aspect of Renaissance art and thought: a notorious example is the unchecked speculations of Edgar Wind which find Neoplatonic themes everywhere.[16]

Foucault offers a route out of this impasse. Neoplatonism can be considered as a complex discursive formation within a dominant *episteme*, with the crucial aspect of this *episteme* being the relation between knowledge and the world, the mode of existence of objects. It can thus be linked with – and yet differentiated from – a complex of discourses and practices: Hermetism, Cabbalism, Natural Magic, the revival of mathematics through the use of Pythagorean and Neoplatonic doctrines, astrology, alchemy, and the search for emblemata. All of these discourses share three decisive characteristics, common rules of formation of statements:

1   Concepts of resemblance, harmony, sympathy, etc., which postulate analogous modes of existence of objects and of the relation between knowledge and the world.
2   A common relation to Antiquity as the authentic source and the prefiguration of knowledge, modern knowledge thus proceeds by *recovery*.
3   Knowledge generates practices of transformation, practices which are not 'technologies' in the modern sense, but involve a distinct relation between subject and the world, a relation in which the world as spirit-existence and the subject as spirit-intellect are brought into harmony.

Thus something very specific is entailed in the notion of 'humanism' in these discourses, something quite different from the modern humanities. Humanism involves subjective and spiritual transformation, and human learning is predicated on the discovery of the relations of resemblance between man, the order of the universe and God.

The highly particular practice involved in such architecture is the transformation of human subjects through geometrically organized space. The essence of this transformation is spiritual, and it involves a privileged place for Church architecture. Medieval constructions also seek to establish relations between man and God, insofar as we can interpret them, but the relation posited in the geometrically planned church is distinct, and is mediated through the experience of harmony. The centrally planned church is thus a power relation of a very specific type: its effectiveness depends on the credence given to the metaphysics of a particular discursive formation.

Taking the Renaissance *episteme* and its central category of resemblance, we can thus see why the centrally planned and geometric church structures of the Neoplatonic architectural theorists have to be considered as statements in a highly particular sense, and why this practice of architecture is a specific one. Further, we can see why, in relation to this *episteme*, we cannot remain at the level of intentions. This is because spatial, geometrical and harmonic relations have significance in themselves; they are not merely the rendering of ideas but the presence of real relations of resemblance effective in the mind through experience.

Structures therefore provide a means of knowledge through experience. The structure is an experience-effect. Churches with certain forms and features can produce effects of piety, the recognition of God through sympathies present in His temples, and the correct rendering through experience of God's plan. In this conception, there is not merely a subjective experience of space, but rather a set of effects which go beyond the building to the world and its Creator. So we can see Alberti means something highly specific by the statement: 'Without such sympathy between the microcosm of men and macrocosm of God, prayer cannot be effective.'[17] For it means we are dealing with the Church both as a statement and as a transformatory device. We are not merely concerned with a 'statement' in an architectural theory, but also with a concrete discourse-practice in architecture. Certain forms such as the circle are regarded as inherently symbolic and spiritually consequential: they are privileged not merely as an aesthetics of 'impressions', but in a doctrine that links experience, knowledge and religious belief.

In order to estimate this discourse as a practice, its own presuppositions cannot be set aside, for to do so is to convert the buildings assessable in these metaphysical terms either into a non-statement or into another statement, just as to view music as a sequence of sound without inherent meaning would radically transform a Monteverdi mass or opera into a statement of another class. The *episteme* of resemblance and the theory of the consequentiality of geometry/harmony cannot be set aside if we are to link architectural theory and 'practice'. To do so is to sever the specific relations of discourse and practice it should be our object to recover.

A good example of such a laying aside can be found in a text to which we shall return in the next chapter, John Hale's essay *Renaissance Fortification: Art or Engineering?*[18] Having attempted to recover Renaissance fortifications from the lumber room in which our own attributions of significance have placed them, to see why fortifications could be an object of aesthetic significance to Renaissance architects and audiences rather than consigned to a 'dirty' province of military pragmatics, Hale baulks at going too far – of moving beyond explicit intentions and acceptable evidence. He objects to the interpretation of pentagonal forts in terms of Neoplatonic theories of geometrical symbolism. He regards this as far-fetched and remarks that: 'It is highly unlikely that symbolism had anything to do with a form found to be practical well into the nineteenth century.'[19] He rather neatly betrays his indifference to the discourses of contemporary practitioners or the claims in relation to practice that follow from them. For them, the 'practicality' of such a design would be no accident but a function of harmony and the intrinsic superiority in the nature of things of certain forms. Again, to remark of the fortress of Palmanova that its symmetry could only be appreciated from the air is to miss the point: structures have significance and consequences because of what they *are*. In the Neoplatonic discourses the virtues of the study of geometrical form, of the planned execution of the purest forms, are evident, but for all the stress on the theoretical training of architects, the discourses undercut any monopoly of intention or narrowly professional training. Certain forms are privileged because of what they are and what they signify, irrespective of origins. Neoplatonic theory provides, therefore, a route to discount 'intentions', to consider structures in their forms and in their effects and not merely through their originating 'ideas'. The same route can be used with allegedly 'practical' architects like Palladio, to ignore intentions and to consider structures in themselves as statements identifiable by reference to a discursive formation, which is more than just the theories in architectural treatises, but less than a spirit of the age.

II Power-Knowledge and the Prison

Having considered how Foucault's methods and concepts can contribute to resolving problems in architectural history, we move on to his later works, *Discipline and Punish* and *The History of Sexuality*, vol.1. We shall consider his treatment of the relation between a new form of power and a new class of specialist structures which both developed towards the end of the eighteenth century. In his later works, the key theoretical innovation is the systematic linking of the categories of power and knowledge to form a hybrid 'power-knowledge'. Foucault regards this both as the consequence and the condition of the rise of forms of 'disciplinary power' from the eighteenth century onwards. He considers such forms the distinctive feature of modern forms of control of and transformation of subjects. *Discipline and Punish* is focused around an account of the development of the modern prison, and it is concerned to challenge a pervasive Enlightenment view of truth and power as inherently opposed forces. Foucault considers this opposition of truth to power to depend on what he calls the 'juridico-discursive' concept of power. In this conception, power is regarded as a possession: it is something that the sovereign subject possesses and other subordinate subjects do not have. The essence of this power consists in prohibition: it is the power to say no, to forbid, to suppress. Power is thus conceived of as fundamentally negative, as a punitive relation between the dominant and the subordinate subject. Power is possessed exclusively by dominant subjects and is a means of holding down and repressing subordinate subjects such that they conform to the will of the former. We can thus see why, in this juridico-discursive conception, power and truth are perceived as in inevitable opposition. Truth must be considered as a means of critique of power and must at all costs avoid the corruption of power, because power is negative and is the exclusive property of subjects who hold others in suppression. Truth allied to power becomes corrupted by it, by the demands of limits to knowledge which must follow from the unfair control of property and from repression. So in the Enlightenment critique of this conception of power, held to be characteristic of Absolutism, power is held to deny, to suppress truth, and to work in darkness and through secrecy. Truth on the other hand is universal and should be the property of all humankind: it should bring enlightenment and promise emancipation and concord.

A very good example of this Enlightenment critique is the Italian penal reformer, Cesare Beccaria, to whom we shall return later.[20] He attacks the tortures and arbitrary and excessive punishments held to be characteristic of Absolutism in the interests of a penal regime based on knowledge and law. In this new regime, punishments are certain and calculable, and law is a guide to action that can be known by all and to which all are subject.

In contradistinction to this essentially negative and sovereign-centred view of power, Foucault argues that in the modern era power is productive of knowledge and knowledge is productive of power. This involves a new view of power and new types of power, of which the most important is 'disciplinary power'. This form of power is transformative of those subject to it and it uses knowledge as a resource in the process. Far from being merely prohibitive, the controls of this new form of power are productive. Power does not merely draw on existing social resources in the form of a levy, but acts to create and multiply resources. Knowledge is a necessary resource of power. Thus power needs definite knowledges in order to be productive.

And, vice versa, power is a crucial resource of certain knowledges. This is because power constructs the 'surfaces of emergence' that make discourses and knowledges able to function as such. Knowledge is thus implicated in institutions and definite power relations. A good example is clinical medicine, which was tied directly to the health care for, and regulation of, the poor.[21] Clinical-observational medicine depended on large numbers of cases being brought into the hospital, on the separation and classification of cases, and on the controls and forms of institutional order which made this possible. Clinical medicine used the bodies of the poor as a resource of knowledge, to be dissected for research and teaching. As a result of a large number of cases gathered together, the clinical observation of disease entities and the examination of the organic structures of cadavers made new knowledge possible. The hospital is not merely a site of care, but a machine of observation – a central institutional condition for the clinical 'gaze'. The new surfaces of emergence in clinical medicine thus depended on definite institutions, on their social and organizational (and not merely their discursive) conditions of existence. In summing up his view of power-knowledge, Foucault remarks:

> If power were never anything but repressive, if it never did anything but say no, do you really think one could be brought to obey it? What makes power hold good, what makes it accepted, is simply the fact that it doesn't only weigh on us as a force that says no, but that it traverses and produces things; it induces pleasure, forms knowledge, produces discourse. It needs to be considered as a productive network which runs through the whole social body, much more than as a negative instance whose function is repression.[22]

Thus Foucault does not merely link knowledge and power while leaving the traditional repressive and sovereign-centred notion of power untouched. Power is not simply a global relation between the sovereign, who is the source of prohibitive power, and the subjects who are subordinate to this power. Power does not proceed downwards from a single centre. Rather, the power relation Foucault is concerned with has no simple centre but is diffused throughout the whole social body in complex networks and diverse relations. He refers to the need for a 'micro-physics of power', considering all the sites of its exercise and functioning and not merely the gross repressive forms associated with the state. Sites like hospitals, insane asylums, schools, and so on, are considered as centres of power-knowledge.

In order to consider such forms, Foucault introduces the concept of 'disciplinary power'. The essence of such power is not repressive force but 'surveillance'. The surveillance of subjects is a crucial mode in which they are transformed. Surveillance requires both knowledges and institutions ordered by knowledge for its functioning. It depends on the isolation and specification of individuals such that its controls can be brought to bear and can effect the work of the transformation and construction of subjects. Individuals are isolated from social collectivities and one another. Their conduct is brought under continuous inspection and subjected to norms of performance, a process Foucault calls 'normatizing individuation'. Subjects are constructed in institutions in such a way that they too become a resource of power: workers in factories, children in the schools of the bourgeoisie, and so on. Subjects are transformed into beings of a particular type, whose conduct is patterned and governed, and who are endowed with definite attributes and abilities. Such forms of power do not merely act upon workers or the poor, but also on the bourgeoisie themselves through education and the transformation of the home.

The model of this form of power based on surveillance, which individuates and transforms, is the penitentiary prison. And the archetypal form of such a prison as a system of power based on surveillance, where individuals are brought under what Foucault calls the 'eye' of power, is to be found in the English social reformer Jeremy Bentham's proposal for a panoptical prison. The Panopticon was a design for a prison in which the conduct of all the inmates and all of its internal space is subject to inspection by the directive staff. The Panopticon is a circular structure in which each of the floors is divided into a series of cells around the circumference; these cells isolate the inmates, and at the centre of the structure is an inspection tower, from which each of the cells on each of the floors can be observed. The principle is that light comes in through the windows or slits on the circumference of the structure such that each of the cells is back-lit. This makes it possible for the observer in the tower to see without being seen. To the inmate, the inspection tower is darkened and he or she cannot see through the slits on the tower into the centre. The prisoner does not know whether he is being observed or not. At any given moment the prisoner must presume himself to be under observation, with the consequence that conduct is governed by surveillance twenty-four hours a day. One person moving up from the inspector's lodge and walking round in the inspection tower can see each of the galleries in the structure. Because Bentham believed in transparency, the inspection tower was to be open to the public, and their gaze would ensure the competence of the warders and the good order of the prison. The custodians are thus guarded in the same way as they manage the prisoners: by inspection.

Bentham called the Panopticon an 'idea in architecture'. Its principle is that the many can be governed by the few, and its object is in Bentham's pithy phrase 'to grind rogues honest'. This 'grinding' takes place through the uninterrupted surveillance of conduct. It should be said that when Bentham refers to an 'idea' here, he means the concept of a structure. The idea is a construction, a space which makes possible both a certain discourse and certain power relations. The Panopticon is both a possible construction and a 'statement' in construction. It is the space and site of a certain form of productive power. The 'gaze' of the inspector in the tower is a form of power-knowledge; it is productive both of controls over subjects and the re-modelling of their conduct, just as the gaze of the clinician in the hospital is productive of observational knowledges.

Bentham's idea did not spring from his own head alone. Foucault treats Bentham's model of such a construction as an example of a supra-individual 'strategy'. A 'strategy' is a definite pattern of means and objectives that can be discovered operating across a number of sites. The prison of which the Panopticon is a model is one of a series of structures embodying the surveillance principle. Bentham drew his initial conception of the inspection principle from his brother's visit to the Military School of Paris, built in 1751. In this school, the dormitories were so constructed that each pupil was assigned a glassed-in cell, and, thus completely isolated from direct contact with his fellows, he could be observed by the supervising master. This made it possible to regulate the extra-curricular conduct of the pupils and to prevent unacceptable sexual practices. This example of the inspection principle was by no means isolated. Diverse structures were being constructed in the mid-eighteenth century with the object of isolating and controlling individuals. Barracks and military hospitals are an example. Separation and inspection had the objective of both maintaining discipline and promoting hygiene, thus preventing the fevers which led to such high mortality in places where military personnel were crowded together. Great attention was paid not merely to separation of individuals and supervision, but also to promoting the flow of air and the drainage of waste. Hence both internal arrangements and structures as a whole were being transformed with regard to the 'strategy' of inspection and separation.[23]

Bentham's Panopticon is distinct in that it is an elegant example of rationalizing the whole structure such that it corresponds to certain demands of use. The whole construction is built around the strategy of inspection. In this it differs from merely setting up devices within an otherwise conventional structure as in the Military School or the systems of wards or pavilions in the military hospitals, which were not wholly subordinated to the inspection principle. In this sense it is a systematically functional architecture: a space organized by certain demands of utilization and worked out rigorously to facilitate them.

We can contrast this functionalism with other structures planned according to a schema. In the centrally planned churches of Alberti and others in the Renaissance, the rationalization of the structure is governed by the very different demands of its producing effects on subjects. The structure reflects a geometrical order, and it is this order that is supposed to have direct experience-effects on subjects. Space here is governed by expressive relations, and it is these relations which are held to impinge on subjects rather than any practice distinct from the structure that utilizes the space. While the structure sustains and validates practices such as prayer, it is not a 'prayer-machine'.

This is one example of a very different way in which a discourse and certain demands following from it are inscribed in a structure. Another example is artillery fortification, to which we shall return in the next chapter. Here again, space is governed by geometrical considerations, but those requirements of patterned space are not primarily expressive. Rather, in this case, the geometrical plan is subject to the demands of creating interlocking fields of fire, and the dominant consideration in the rationalization of the ground plan is that there be no dead ground which cannot be observed and swept with gunfire. Given the central role of the geometrical rationalization of space it is not surprising that it was Italian Renaissance architects who developed the bastioned trace. It is possible that some of the architects involved in the central innovations may have subscribed to Neoplatonic theories. This may have facilitated their break with previous practices of fortification and also with the very different models offered by Antiquity. Classical fortification in no way resembles artillery fortification. Renaissance military architects were thus not simply 'returning' to classical Roman models like Vitruvius.

But geometricization serves another function in the fortress from that in the church, one which certainly does not exclude expressive relations but which must accommodate them in the course of meeting military demands. In the centrally planned church, the relation of the subject to God is very different from Bentham's inmate to the inspector in the Panopticon. The space of the church does not facilitate God's inspection of the subject. Rather, the relation is the other way round, in that it is the lesser subject perceiving in the spatial order of the church the eternal and unchanging nature of the greater subject, God. Transformation is not effected by power relations.

Similarly, the spatial formula of the fortress is primarily directed not inwards towards the subjects of the city, but outwards. Observation and inspection are primarily directed outwards towards the surrounding ground to be controlled by fire. Certain fortresses and citadels obviously did serve to overawe the towns they enclosed or adjoined, such as the Spanish Citadel at Antwerp. Street plans sometimes did reflect the demands of the assembly of troops and the limitation of damage from bombardment, as was the case with Palmanova. But there was no simple and direct relation between the bastioned trace and the town plan or the social relations within the walls. A perfect bastioned trace like Antwerp or like Naarden in Holland could thus enclose either a cowed populace or a free citizenry. These examples, the centrally planned church, the bastioned fortress and the penitentiary prison, show that discourses concerned with the rationalization of space can lead to quite different forms of 'statement-structure' and involve quite different functional principles in rationalizing space.

Prisons existed long before Bentham and long before the reform measures that led to the large-scale construction of penitentiary prisons in Europe and America from the late eighteenth century onwards. But the prison is transformed into the 'penitentiary', and this change of function involves a change in structure and the considerations acting on it. The first consideration involves the spatial demands of facilitating the inspection principle. This leads to as radical a relation between structure and fields of vision as an artillery fortress, although for very different functional demands. The second consideration is that the prison sustain a rigid timetable which affects every aspect of the life of inmates and that it facilitate the segregation of individuals and classes of offender. The 'strategy' embodied in the new type of prison is that it transform the conduct of its inmates through governing their behaviour. It is a penitentiary, the aim of which is to reform criminals and to bring them to a full cognizance of their guilt. Previous prison structures were sites of incarceration or detention for those awaiting execution or trial, or as a pressure to redeem a debt.

Here we shall consider two examples of prison structures to contrast with the new penitentiary regime whose model is the Panopticon. The first is George Dance the Younger's design for the new Newgate prison, and the other is the world of imaginary prisons in Giovanni Battista Piranesi's *Carceri*.[24] In Piranesi's case his prisons are an imaginary architecture of *supplice*.

Supplice is the form of exemplary punishment meted out by the monarch under the *ancien régime* for a regicide, parricide, traitor or other serious malefactor. The king rules the state and the father the family: royal justice thus regards patriarchal power as a vital part of the political order. Such crimes were therefore regarded alike as *lèse-majesté*. It is an affront to the power of the sovereign and is countered by a demonstration of the sovereign's dominion in the systematic destruction of the body of the offender in torture and execution. *Supplice* thus fits directly with a conception of power and repression and a capacity exclusively possessed by the sovereign. *Discipline and Punish* opens with a contrast between the spectacle of the execution of a regicide in 1757 and a prison timetable for a juvenile reformatory eighty years later. These contrasting examples show two quite distinct regimes of punishment. The *Carceri* are an imaginary architecture that fits exactly with this exemplary and savage punishment, as much as Bentham's Panopticon is an imaginary figuration of the new penitentiary prisons (Illustration 1).

Illustration 1
G. B. Piranesi, *Carceri d'invenzione*, c. 1761, Second State VIII
(*The Prisons* (*Le Carceri*); Copyright © Courtauld Institute)

In the illustration, wretched individuals groan under instruments of torture, and tiny figures are lost amidst the lattice work of bridges, the immense machines and vast decorative features. The prison is a grotesque theatre for torture, an imaginary structure which intimidates subjects by its bulk and monumental brutality. These imaginary prisons have no rationalized or evident plan. Rather, they serve to make arbitrary power expressive and visible through the sheer mass of the structure, which dwarfs the inmates, and through the darkness which pervades all despite the immensity of the internal space. Such prisons are sites for torture, incarceration and exemplary punishment, and their form is correspondingly monumental and expressive. They are quite different from the ordered cells pervaded by light of the Panopticon.

This view of the *Carceri* is closely influenced by Foucault. The Italian architectural historian, Manfredo Tafuri, in *Architecture and Utopia*, interprets Piranesi very differently.[25] For him, the *Carceri* are not an imaginary repetition of the horrors of the *ancien régime* but, on the contrary, an anticipation of the alienation of modern man in the formless space of the city created by capitalism. He says as follows: 'And Piranesi translates into images not a reactionary criticism of the social promises of the Enlightenment, but a lucid prophecy of what society liberated from the ancient values and their consequent restraints, will have to be.'[26]

Even allowing for Tafuri's eminence as an architectural historian, it is difficult see how the construction he puts upon the *Carceri* can be sustained. First, I cannot see how Piranesi's iconography has modernist overtones, how in the images he presents there is any actual anticipation of the modern industrial city. What subsequent artists and architects *made* of Piranesi is another matter. The *Carceri* and the *Campo Marzio* reconstructions serve as materials for later readings and practices. But Tafuri says much more than this if we read him to the letter. In effect, he attributes an inherent modernist aesthetic effect to Piranesi. Second, Piranesi can be illuminatingly interpreted by bringing to bear the suppositions of eighteenth-century reformers like Beccaria about torture, incarceration and arbitrary power.

Piranesi's prisons are nothing less than a picture of the darkness the Enlightenment critics perceived to be the essence of the *ancien régime*: they are a gloomy stage for arbitrary punishment, for the excesses of torture and injustice. They are in that sense not a 'reactionary criticism' of the Enlightenment, since there is no gloss that permits them to be considered as a challenge to the reformers. Rather, they are the *image* of what reformers found repellent in the prisons and tortures of the *ancien régime*. To say that 'In the *Carceri* we are already in the presence of an anguish dominated by the anonymity of the person and the silence of things' is to treat the *Carceri* as an empty, silent space of alienation.[27] But it is a full space, pregnant with the darkness of arbitrary power and the anonymity of the person is that of his helplessness before despotism, not modem capitalism.

To call the *Carceri* an imaginary architecture of *supplice* extends the meaning of *supplice*, for the closed space of the prison is not the public exemplary space of the scaffold. But the analogy holds because the *Carceri* are a massification of the dungeons and torture chambers of the Inquisition and the Absolutist State. The vast internal space of Piranesi's prisons turns them into a theatre equivalent to the public scaffold. They are at once a closed and dark space and, at the same time, an immense planless space open to the gaze of the spectator and expressive of an awesome arbitrary power. They both enclose the victims, forever isolating them in the grip of repressive power, and also admit the spectator as a voyeur. They combine as images the dungeon and the scaffold, the secret places of incarceration of the *ancien régime*, and the public brutalities of exemplary punishment. They both horrify the spectator and make him complicit with a guilty secret.

We now turn from Piranesi's imaginings to the practical demands of construction. The traditional function of the prison was to detain, and its internal spaces were not rationalized according to any functional scheme of use. This was because there was no conception of a 'regime' such as we find in the notion of a timetable and in the surveillance necessary to make prisoners conform to it. In the purely custodial prison, prisoners were neither isolated one from another nor from the outside; commonly they could purchase food and receive visitors. Privileged noble and bourgeois prisoners were permitted to re-create their domestic arrangements within the prison, at a price. Insofar as this type of building's function concerns its form, it relates primarily to the facade rather than to the organization of its internal spaces. The custodial prison was often monumental, symbolizing its strength and solidity, but its plan was not subject to the demands of inspection. Dance's design illustrates this well (Illustration 2). It is immediately prior to Bentham's proposal for a Panopticon, but it embodies a completely different 'idea in architecture'. It is dominated by a massive facade, visible from the street but not to the inmates. It was designed to impress passers-by. Within, it is divided into a series of squares. It is characterized by numerous dead angles and has no principle of circulation such as minimizes the demands for inspection. Its arrangements do not permit easy isolation and classification of inmates. As such, it is an unpoliceable building. But it was not designed systematically to regulate conduct, merely to contain prisoners. Its exterior

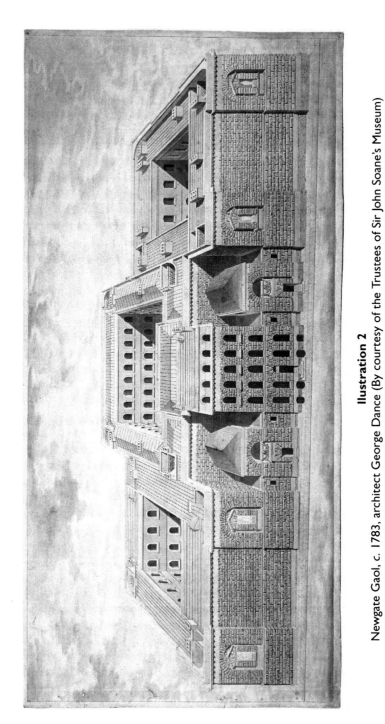

Illustration 2

Newgate Gaol, c. 1783, architect George Dance (By courtesy of the Trustees of Sir John Soane's Museum)

symbolizes its functions: to detain before execution. It is a preliminary symbolism to the scaffold, and designed to intimidate.[28]

Foucault's concept of disciplinarity thus enables us to comprehend important differences in a certain class of structures. It enables us to see the Panopticon in terms of an architecture immersed in discourses and pursuant of strategy, as a form of power, rather than in terms of style. Newgate can be viewed in terms of conventional considerations of style and also found wanting as a device for a strategy. The one possibility is closely connected with the other. Conventional considerations of style and the demand for intimidating facade can happily coexist. Inspection implies a new organization of space, one in which style is secondary. A Panopticon could be built like a large shed. Foucault's concept enables us to fully appreciate the difference between these two 'ideas'. It links architecture to the functioning of institutions of power/knowledge and, thereby, provides us with another measure of structures than styles or technical solutions to constructional problems.

Bentham's Panopticon was never built, but it is not an irrelevancy, a mere idea, for all that. This is because many prison structures did systematically pursue the demands of the inspection principle and of an internal reformatory regime. Radial and star plans, rows of cells in galleries and inspection towers are all testimonies to the relevance of Foucault's emphasis on Bentham's 'idea'. Prison regimes attempted to isolate and transform, as in the case of the Auburn and Philadelphia systems in the USA. The Auburn Prison in New York was based on the system of solitary confinement but associated silent work. The Philadelphia system was based on both solitary confinement and isolated work. Prison regimes have never worked as the reformers hoped, and the prison has never succeeded in its apparent task, reform. Again, these failures do not undermine the centrality of the prison as a means of comprehending disciplinarity.[29]

Quite different constructional schemes were also attempts to pursue a disciplinary strategy. For example, the Retreat at York constructed by William Tuke was purpose-built as an insane asylum.[30] Its disciplinary mode is quite different from Bentham's inspection principle, but also embodies the strategy of 'normatizing individuation'. The Retreat was constructed to sustain an architecture of impressions but one very different from Alberti's churches or Newgate Gaol. For the impressions created by architecture were at the service of a transformative regime which is disciplinary. The Retreat combined the necessity of detaining the insane with a 'domestic atmosphere' (Illustration 3).

The patients were deceived by bars concealed as ordinary domestic sash windows, and by walls which are hidden by the landscaping of

Illustration 3
Exterior view, The Retreat, York
(By courtesy of The Retreat, York)

the grounds. Discipline proceeded not through inspection by means of the functional organization of visibility, but via surveillance through domesticity. The restraint of the mad was to be achieved through the patterning of conduct on the domestic normality of 'family life'. Deviation becomes visible by its gross departure from ordered gentility. Surveillance works through a different mode and architecture is subordinate to the demands of the domestic management of the insane.

These demands could be multiplied in relation to the architecture of hospitals, schools, factories and so on. This section has concentrated on the architectural consequences of the inspection principle, but Foucault's concepts offer the means to reassess and analyse the mass of new special-purpose structures created from the nineteenth century onwards. One could use Foucault's concept of power-knowledge to analyse domestic housing, in particular the need to construct spaces for the formation of 'family life' among workers and the regulation of the sexuality of family members. Many interesting insights are to be found in this regard in Foucault's *History of Sexuality*, vol. 1, and in Jacques Donzelot's *The Policing of Families*.[31] This would stray from architecture proper into the whole field of governance of social life.

9

The Defence of Places: Fortification as Architecture

From Castles to Bastions – The Advent of Artillery Fortification

The millennium has led us to reflect on the character of the last 1,000 years in most major fields of endeavour. In architecture one observation can be made about European buildings for the greater part of that time: two classes of structures stand out for their scale, their durability, and the investment and effort expended upon them – churches and fortifications. Crudely put, Europe invested in the means of physical and spiritual security. Churches were a way to salvation and thus a defence against eternal damnation. Architectural historians have lavished their attention on churches, and so has the heritage industry. If we consider fortifications, the situation is quite different and rather curious. For the first 500 years the main form of fortification was the castle. These structures are regarded as romantic and picturesque, much visited by the public and expensively maintained by heritage bodies. In the early sixteenth century castles were supplemented or replaced by artillery fortification, most modelled on the *trace italienne* (a polygonal structure with arrowhead bastions covering the curtain walls of the faces). The bastioned fortress survived for well over three centuries – from the 1530s to the 1850s – as a viable means of the defence of places. However, the bastioned fortress and the more modern fortifications that replaced it have never enjoyed the same degree of interest from architects or architectural historians, and until recently they were ignored by the heritage industry and the general public.[1]

The reasons are not hard to find. Many of these structures are difficult to identify, since they consist in the main of earthen ramparts that barely show above a ditch covered by a *glacis*. Often they have become city parks, with mature trees further masking their features. In other cases their traces mark the city with a distinctive feature: in Vienna the Ringstrasse, in Paris the *Périphérique*. But the fortifications themselves have been demolished. In all cases the shape and symmetry of the bastioned trace is almost impossible to appreciate from ground level. Consider Naarden (Illustration 4) or Palmanova, two well-preserved examples, the symmetrical plans of which are revealed only by an aerial shot.

We saw in chapter 8 that J. R. Hale raised the question of this neglect, but in a form dominated by aesthetic considerations: 'In the mainstream of architectural history fortifications are accorded but a fitful or embarrassed attention. They are historically important, but are they, can they, be beautiful? Are they a proper concern for the historian of art, or should they be left to that perhaps drabber figure, the chronicler of engineering?'[2] Hale recognized that Renaissance polymaths would have regarded the question as meaningless, but he never wholly escaped from its clutches.

There are several reasons to refuse this question and to pose other more pertinent ones. First, architecture is not just about art: it is also about power, control and social significance. Europeans lived in an urban world circumscribed by walls that defended, controlled and often dominated them. Fortifications were a realm of power technique, not just of military engineering. They facilitated the inspection and control of populations. At night the gates were closed, and by day those entering and leaving were subject to inspection by guards at the ornamental gates. In many cases residence depended on the will of the governor, and the governor or the town council could control building within the walls and in the suburbs on grounds of defence. Many fortresses were planned towns, built anew or reconfigured with defence but also social control in mind. The history of fortifications as power over civilians remains to be written, but it is a vital part of the European experience of urbanism. These controls were as real if the walls enclosed a self-governing republic like Lucca, over one of the gates of which was inscribed the word 'Liberta', or if they overawed a rebellious citizenry as with the Duke of Alva's citadel at Antwerp.

Second, artillery fortifications mark a radical departure in the history of architecture. As we saw in the previous chapter, they are the clearest example before the penitentiary prison of space rationalized according to the demands of a functional programme. In chapter 8 we saw that Michel Foucault argued that the panoptical prison subjects the structure to the rationalized demands of the inspection principle and to the requirement of a regime of control and reform of the inmates initiated by a new conception of incarceration as transformation of

Illustration 4

Aerial view of Naarden (Copyright © KLM Aerocarto, Arnhem. No. 38079)

men's souls.[3] Likewise, we saw that Rudolf Wittkower demonstrated the principle of the rationalization of space according to a programme also underlies the centrally planned churches of the Renaissance.[4] The bastioned fortress was subject to as radical a domination of the structure by the spatial demands of its form of use as the Panopticon. Artillery fortification in its developed form was governed by geometry, with space being dominated by functional demands, and the resultant structures are consequences of this logic rather than of stylistic considerations. The Renaissance fortification engineer subjected the whole space beyond the walls of the city to rationalization. The *glacis* screened the bastions and curtain walls from hostile artillery fire. The bastions gave interlocking fields of fire over a kilometre or more of open ground and also along the faces of the adjoining bastions and curtains, thus creating a zone swept by artillery in which there is no dead ground. The Renaissance fortress is thus of considerable interest as an example of architectural form.

Third, the Renaissance fortress teaches us a general lesson about the history of design and technology. Although the artillery fortress is an example of a structure rationalized according to a certain programme of use, it by no means follows from this that the *trace italienne* is an example of the long-discredited axiom that 'form follows function'. That would imply a simple linear relationship in which function defines form and is causally prior to it. Here, in the case of the fortress, function and the form chosen to accomplish it are intimately and reciprocally connected. There was no necessary reason why the geometrical constraints of artillery fortification should result in the form of a bastioned trace consisting of arrowhead-shaped structures flanking each other and the curtain walls. Other systems were possible, as examples from leading artists like Michelangelo (Illustration 5) and Dürer indicate.[5] The saw-tooth design of the *tenaille trace* is equally effective in providing converging fields of fire. In the late eighteenth century experts like Carnot and Montalembert returned to Dürer's idea of multi-level gun towers as the key to new systems of defence. The bastioned trace was a consequence of the prevailing ideas of how to rationalize space. Regular polygons were the geometrical solution likely to be preferred by Italian Renaissance intellectuals to the problem of interlocking fields of fire. It also answered to a practical consideration, largely ignored today because architectural history and military history are generally written in splendid isolation one from the other, that artillery was extremely scarce until the very end of the sixteenth century. Small bastions make economical use of the available guns against threatened curtain walls. The history of the development of the bastioned fortress is thus very different from a simple and inevitable engineering solution.

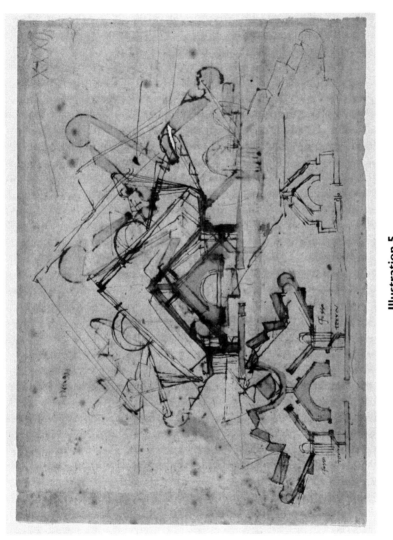

Illustration 5

Designs for fortifications, Florence, c. 1528, Michelangelo (Copyright © Scala Picture Library)

There was a range of other spatial systems, and thus the choice of one technology over another cannot be understood in purely technical terms. The issues at stake are wider than art or engineering: they are intellectual, political and economic. The influence of Neoplatonism on geometry and the periodization of the growth of the English and Swedish iron industries are perhaps more pertinent to answering why Renaissance fortifications developed as they did, than the option of regarding them either as art or as engineering.

Lastly, Renaissance publics *did* have the means to appreciate the symmetry and system of the new fortresses. Printing, a technology developed contemporaneously with the gunpowder artillery that made the new investments in city walls necessary, made possible splendid engravings. Books were available to prosperous citizens showing the cities of Europe and their fortifications. Braun and Hogenburg in the mid-sixteenth and the Merian brothers in the mid-seventeenth centuries offered plan views of the bastioned fronts of Europe's major cities.[6] Artillery fortifications were a sign of modernity, and their aesthetic qualities could be appreciated in full, in a way a casual tourist today cannot. Kings and city councils took pains to enhance the experience of the fortifications for the citizen or foreign merchant passing through the walls. Elaborate gates, mostly in the style of classical triumphal arches, showed off the paraphernalia of Mars. In the main, the gates were the one element in which considerations of style had significance rather than the considerations of artillery sight lines. Thus the aesthetic and symbolic experience of the fortified place was quite different and also far more intense in the Renaissance than it is today. Central to the question of fortification as 'art', is 'for whom?' The answer in our aesthetic, which tends to exclude the practical, is probably not. But for Renaissance contemporaries, fortifications could certainly be beautiful.

The artillery fortress is the built environment equivalent of Marcel Mauss's 'total social facts'. Various aspects of life are at once combined in such structures and they require several disciplines to understand their true import.[7] Architectural, military and socio-economic histories need to be combined to explain how the fortress and the fortified city functioned: no single one will be sufficient. It is necessary to integrate architectural and technical with military history, in order to explain how fortifications were used. The fortress is part of an ensemble of means of fighting, including weapons, tactics, military skills and strategic objectives. One cannot appreciate it as a building unless one takes that into account.[8]

In the greater part of the millennium, sieges far outnumber battles: the defence of places is a central part of war and their capture the principal strategic objective. Certain simple continuities impose the inevitability of sieges as the dominant form of warfare, from the Crusades until Napoleon. As we have seen in chapter 6, one might consider this a kind of military *longue durée*. One of the chief difficulties is the fact that armies could not keep the field throughout the year. An army could march all over the country of a theatre of operations and yet have to withdraw without effect unless it could find winter quarters. These would inevitably be in a defended place, and the invading army could not acquire that without a siege. Feudal armies, moreover, seldom had obligations of service that would extend beyond a short campaigning season. Second, we have seen in chapter 6 that the economic limitations on the size of armies through most of the millennium, the poor condition of roads, and the limited food surpluses to be had from the countryside into the eighteenth century, meant that political objectives had to be confined to the capture of at most one or two key places leading to the control of a region or province. Warfare could seldom be decisive save by steady attrition. Witness the long Muslim struggle to remove the European invaders from Outremer, the Hundred Years War over the English attempt to build an empire in France, and the Eighty Years War in which Spain sought to subdue the Netherlands. Cities were means of domination of the surrounding countryside, as were major castles. Hence in all but the small handful of pacified regions in Europe, urban space had to be defended. Sieges were part of the normal experience and expectation of urban dwellers, and fortifications were for most of them a welcome source of security.

The continuity in the military and social role of defended places between 1000 and 1800 is in contrast to the fundamental discontinuity in their form. In the fifteenth century defences based on high walls began to give way to ones in which vertical surfaces had at all costs to be screened against artillery. We tend to regard the walled place, castle or city as ancient, going back to the sieges of the Assyrians and the wars between cities in Hellenic Sicily. But the perspective of the millennium gives us a new focus. Elaborate stone fortifications were actually quite recent in most of medieval Western Europe when they were rendered obsolete by gunpowder in the fifteenth century. They were also products of a rapid evolution, being highly sophisticated and in no way inferior to their successors, either in matters of architectural technique or military function. From the sixth to the tenth centuries AD in Northern Europe, stone buildings were a rarity. Most of Europe was too poor and too de-centralized to copy or even to conserve Roman achievements and legacies.[9] Before the tenth century defences were based on earth ditches and wooden palings. Motte and bailey castles were effective against raids, and few pirates or local feudal foes had the means to mount a regular siege. As feudal rule expanded eastwards into Germany, the Baltic coast and Poland, and westwards in the Norman Conquest of England, it secured its control over new manors with these earthen defences.[10]

Stone castles are an index of centralization, of new monarchies and empires, just as Roman and Byzantine fortifications were. In England royal castles strengthened the power of the king over barons and subject Saxons alike. In Syria the great crusader fortresses like the Crac des Chevaliers, Beaufort and Soana (Sahyun) served the dual purpose of protecting feudal power by overawing the locals from whom revenue was extracted, and of preventing reconquest by the Muslims by forcing their field armies either to conduct a successful siege or to retreat. These fortresses were difficult to overcome, especially in an area where water supplies and surplus food were scarce, and they represented spectacular achievements for their builders, the feudal lords of Outremer and the military orders of the Hospitallers and the Temple. In Wales the great coastal castles of Caernarvon, Harlech and Beaumaris secured the English conquests.[11] They served as a base for offensive operations and also offered a highly defensible site which could be re-supplied by sea.

Medieval castles were frequently strategic in their location and often part of a plan of expansion and control. They were means of domination over captured territories and bases of resistance against forces far larger than could be mobilized by a local feudal lord. Feudal lords built in stone too; often great lords rivalled the king in power and, in areas where the economic growth of the twelfth and thirteenth centuries created considerable surplus wealth, they could build substantial castles on their domains. Cities also bought rights of self-government and fortification. In Northern Europe most cities were founded after the year 1000 and became substantial centres of wealth with the twelfth-century renaissance. In poor frontier areas, small local stone fortifications, for example, peel towers in the Scottish and English borderlands, were essential in societies where raiding warfare was endemic. Even in cities threatened by inter-clan strife, stone towers were built to protect urban residences. The remains of this once common phenomenon in Italy can be seen in San Gimignano today.

The fact remains that sophistication is closely connected with centralization and with economic growth. The new sophisticated fortifications of the twelfth and thirteenth centuries are a departure in Europe, so much so that it was often supposed that they were a form of technology transfer from the Muslim world as a result of the lessons learnt by the crusaders. This has long been discredited.[12] A society that could build the great cathedrals could build castles too. Crusader strongholds were not copies of Byzantine or Muslim strongholds, and the sudden achievement of more complex structures in Europe owes far more to changing political and economic factors than it does to influences from Syria.

The castle in its developed form deliberately created a favourable imbalance between the forces needed to defend it and those needed to besiege it. The English could thus hold out in their conquests in France with relatively thin garrisons and a small field army that could be mobilized from the garrisons to threaten besiegers. Concentric lines of defence, each overlooking the other as at Crac in its developed form, or Beaumaris, were defended primarily by firepower, by crossbows firing from numerous covered arrow slits. The knights of the garrison in normal times held the rent-paying local territory in check; they might join the field army (as was typically the case with a major Muslim invasion in Outremer), or they would hold vulnerable spots like gateways or breaches during a major siege. The medieval fortress thus projected its power outward. At its most developed, it relied on firepower as much as the fortress of the sixteenth century. Most castles made extensive use of guns in the late fourteenth and fifteenth centuries. Round towers offered flanking fire along curtain walls by means of bows and guns.

The defeat of the English in France, finally expelled in 1453, and the fall of Constantinople in the same year to the guns constructed by a Christian renegade for the Turks, were the crisis points in the traditional system of fortification.[13] Yet they provoked no decisive response in the way fortifications were built. Castles retained their form and further adapted to artillery. Salses Castle near Rousillon, built in 1498, is a fortress adapted to artillery: its walls are 18 metres thick, their profile lowered and rounded to deflect cannonballs, and its towers pierced by embrasures for guns. But it is still a castle.[14] The invasion of Italy by the French Army of Charles VIII in 1494 had a more profound impact. The walls of Italian castles and cities fell with great rapidity. The English defenders at the end of the Hundred Years War were often too few to mount an active defence, allowing guns to be brought very close to the walls, and the English lacked the field forces to relieve their besieged places. Equally, many Italian walls were weak, ill-maintained and poorly defended. Charles's guns were far more mobile and powerful than those with which the Bureau brothers had cleared France. Like them, they used iron shot, making possible a lighter cast barrel, but they were mounted on new and effective field carriages.

As Pepper and Adams demonstrate, it took some eighty years for an effective bastioned trace to become the model for future fortifications, from the fall of Constantinople in 1453 to the Fortezza da Basso of 1533 by Antonio da Sangallo Jr., which is the first fully systematic use of bastions to form a complete trace.[15] In the meantime, powerful and effective fortresses were built, adapting to artillery but not utilizing systematic flanking fire from bastions. Some examples follow. Sassocorvaro (1474) is relatively small but with a thick front face and a beak-like projection between two round towers. Sarzanello (built by Francesco Giamberti, founder of the Sangallo dynasty of fortress builders in 1502) combines a triangular fort, based on three round towers, with an early form of ravelin covering the most threatened curtain wall and itself overlooked by a traditional tower-keep. The Rocca at Ostia (1483–6) was built by Baccio Pantelli, and like Sarzanello was an influential design. Poggio Imperiale (1495–1513) by Giuliano and Antonio da Sangallo has proto-bastions, as does their fortress at Nettuno (1501–3). Many of these sites were in hilly country or for coastal defence. Within the conditions of the late fifteenth century they were effective designs, particularly since before the invention of an efficient arquebus, and the presence of a good deal more artillery, low-lying fortresses were highly vulnerable to being taken by storm.

In the treatises of Filarete and Francesco di Giorgio Martini, there are clear attempts to rationalize space and impose a coherent ground plan.[16] Filarete's plan for the ideal city of Sforzinda shows that options other than the bastion were available. Based on the symbolic geometry of the square in a circle, it offered a version of the *tenaille* trace. This permits flanking fire just as effectively as bastions, but its great disadvantage is that it cannot easily be adapted to irregular sites. When Francesco di Giorgio built the Rocca at Mondavio (1482–92) (Illustration 6), for example, he adapted his geometric ideas to a confined and hilly site, building a relatively conventional strongpoint complete with machiolations.[17]

The point is that one should not examine such designs teleologically, as if they were a search for the perfect solution – the bastioned trace. They were effective into the first three decades of the sixteenth century, and adequate to withstand the artillery of their day, given the constraints of site and possible lines of attack. One might question whether permanent fortifications were a necessary solution at all. Improvised earthworks before medieval walls were extremely effective, and almost as efficient were retrenchments within them once a breach had been made. The problem with relying on temporary fortifications is that they involved a great deal of labour, most of which

Illustration 6
View of the keep and the support tower of the Rocca at Mondavio by Francesco di Giorgio, built 1482–92

might have been more profitably spent digging and building more permanent ones. Michelangelo proposed temporary defences for the old walls of Florence, achieving interlocking fields of fire without the arrowhead bastion.[18] Viollet-le-Duc offers striking illustrations of such temporary positions and also attempts to reinforce old town walls with new bastions at Metz, Augsburg, Frankfurt am Main, etc.[19] Pepper and Adams show how Siena, short of resources, strengthened its medieval walls with modern bastions at a few key sites, how the siege of 1554–5 was protracted by temporary fortifications and retrenchments, and how a weak place like Montalcino might be defended by such means against all the odds.[20]

Artillery remained scarce, even in the mid-sixteenth century.[21] This was inevitable given that most cast guns were made of bronze. Cast iron was still fragile: the properties of English and Swedish iron were not yet fully exploited.[22] Bronze casting was expensive. Most fortresses were unlikely to face a full royal siege train. The bastioned trace helped with this artillery shortage since it maximized flanking fire. Guns could be concentrated into the one or two bastions likely to be attacked, provided they were big enough and accessible enough. Antonio da Sangallo Jr.'s bastions at the Porta Ardeatina in Rome

(1535–42) show an attempt fully to exploit flanking fire: the double bastion provides eight embrasures to flank the curtain wall. Such a scheme could not be extended to all curtains; it was too expensive to build and to arm. A more practical, if less elegant and less apparently 'teleological' structure, is Baldassare Peruzzi's bastion (1527) at Porta San Viene in Siena.[23] The bastion concentrates the limited artillery available in a three-tiered casemate. In conditions of artillery shortage, weak places or 'intermediate' designs could prove militarily effective. Vauban was still 150 years away.

Only later, when artillery become plentiful, would the broad arrow-head bastion, with a wide platform on the curtain walls for moving guns to the threatened flanks, become the norm. There is a great difference between the small bastions of the Sangallo or Peruzzi, which emphasize flanking fire, and the big structures of Coehoorn or Vauban, which give platforms for guns to dominate the whole space beyond the *glacis*.

The bastion developed in Italy, not least because architectural theory, the geometric rationalization of space, and the symbolic value attached to symmetry were all highly developed there. The bastion was not the only possible geometric solution, nor were early bastions effective in the way the fully developed traces of the late seventeenth century were to be in bringing a significant volume of fire to bear on every inch of threatened ground. The logical fire plans possible with early bastions were largely irrelevant, since even major fortresses possessed at best a few slow-firing guns. Geometrically elegant, the bastion was adapted and was adaptable to a world of limited military and financial resources.

Monuments and Ruins – The Fortress as Symbolic Architecture

Buildings seldom have 'meaning' in any obvious or simple way: they are just *there*. As Nelson Goodman argues in one of the most acute comments by a philosopher on the status of built environment, buildings do not as such denote: they 'do not describe, recount, depict or portray'.[24] They are neither like novels, plays or operas, which narrate, nor like paintings or sculptures that can represent. Buildings occupy space. They are much bigger than we are and we can seldom see all of them at once, and they are made of materials that are not in themselves significant (that is, they do not have value as signifiers in the way that words, for example, do in a play or novel): stones, bricks, wood, concrete and steel.

To return to John Hale's question: art or engineering? Nelson Goodman has a challenging answer to the issue of the nature of art. Art is not a matter of intention or aesthetics. Most art is bad. It may try to be or claim to be beautiful, but it isn't. What differentiates art is not beauty as such, since a failed work may be judged to be ugly, but the attempt to make its materials signify or symbolize in some way that *could* have aesthetic value.[25] Buildings symbolize either by being what they are, in that they do not represent but exemplify, or by providing locations for symbols. For example, churches exemplify by being built in the shape of a Roman or Greek cross, or they are centrally planned so as to present the symmetry of the macrocosm in the order of a constructed space. Likewise, churches provide the location for representative media: niches for statues, walls for frescoes, windows for stained-glass pictures, and so on.

What might this have to do with the fortresses of the Renaissance? The answer is that even if we accept that buildings have 'meaning' in complex ways that are mostly different from the other arts, it does not follow that we should regard the fortress as especially meaningless and think of it in purely utilitarian terms.

Fortresses are also not 'engineering' pure and simple because – and not in spite of – the fact that they are military technologies. Technology is only a part of the ensemble of those things that make up war. As we have seen in chapter 4, war is a contest with a moral dimension. Fortresses depended on the people who were their besiegers and defenders, on how brave, how loyal, how competent, and how resourceful they were. A poor place in a weak condition of defence might still be held, or a strong one carried. Naarden, a pivotal and strong place, surrendered to the Spanish in 1572 without a fight and was brutally pillaged by the Duke of Alva's troops. It was refortified in 1668 and bluffed into capitulation in 1672, remodelled by Coehoorn in 1674–85, and surrendered to the French in 1795.[26] Was Naarden a 'weak' place? On the contrary, after 1685 it was a well-developed model by a master of the art of fortress architecture second to none. Thus it was often difficult to draw lessons from this military history of success and failure, and to judge what was the best 'engineering' solution.

If the role of engineering is ambiguous in the military history of the early-modern fortresses, in contrast the place of art is clear. War is not just technique, a clash of forces the outcome of which is given by the capacity of the weapons on the respective sides and decided by the resulting casualty lists.[27] War is also symbolic, and symbols affect the capacity of the soldiers and civilians to fight and to suffer. They also help them to *understand* war, both as conduct – to see models of bravery, competence and endurance – and in terms of placing themselves, knowing where they are and why. The fortress is no exception to this logic. Buildings do not readily narrate. But siege warfare needed to place soldiers and civilians within symbols, not merely to write or speak about buildings in war, but to symbolize what mattered through the buildings themselves.

Siege warfare in the gunpowder age was grim and demanding. Soldiers were isolated in small groups – on the covered way, at an embrasure, in a casemate – unaware of action elsewhere. Hence it was important both that they should be motivated and that they should know their place within the whole. Such fortresses do not by their form encourage the symbolic, and they provide few sites for symbols: they consist of earthen parapets, sunken walls, ditches, underground passages, and so on. How was the soldier to identify with a structure that aimed to minimize visibility? How could the fortress be made symbolic and also intelligible?

Alberti, in *De re aedificatoria*, understood the function that monuments had played in Antiquity: they symbolize the glory of the city, its heroes and its chief families. The monument is honour in stone, its purpose to signify glory and to stimulate *virtú* in its beholders: 'Would not all these monuments to the past provide numerous occasions to recall the deeds of great men, and so provoke conversation that itself serves both to make the light of the journey and to enhance the reputation of the city?'[28] As with the passage along a military road, like the Appian Way, so too on entering the city similar thoughts occur to the traveller as he beholds the gate. Alberti asserts that a gate should be adorned like a triumphal arch since, like the arch, its function is monumental and it symbolizes power and glory.[29] The vast majority of city and fortress gates in the early-modern period were built like triumphal arches, provided with niches and adorned with statues, and covered with representations of the paraphernalia of war. This was often counterproductive in strictly military terms, since it provided a larger and more conspicuous target. Gates were the weakest point in any fortress, yet such elaboration and ornament did nothing to strengthen them in a technical sense. They did, however, provide the most ready site of symbolic power in the artillery fortress. In this respect they were like the entrance doors and the niches immediately surrounding them in a medieval church or cathedral. Soldiers and citizens passed daily through the gates; they saw what was expected of them in these temples to the heroic. They saw there glory that was often hard to find at the bottom of a ditch. The gate was part of an entire system of military ritual and political theatre. The Renaissance is the high point of the procession, the symbolic entry into a city or fortress-palace by the sovereign or prince.[30] The bare spaces of the *glacis* provide an external site for such a theatre, meeting the sovereign or his representative and ceremonially conducting them into the city. The eighteenth and nineteenth centuries are the high point of the parade, when standing professional armies march past in garrison towns like Berlin or Épinal. The parade ground becomes an integral part of the fortress, and the avenues and the squares of the city a space for parades. Conceived in part practically by city planners, radial roads and squares forming places of assembly and ready routes to threatened places on the walls, the fortress-city becomes also a means to symbolize military power.[31]

The soldier saw the royal arms and wreaths of weapons upon the gate and experienced the show of glory in a parade. These things symbolized what was honourable in war. They helped to moralize the soldier into his profession. Bastions were almost invariably named, as were the curtains in most cases. This was because they are virtually identical, and only in this way could soldiers readily place themselves within the all-too-regular geometry of the fortress. The King's Bastion at Gibraltar, for example, was the site of a heroic defence during the Great Siege and thus its name served to remind soldiers that they stood on ground with symbolic value. Officers and fortress engineers had access to geometric plans, but also to detailed scale models. In northern France or the Netherlands from the seventeenth century onwards, military professionals had precise representations of the fortresses they were defending, including removable cut-away sections of casemates, counterscarp galleries, etc. Such models had originally been developed by Renaissance architects in order to sell the 'concept' of a fortress to princes and generals, and as an aid to mapping out the geometry of the fortress on the site. From the sixteenth century onwards, elaborate textbooks of the art and engineering practice of fortification were written and published in steadily increasing numbers, each author proposing a 'system'.[32] Even secret state handbooks, like Vauban's *Treatises*, were eventually put into the public domain by pirate publishers. Thus both the common soldier and his superiors, the garrison officers and military architects, could relate to the fortress, the former symbolically and through relatively straightforward devices of placing, and the latter through more elaborate models and representations.

The fortress was monumentalized, and enriched with symbols. As we have seen in chapter 8, to Renaissance intellectuals the *form* of the fortress also signified, since geometry had a symbolic value then that it has lost today. Symmetrical form, regular polygons, were not merely conventional geometric figures but examples of the order inherent in the universe. To a moderately well-read architect or a philosophically inclined layman, the fortress meant more than it does to us today. Today, a well-informed modern person may know what sixteenth-century adepts thought, but they do not themselves think it or believe it. Buildings have meaning, but they have more meaning in some intellectual contexts than in others. The symmetrical form of the bastioned trace was held to be strong because its fields of fire interlocked effectively, but that very geometrical order showed its connection with the innermost nature of things.[33]

Symbolism had a military value. The fortress had monumental aspects, just as the classical city conceived by Alberti did. Its monumentality could contribute not merely to its military, but also to its political effectiveness. Symbols inspired loyalty and also intimidated populations who might resent the rule of a foreign state or dynasty. Ruins are the opposite of monuments. The besieged fortress could become a ruin. In most cases damage was localized to a couple of bastions and a curtain wall. A practicable breach was sufficient to force a defending garrison to capitulate. This damage was rapidly repaired, as the besiegers typically sought to annex and to use the place themselves. In some cases, however, defeat led to demolition. The fortress was a threat to free citizens or an obstacle to free passage. The demolition of the citadel of Antwerp is an obvious example, one that proved ultimately ineffective as the Spaniards prevailed over the citizens' aspirations to freedom. Another example is the destruction of the Huguenot fortresses in France during the victory of the monarchy, culminating in the siege of La Rochelle in 1628.

The ruins of bastioned fortresses built mainly in earth are not picturesque or readily identifiable. Unlike medieval castles that became militarily obsolete and then served as the residences of princes and nobles, early-modern fortresses were mostly not allowed to crumble into romantic decay. They were either modernized or replaced. Bastioned fortresses constricted cities and limited the growth of the central core. Suburbs were a menace to fortifications, and had either to be kept at a distance or themselves expensively fortified. Cities like Paris or Antwerp had successively to slough off and rebuild new fortified enceintes until the ground to be enclosed become too extensive for a continuous fortified trace. A glance at photographs of the fortifications of Vienna in the mid-nineteenth century demonstrates how they constrained the growth of the central city and contributed to its well-known overcrowding and housing shortages. The fortifications of the 1704 Linienwall stood where the Ringstrasse does today. The fortifications were dismantled: they left no picturesque ruins, merely their trace in the ring.

The siege of Sebastopol in 1854–5 brought the techniques of three hundred years of warfare to a culmination. Pre-industrial weapons were allied to the semi-industrialized productive power of Britain and France, resulting in hundreds of guns firing upon two principal works – the Malakov Tower and the Redan. Both were reduced to a shambles in the course of the siege, and endlessly rebuilt, repaired, improvised and extended by Russian work details under the energetic direction of General Todleben.

The guns at Sebastopol were, however, highly evolved versions of the weapons with which the Sangalli or Vauban would have been familiar. The most powerful cannon in 1850 could fire a ball of approximately 31 kilos maximum weight over an absolute effective range of about 1½ km; the typical heavy weapon of 1600 was capable of about half that performance. From the 1860s onwards the Industrial Revolution transformed the iron and steel industries and with them the artillery that could be brought to bear on fortifications. By 1880 powerful mobile howitzers could fire explosive shells of about 100 kilos over about 6 km on high-angle trajectories. This would shatter any existing bastioned trace fortress, including existing bomb-proof shelters. By 1914 Germany possessed 420 mm siege howitzers firing shells of 1 metric tonne, and Austria 305 mm weapons.

Fortresses evolved in an attempt to cope with this rapid development of artillery. Cities like Paris were refortified with rings of forts some kilometres from the centre. Antwerp was twice refortified, with a ring of twelve forts 4 km from the original walls in 1860–4, and with a new ring which was built between 9.5 and 14 km further out between 1878 and 1898. There were further additions and interval redoubts up until 1914.[34] Antwerp was intended as a 'National Redoubt' or armed camp into which the Belgian field army could retreat. Belgium also built barrier fortresses at such cities as Liège and Namur. Liège was defended by twelve forts built in a ring in the 1880s. Similar fortresses were to be found at Verdun in France, Metz and Thionville in German-occupied Alsace-Lorraine, and Przemysl in Austrian Poland, for example.

The most radical proposals, like those of M. Mougin in 1887, envisaged an entirely subterranean fort defended by retractable iron-armoured cupolas. In effect this was a vast sunken concrete block. In fact, Mougin was less engaged in practical design than in making marketing copy for the products of the Saint-Chamond iron-making and armaments firm of which he was a director. As Sir George Sydenham-Clarke – an acute English observer – pointed out, such forts could easily be overrun or blinded.[35] He was equally scathing about other fortification systems based on a regular plan and fixed works, including those of the most prolific and distinguished military engineer of his era, Henri Brialmont. Brialmont, who fortified Antwerp and Liège, constructed regular geometric forts that in the latter case were mostly triangular in trace. He relied at Liège for means of defence on heavy guns in armoured cupolas, concrete bombproof shelters and barracks, underground passages between the works, and counterscarp galleries flanking ditches for close-in defence. He tried to modernize the traditional fortress trace, to harden the fort against the new artillery and to add to it the materials and products of the industrial era: concrete, steel and heavy guns.[36]

Designs like Mougin's make use of and, indeed, anticipate mass concrete construction; they utilize mechanical services for lighting, ventilation, elevators, etc., and thus represent one of the first uses of modern industrialized building materials and the new architectural forms they make possible. They were early forms of architectural modernism.

Brialmont was an able engineer, but the industrialization of war made the fortress an even harder place to present symbolically to the soldier or for him to understand in combat. The concrete forts were damp and cold, the passages dark and often tortuous. Soldiers were stationed at positions remote from one another in steel turrets with limited vision, in concrete blockhouses, or on open slopes exposed to artillery. The fortress had become more like a tomb than a monument. The despersion and enclosure of the garrison, their virtual invisibility and troglodyte existence, undermined the means to an effective defence. The symbolic role of the fortress was often reduced to the despairing one of carving or painting slogans on the walls and archways of the casemates. Thus French forts had posted in prominent places: 'Better to be buried beneath the ruins of this fort than to surrender' – a gospel of despair rather than an effective stimulus to military *virtú*.

The 'places' to be defended were now huge, no longer readily recognizable towns. Cities had become big, and the increased range of guns demanded the protection of an area of many square kilometres. The city and its defences now made even less coherent sense: the fortifications were harder to endow with symbolic value. Most of this vast effort and expense had been in vain, a last attempt to ensure the traditional defence of places. In effect, the new forts were large concrete targets, regular in shape, plotted on maps, and easy aiming points for controlled artillery fire.

The new fortresses were rapidly turned into ruins. Unlike the old siege techniques, the new methods used big guns that could only smash and shatter. The places in question were mostly obstacles to military advance. In the case of the Belgian forts in 1914, they were in the way of the German march to outflank the French. Hence their destruction sufficed, and their occupation and repair could have little or no purpose. They were no longer the primary objects of the military campaigns as fortified places had been in the warfare of the earlier centuries.

The great guns smashed the Belgian forts. The big shells tore concrete apart, and battered and overturned the armoured cupolas. The men inside were terrified and rendered helpless by the noise, the concussion, the smoke and the shock. There could be no prospect of a brave defence: the forts were built to resist shells a fraction of the weight of those falling upon them. The spectators in other forts, as yet unbombarded, had little option but to surrender before the guns switched target. Brialmont's elegant and economical designs had become unpicturesque ruins, merely grotesque shapes of twisted steel and pulverized concrete, over which the Germans clambered as military tourists.

In 1914 the remaining forts in France were mostly abandoned. The guns were removed from the cupolas to be put to better use. In 1916 the Germans cynically chose to attack Verdun – not to capture the place, but to force the French to defend it because of its historic and symbolic value. The plan was to bleed the French Army to death by bombardment, creating the conditions for a collapse of French morale. *Both* armies were bled white at Verdun. The French held the place and the 1870s forts played a key part in the struggle. Forts Douaumont and Vaux were fought over repeatedly, shelled until they became mere traces of their original shape in a sea of mud.[37] The French concrete, unlike the shoddy work by Brialmont's contractors, turned out to be first class and able to withstand heavy shelling, and the casemates of the forts became shelters. In the ruined forts, soldiers performed feats of heroism by enduring and surviving. A well-known picture of exhausted, mud-caked soldiers at Mass in Fort Douaumont shows the barely legible remains of the slogan, 'Better to be buried beneath the ruins of this fort than to surrender'. The brittle exhortation of this early Third Republic slogan has become mocking and meaningless. The men are heroes because they have survived the intolerable, their virtue is just to *be* there in a war devoid of glory. Verdun did become a symbol, defended for its purely symbolic value as a matter of national pride. It then became a new national symbol of stoic, almost unmilitary, courage. Douaumont and Vaux became part of the mythology of France's sufferings and as such they 'mean' this with diminishing value today.

10

The Defence of Places: From Sieges to Silos

Siegeworks: A Provisional and Anti-Architecture

The fortress is a non-object for modern mainstream architectural history and theory. Writing on the subject is sparse, specialized and marginal to architecture discourse. Certainly there is a reason for this in that fortresses are no longer built by architects; the construction of fortifications had become a specialist province of the military engineer by the mid-seventeenth century. However, a similar situation has not stopped intense thinking and writing about other structures that are hardly a common part of architectural practice today, such as Gothic cathedrals or Palladian villas. In an interesting and thought-provoking book, *Buildings and Power*, Thomas A. Markus analyses building-types in terms of their specific uses, their social context and the discourses that surround them.[1] Fortifications are absent. Yet his key period (the nineteenth century) is an age of extensive change in fortress design and large-scale building, and the fortress is a primary example of the relationship between buildings and power. The reason is that architecture has become a pacific profession. War is literally out of sight and, therefore, out of mind.

If the artillery fortress as a permanent structure is neglected in archi-tectural history, its *use* in war receives even less attention. This neglect is also true to a considerable degree of most military history up to the last couple of decades. In one sense military historians knew that, in the period 1500–1800, the siege was the dominant form of warfare and that sieges outnumbered battles by a factor of ten to one. Yet the attention that historians gave to battles rather than to sieges is of a reverse order. Battles, of course, are dramatic and finite actions, and they are apparently easy to narrate.[2] Sieges, by contrast, are mostly protracted, episodic in their conflicts, and often unsuccessful in outcome. Battles attract military historians of the traditional type because, following Clausewitz, they see them as the decisive form of war, and sieges as merely local forms of action that are inherently indecisive. This viewpoint is profoundly inaccurate and anachronistic, projecting back Napoleonic assumptions into a very different military system. The attack and defence of places was a central component of early-modern warfare. Without sieges places could not be captured and, therefore, territory could not be held. Thus the battle of Rocroi (1643), where the French smashed the Spanish Army of Flanders, was as decisive a victory as one could expect – except that it did not end the war. As Geoffrey Parker comments: 'Although defeated in battle, the Army of Flanders still controlled numerous fortified towns, each of which had to be starved into surrender.'[3] Spain did not make peace with France until 1659.

Artillery fortifications and the *trace italienne* made what had always been the difficult art of besieging a defended place even more complicated. Cannon had to be brought close to the walls to realize a decisive breach; bombardment might begin at 300 metres but was seldom effective unless it could be brought within 100 metres. As such, the guns and gunners were vulnerable to enemy fire from the fortress and to sorties by the besieged. The besiegers thus had to behave as if *they* were besieged and to erect fortifications that were often as elaborate, if temporary, as those they confronted. Sieges thus involved an immense amount of digging. They created ephemeral structures that are fascinating in their own right but that have been ignored by architectural historians.

Disposable architecture is not just a 1960s invention. Consider, for example, the plan of the Turkish trenches at the siege of Vienna in 1683[4] (Illustration 7). They are constructions as remarkable and inventive as anything designed by the 1960s radical architectural group Archigram, and yet just as throwaway as the latter's walking cities. These trenches have vanished under suburban Vienna, but often the trace of similar works can be seen as lighter patches in the soil in aerial photographs of older towns that have not grown considerably beyond their original walls.[5] However, the main sources today for examining such siegeworks are the military textbooks of the period, and contemporary engravings that illustrate sieges. The spider's web of earthworks reaching towards and menacing the ramparts obviously caught the imagination of contemporaries, who were eager to record them before they vanished without trace. Thus the besieged fortress generated a temporary structure as elaborate and as costly in human effort to create as itself.

We have seen in chapter 9 that, until the late sixteenth century, guns were relatively few: thus fortifications were often able to survive

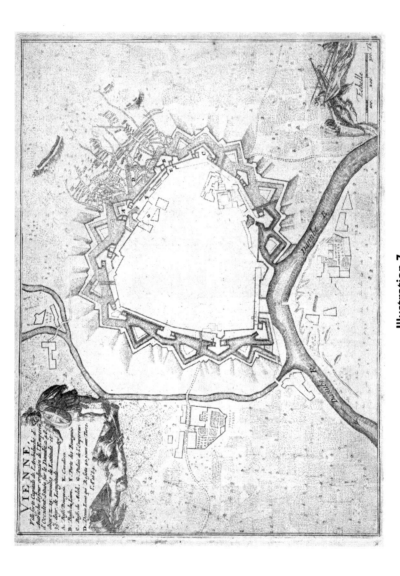

Illustration 7

Part of the Turkish trenches during the siege of Vienna of 1684 (*Les Forces de L'Europe*, N. de Fer, 1695; Copyright © British Library)

battery by guns, and sieges were very prolonged.[6] The result was that the besiegers had to be prepared to sit it out. In most cases their logistics could hardly cope, and they therefore had to dig in and hope to accommodate and feed themselves as best they could.

The danger of a relieving force to the besiegers was acute. The besieged place had to be cut off from relief, completely encircled to prevent sorties by the besieged forces trying to obtain supplies or to link-up with a relieving force. The besiegers themselves had to be protected from attack in the rear, because they were exceedingly vulnerable if a strong relieving force did arrive. In 1683 the Turks were caught before Vienna by the relieving Austro-Polish Army, and scattered. Their elaborate trenches faced only one way. They had not made rear defences and their camps were unprotected.

A prolonged siege thus required even more complex temporary fortification works by the attackers than was strictly necessary to effect a breach. Only one bastion needed to be broken into to make the fortress technically liable to surrender under the prevailing codes of war. To do so required an elaborate network of saps (trenches zigzagging towards the walls), parallels (lines of trenches facing the walls which served both for communication and secure assembly points for an assault), and fortified gun batteries giving off from parallels. All these trenches were elaborately revetted with planks and wattle panels, and the parapets reinforced by wickerwork baskets filled with earth, called *gabions*.

This in itself was digging enough. Often commanders were unclear as to how long a place could last, and whether they had the labour force or the logistics for a prolonged siege. If they did expect to sit it out, then they created much more elaborate works. In addition to the front to be attacked, the whole place was encircled by trenches with strong points at intervals in them, called lines of circumvallation. These works cut off the place from the outside. These strong temporary fortifications were then mirrored on *their* outside by lines of countervallation, to protect the besiegers should they in turn be besieged. The cost of all these works was enormous and they could only be justified if the place in question was pivotal. Prolonged sieges were unpopular: they involved investing forces in long periods in damp trenches, often without adequate food or shelter. Besieging armies often suffered from the ravages of disease or mutinied for lack of food or pay.[7] The reasons why armies could not keep in the field were the self-same ones that made long sieges a difficult option to contemplate.

Well into the seventeenth century, most states lacked the means to conduct sieges 'scientifically'. Armies were composed of temporary mercenary forces raised by military contractors. Spain's army was for long the exception. The manpower to dig was often limited to the summer season before the harvest. The fiscal base of most states was fragile. Cannon were in limited supply. Thus the temptation to try to settle a siege quickly by battery and storm was great. The economics of regular sieges told against them – particularly as many failed. Fortresses could be carried by storm on occasions. Methodical sieges became the norm only when the resources to conduct them were widely available: larger armies, more secure finances and more guns. Then method could commonly be applied to siegework, and the siege engineers like Coehoorn and Vauban could devise systematic ways to conduct sieges. Both used the spade more than any specifically military implement, relying on vast amounts of digging to bring guns to the walls in a relatively short time (in Vauban's case twenty-one days after opening the first trench).[8] Greater resources allowed for greater method, and far shorter and more decisive sieges. The 'unsystematic' period involved either long struggles to starve a place into submission, or violent – often bloody and ineffective – attempts to take places by storm.

Just as with the evolution of the bastion, discussed in the previous chapter, we should not view siege technique teleologically, as if soldiers in the earlier period were simply less able and observant than Vauban and failed to hit on his 'solution'. Their choices as besiegers were frequently highly circumscribed.

Inevitably, in the siege of most defended places, enemy soldiers and local civilians came into contact. Early-modern societies in Europe were concerned to regularize their affairs by law, especially in the relations between friend and foe, between conquering states and subject peoples. War was governed by norms, and they were abided by perhaps more frequently than the laws of war are today. The laws and customs of war were also part of the way in which soldiers and civilians related to the fortress symbolically. They were part of the way combatants and non-combatants understood war and their place in it.

War was a normal part of human affairs and thus part of natural law, that is, the common understanding of the basic rules of conduct that applied to all humanity whether or not they were subject to the laws of a given state. By the seventeenth century such rules were well-established, for example, in the *De Jure Belli ac Pacis* (1625) of Hugo Grotius.[9] Grotius held to the Roman view that a combatant defeated in war had forfeited his life: surrender puts one at the mercy of one's captor. The captor could demand ransom or enslave the captive. As applied to sieges, the laws of war were clear and commonly accepted by Europeans. The besiegers would formally call upon the besieged to surrender. If they did, then the civilians became the subjects of the besieger's prince and their lives and property would be guaranteed, subject to legitimate exactions and billeting. This is why many commercial towns in the sixteenth century in the Low Countries submitted to the Spaniards; had they not done so, they would have been treated as rebels against the Crown. The requirement applied in Flanders as much as it did in the New World. Once a practicable breach (that is, a hole in the walls that could be stormed) was opened, then the besiegers could legitimately require the garrison to surrender. Having defended the place honourably, the defenders could leave with their colours and arms, and were given free passage on the understanding that they took no further part in the conflict. If they refused the offer of honourable capitulation and continued a defence, then if the fortress were stormed their lives and goods were forfeit and they were at the mercy of the victors. The victors after a bloody assault were seldom merciful, and officers in any case could hardly control their troops once they were loose in the town. The prospect of rape and plunder was one of the few incentives for soldiers called upon to risk their lives in storming a breach.

Citizens of fortified places were subject to military law in the case of a siege. They had the comfort of knowing that they were within the walls and not subject to the exactions and abuses of the besieging army outside. However, besieged citizens were expected to provide for themselves in the main, and if food ran out, or prices rose beyond the pockets of the poor, then the civilian population starved. Governors had draconian powers. During the 1554–5 siege of Siena the French garrison commander, Blaise de Monluc, turned out 4,000 of the civilian population at the end of February 1555 as 'useless mouths'. Monluc confessed in his memoirs: 'These poor folk made their way towards the enemy, who merely chased them back to us . . . But we remained firm, and the agony lasted for eight days. The refugees had only grass to eat, and more than half of them died, for the enemy helped to kill them off and very few managed to escape.'[10] Sixteenth- and seventeenth-century warfare was quite as horrible in its own way as anything in the twentieth – allowing for greater resources and greater technological killing power today. The impact of a siege was felt not only within the walls. Not for nothing was the army official charged with raising contributions from the occupied populations in the German lands called the *Brandtmeister*. An observer commented towards the end of the siege of Siena that for 10 miles (18½ km) around the city 'there was not a wall standing, while the country was infested with dogs devouring the corpses'.[11]

What citizens feared above all was a general bombardment, rather than a methodical attempt to breach the walls with cannon. By the mid-seventeenth century, effective mortars could lob explosive or incendiary shells over the walls and into the interior of the fortress or city. Against a determined defence this would not suffice: it could only reduce the place if the civilian population forced the governor to surrender and open the gates. Bombardment was widely regarded as a brutal and generally unjustified attack upon civilians. The Swiss jurist, Emerich Vattel, claimed in 1773 that: 'it is only in cases of the last extremity, and with reluctance, that good princes exert a right of so rigorous a nature'.[12] Nevertheless, even in the apparently restrained eighteenth century they took place. In 1747 the French savagely bombarded and then pillaged Bergen-op-Zoom in what was widely seen as an act of militaristic barbarity.

The trenches that served to besiege the classical artillery fortress had a second and even more elaborate role as infantry weapons became far more effective in the nineteenth century (as we saw in chapter 6, by the 1880s rifles could fire ten times faster than, and with about ten times the effective range of, the muskets of the Napoleonic Wars). The American Civil War proved that entrenched infantry could hold out against powerful forces and heavy bombardment in temporary fortifications. Vicksburg held out for 213 days against vastly superior forces and surrendered only because food and ammunition were running out. The same thing occurred in 1877 when a small, ill-equipped Turkish force defended the village of Plevna in Bulgaria against a whole Russian army for 142 days, and had eventually to be starved into surrender.

Sir George Sydenham-Clarke, in the first edition of his textbook on fortification in 1890, drew the obvious lesson for examples like these: permanent fortifications were largely obsolete and at best an expensive luxury, since improvised field fortifications were as effective, if not more so.[13] At Port Arthur in 1904–5 the Japanese suffered at least 60,000 casualties storming the Russian fortress in successive bloody assaults. Repeating rifles and machine guns made attacks in the open, in daylight by large formations, all but suicidal.

Generals and strategists realized that warfare would be much more difficult and that armies would face a lethal zone of about 1 km across which they would have to advance to take a position. The Polish banker and amateur strategist, Ivan S. Bloch, argued in the 1890s that repeating rifles and machine guns had made warfare counterproductive: 'Between the combatants will always be an impassable zone of fire deadly in equal degree to both the foes', and 'everybody will be entrenched in the next war. It will be a great war of entrenchments. The spade will be as indispensable to a soldier as his rifle.'[14]

In 1914 the German Army could destroy the Belgian fortresses effortlessly, but it could not subsequently prevail against improvised

English and French defensive positions. By October 1914 the Western Front had stabilized into a continuous system of improvised trenches confronting one another from Dunkirk to the Swiss border. It was to remain thus for four years. The 'new' trench systems were simply versions of the saps and parallels of the old siegeworks. Over time they became more and more elaborate, and concrete bunkers began to appear as the core of the strongpoints. Essentially, a sixteenth-century technology was adapted to the demands of industrialized warfare. Above all, the main difference lay in the *numbers* of men at the front. Modern industrial societies were productive enough to release large numbers of men, whereas from the sixteenth to the eighteenth centuries ratios of soldiers to overall populations were low. The mass armies in Western Europe were relatively well-fed, well-supplied and well-cared for by modern medicine and public health. Conditions that would have starved and exterminated by epidemics whole armies in the seventeenth century were tolerated for the better part of four years by most First World War mass armies. Given the modern industrial system, what mattered was productive capacity and logistics, not the type of weapons. As we saw in chapter 6, the improved rifled muskets of the American Civil War were quite capable of producing a long stalemate.

By 1914 the 'place' to be defended was no longer a city, but a country. France was in one sense besieged by the Germans, but in another it was the Allies who were forced to attack in order to evict the occupiers. Trench systems proved almost invulnerable, even when millions of shells were fired at them. In Flanders the heavy shelling destroyed the natural drainage and made forward progress by the Allies all but impossible. Casualties were enormous: on the first day of the Battle of the Somme in 1916, the British Army suffered 50,000 casualties.[15] Machine guns and concrete bunkers made it easy for defenders to hold the front line at lower cost. Machine guns were not miracle weapons: they just thinned out the firing line so that fewer defenders were exposed to enemy artillery. The trench system, a simple design solution to sixteenth-century siege-craft, easy to implement with simple tools and unskilled labour, proved resistant to hundreds of thousands of high-explosive shells falling on relatively few square miles. Architects had a limited role in this; trenches had become part of the 'folk wisdom' of the military and the digging of them was close to the unskilled labouring that most soldiers had done in civilian life on farms, at building sites and in factories. The shapes the trenches copied were first determined by Renaissance intellectuals for the fortress built in stone, and were then mirrored in the earth by the military engineers who conducted sieges. Four hundred years later they were still in use: an architectural legacy that almost no one saw as such.

Bunkers – National Styles in the Architecture of Aggression

At the end of the First World War the defence of places had come to mean one thing: the only 'place' that could be defended against the new weapons – long-range guns, aeroplanes and tanks – was the national territory. That could only be done by creating strong continuous linear fortifications on the most threatened frontiers. The improvised linear defences of the recent war had proved remarkably strong. Germany had in the end surrendered because of the consequences of a long total war: the heavy casualties of a war of attrition on the battlefields, and the civilian hunger caused by the demands of the military and the Allied blockade.

France was in a real sense the loser in 1918. It was economically exhausted and its manpower depleted. When Germany chose to reassert itself its productive power was much larger, and there were some 70 million Germans to 40 million French. By the mid-1930s Germany would enjoy its greatest advantage as there would be a sudden drop in the number of French conscripts available.[16] The French were convinced that the new technologies made a surprise attack more possible. Tanks, aeroplanes and motorization could facilitate a sudden *coup* before French reserves were mobilized. The experience of Verdun had shown that deep concrete works could save lives, and that protected communications were essential: Verdun's sole lifeline, the *Voie Sacré*, had been under constant artillery fire. The French reoccupation of Alsace-Lorraine revealed valuable technical lessons from the German fortifications built in the 1910–14 period. The new German defences at Mutzig, Metz and Thionville were actually very different from the classic ring fortress made up of detached works with a regular trace, as they were based on the *feste* or fortified group principle. A *feste* consisted of irregular groupings of detached artillery and infantry blocks that were mutually supporting and adapted to the terrain. Well concealed and linked by tunnels, the new system was much more difficult to identify and bombard.

The French decided to screen their frontier with Germany in the 1920s, well before Hitler. The objective was to prevent a sudden attack, allowing French reserves to mobilize. The field army would then reinforce the fortifications, but the strong fixed defences would also make possible the release of a substantial mobile force that could come to the aid of Belgium. The French were determined to avoid a repeat of 1914, when they had suffered huge casualties attacking the German defences in Alsace-Lorraine and then found they had inadequate forces to counter the German invasion of Belgium. Thus the new fortifications, called the Maginot Line, were not strategically irrational as is often asserted – even if they did amount to re-fighting the last war.

In fact the new mobile warfare made possible by tanks and trucks did require fortifications to check it. The *Blitzkreig* was invented in the 1930s and was indeed intended to break through before the enemy could marshal reserves. The greatest armoured battle of the Second World War, at Kursk in 1943, revolved around dense fortified belts on the Russian side. The Maginot Line was a unique attempt to create a permanent defence system in peacetime that could defend a frontier throughout its threatened length. Previous linear defences had never had this ambitious aim or the means to carry it out. The Dutch Water Lines of the sixteenth and seventeenth centuries were national redoubts, lines of fortified towns along water obstacles designed to keep the enemy out of the inner core of the country.[17] We have seen in chapter 4 that the Roman *limes* and the Great Wall of China were border control systems, designed to exclude barbarian 'economic migrants' and to channel major incursions. They were screens, not a system of rigid defence at the frontier.

The Maginot Line was an immense constructional and technical achievement. It included underground power stations, air conditioning, underground railways, highly mechanized systems, and an extensive network of deep tunnels (Illustration 8). There was, however, a considerable contrast between the engineering scale of the works and their high cost, and their fighting power, which was modest. The total number of guns of 75 mm and above in the defences from Luxembourg to the Swiss frontier was only 344, and the maximum range under 10 km.[18] In 1940 the line functioned until the French Armies, outflanked by a thrust through the Ardennes, were forced to surrender. Although designed with 1918 in mind, the line, suitably supplemented by the field army, was an adequate barrier. Likewise, the Americans found the old German fortifications at Metz that the French had incorporated into the reserve portion of the line a formidable obstacle in 1944.[19]

In the 1930s the Germans decided to copy the French and create their own linear system, the Westwall. Its purpose was to contain any French offensive long enough for a *Blitzkreig* attack to succeed against Poland. Mobile warfare and fortifications were thus not in opposition. Both the Germans and the French saw them as complementary in their

Illustration 8
View of the Maginot Line, showing tunnels, 1939
(Copyright © Imperial War Museum)

strategies. Tanks were still relatively weak: they were small and easy to obstruct by ditches and barriers, and armoured with thickness of at most 30 mm and usually 14 mm or less, and therefore highly vulnerable to light anti-tank guns. Aircraft were useless against well-concealed bunkers with 1.5 metres of reinforced concrete cover. The Westwall was a vast propaganda success, being portrayed in German newsreels, photographs and articles as much more extensive and powerful than it really was. It included no deep works, but was just a network of small surface bunkers. The photographs of deep tunnels were actually taken in the Czech frontier defences that the Germans occupied in 1938.[20] The distinctive feature of the Westwall was the 'dragon's teeth' anti-tank obstacles, concrete sectional pillars that marched over hill and dale like the classic Chinese walls north of Beijing. As the French were deterred from attacking in support of Poland in 1939, the Westwall, both real and imaginary, proved effective.[21]

Illustration 9
Pillbox disguised as a removals van (Copyright © Imperial War Museum)

In 1940 the Germans were on the Channel coast and Britain was faced with invasion. The response was a flurry of improvised building of defensive works (Illustration 9). Most of the bunkers were poorly sited, badly built, and of even worse design. In effect they were death traps. Even the GHQ defence line systems back from the coast were nowhere near French or German standards for small works, let alone large complexes. In both the French and the German cases the defences benefited from uniform design, direction and supervision by competent central organizations led by able engineers – CORF (Commission d'Organisation des Régions Fortifiés) and the OT (Organization Todt). When they did not look like public lavatories gone astray, English bunkers were often got up in droll camouflage as carousels, railway wagons, and so on. It is hard to imagine that they were built by a people seriously fearing an invasion: they certainly appear to be more of a displacement activity than a rational form of defence.[22]

By 1942 it was obvious to the Germans that they faced a serious threat of invasion from the west. Their response was the Atlantik Wall, the most ambitious scheme of fortification ever undertaken.[23] It was to run from the North Cape to the Spanish border. Its construction was partly entrusted to navy engineers for the most elaborate naval gun emplacements, but mainly to the OT. In Fritz Todt and Albert Speer, the OT had as its heads a leading civil engineer and a competent, if grandiose and unimaginative, architect. Xaver Dorsch was Director throughout, and along with Todt a sometime member of the Sager and Wörner civil engineering practice in Munich. The Atlantik Wall was thus built to high civilian design and construction standards, supervised by the leading experts in poured concrete. The Wall, far from being an improvised military field fortification, was the grandest of *grands projets* and can be considered as possessing great architectural merit in the detailed design and siting of its fortification and bunkers.

The Wall was a failure, but the OT and Speer were not to blame for that. Hundreds of thousands of tons of concrete and many heavy guns were wasted on the fortifications in Norway (principally at Narvik) and in the Channel Islands. Had these heavy batteries been sited in Normandy, and had the divisions wasted in Norway (twelve divisions formed the garrison there, as many as were deployed from the Bay of the Siene to Bordeaux) been posted on that coast, then the Allied invasion might well have failed. The commander of the defences, Erwin Rommel, a Panzer general, was absolutely clear that the only chance was to beat the Allies at the water's edge and not let them gain a foothold. The reason was simple: not only was 75 per cent of the German Army in Russia, but an even larger proportion of what was left of the *Luftwaffe* was either on the Eastern Front or defending the Reich from Allied bombers. On 6 June 1944 the *Luftwaffe* managed only about 200 sorties, as against several thousands by the Allies in the area of the invasion. Logic dictated that the Allies could land only within fighter range of England in Normandy or the Pas de Calais – other defences were basically a waste of time. Once Allied air power was established on the continent, German Armies would be unable to move. Logic, however, was in short supply, since Hitler dictated strategic priorities. German engineering brilliance and tactical skill could not compensate for the misallocation of resources. As Paul Virilio points out, the German need to stand on the defensive on the Atlantic littoral was a direct consequence of their expansionary drive. They had conquered France, but were forced to keep the vast bulk of their armies fighting deep inside Eastern Europe.[24] Concrete was thus an attempt to compensate for weakness, to shelter forces that were inadequate to their task without this defensive cover.

The scale of the works remains breathtaking, and so too does the beauty of many of the structures. The coastal observation towers are particularly remarkable: they combine starkness and fluid grace. That they were built to defend an evil regime matters, but it cannot be used to deny their aesthetic qualities. Paul Virilio was among the first to appreciate those forms in his *Bunker Archaeology*, the first version of which was published in 1967.[25] Keith Mallory and Arvid Ottar's *The Architecture of Aggression* was clearly inspired by Virilio, but is a much wider historical survey, ranging over the whole field of twentieth-century military building and including air-raid shelters and pre-fabricated huts.[26]

The Atlantik Wall included bunkers of diverse shapes and functions: gun casemates of varying sizes, shelters, observation posts, etc. (Illustration 10). Closely associated with it were the massive bombproof submarine bases at Brest, Lorient, Saint-Nazaire, etc. (Illustration 11). Much of this remains, and increasingly the architectural merit of these structures is being realized. Often bunkers have been compared to Le Corbusier or to Brutalism: Mallory and Ottar have shots of the Hayward Gallery in their book. There is, however, a more obvious and striking parallel in this case, German Expressionism and the work of

Illustration 10
Radar and observation tower, L'Ancress, Guernsey – part of the Atlantik Wall defences, built 1942 (Copyright © Architectural Association Picture Library, Roger Bennett)

Illustration 11
Submarine pen at Bordeaux, built 1941
(Copyright © Architectural Association Picture Library, M. Hargreaves)

Erich Mendelsohn in particular. If one compares his sketches for the Einstein Türm, for high-rises and for the new town on Mt Carmel, the similarities are remarkable. The Einstein Türm itself on its hilly site could, in misty weather, be imagined to be on the edge of the Atlantic rather than in a science park outside Potsdam.[27]

By 1944 the Reich itself needed fortifying. The Germans built on a scale and with a degree of monumentality and permanence that seem quite out of keeping with a nation on the verge of defeat.[28] Large 'flak towers' and massive air-raid shelters were common in major cities like Berlin, Hamburg and Vienna. In the countryside the SS built underground factories of considerable size; this involved shifting huge quantities of earth and rock in their construction.[29] As we shall see below, Britain and Germany adopted very different philosophies of civil defence.[30] If one compares the Nazi batteries at Sangatte with the English heavy batteries at Dover, the latter are thrown together and covered with corrugated iron sheeting, whereas the former are buried in vast concrete shelters and protected with heavy steel revolving shields. The difference is that the English were pragmatic and confident that the war was temporary, while the Germans were convinced that war was an integral feature of the new Reich and that its structures should embody that permanence and dignity. Where the English

were inventive was in unorthodox engineering solutions, such as in the
sea forts to provide anti-aircraft defences to cover gaps like those in
the Thames and Mersey estuaries, and in the prefabricated floating
Mulberry harbours for the Normandy Invasion.[31]

Thus there are quite different 'national styles' in response to war.
The English are utilitarian, and yet committed to using resources carefully for the duration of the conflict only. The Germans build as if they
are constructing the monuments of a thousand-year Reich, as if these
structures are central to their culture. But can there be national styles
in bunkers? Paul Virilio sees the bunker as a monolith and he argues
that all such concrete masses are essentially the same:

> When we show interest in ancient armour, the ornaments and figures indicate
> clearly the origin and style – Italian, French, etc. – but here hardly anything
> survives of this form of identification, the omnipotence of arms volatilized
> what was left of aesthetic will. If a few details still allow French fortifications
> to be distinguished from German ones, this concerns only problems of imple-
> mentation, of the influence of different types of plans in one country as
> opposed to another for a short time yet. With the bunker the diversity of for-
> tifications fades away; with it the essence of surface entrenchment systems will
> disappear.[32]

A bunker is a bunker is a bunker? This would seem obvious, and
entirely consistent with Virilio's conception of the bunker as a monolith. Yet this is a curiously short-sighted view for someone who took
the photographs in *Bunker Archaeology*. There, Virilio shows a won-
derful eye for the architectural features of the Atlantik Wall bunkers,
above all for their relation to site, and for the combination of monumentality and fluidity in their features.

Why this view is inaccurate is because of – rather than in spite of –
the fact that bunkers rely for their strength and solidity on mass concrete. When set, concrete is monolithic and massive. But when it is
poured into shuttering it is a fluid and plastic medium, making possible many varied shapes. It thus allows for imagination and design.
French bunkers and German bunkers are different in their forms,
despite both countries' engineers having high skills in concrete construction. Indeed, it was those very skills that made possible fluid and
coherent – but different – design approaches. English bunkers either
avoid the possibilities of the medium, using concrete in a utilitarian
and unimaginative way as if it were rigid from the beginning, or they
are entirely whimsical, presenting them through camouflage as if they
were something else. Bunkers differ in the way their mass is handled,
and in their relationship to the surrounding landscape. This can
change dramatically if they are uncovered, for example, by the erosion

of sand dunes. This may enhance their effect, revealing the mass hitherto concealed, or it may make them appear absurd, like overgrown beached turtles.

As Virilio argues, bunkers are not founded: they do not rest as a superstructure on foundations. Their own mass provides their foundations, often with an 'apron' of concrete at the bottom to prevent bombs or shells dislodging them from the terrain. Most bunkers are built or dug into the terrain as far as is consistent with their functions. Thus in a way Mougin's fort mentioned in chapter 9, for all its impracticality, anticipates the logical tendency of fortifications based on mass concrete, as it is an entirely subterranean concrete block. Yet bunkers had to reveal themselves – as with the massive casemates for the guns of battery Lindemann at Sangatte or with the huge submarine pens at Lorient and Saint-Nazaire, for example. The latter structures are simply too big to bury, even if this were consistent with admitting submarines. They take up the space of a city block. They rely for their defence on the simple bulk of mass concrete, with large burster slabs on the roof and thick retaining walls. The U-boat bases are impressive by their very bulk, but also by the consistency of their treatment. They are as close as any structure can get to the monolithic, and they are virtually indestructible.

Can the bunker become a ruin? It was easy for castles to do so, to become picturesque. This did not really happen to the vast majority of artillery fortifications: they have either been dug up or ignored. Mass concrete is difficult to dispose of. Many of the biggest structures are still there because in an urban environment their demolition would be noisy and inconvenient. But this does not mean that bunkers will become 'ruins'. They remind us of a war that was far from heroic. As Virilio says, most people find them sinister, as if they give off an 'aura' of fear and dictatorship.

Bunkers obviously fall into disuse and disrepair, but they don't really become ruins. They are, as blocks of mass concrete, still *there*, just as they were. Damaged bunkers that reveal the scars of war are not 'ruined' either. Although pitted with shell holes they retain their form, and the damage – far from softening them and rendering them picturesque – makes them look seedy and even more sinister. Uprooted bunkers often look absurd because essentially they are 'out of place'. But that does not make them ruins, just useless and incongruous.

There are exceptions to this. Bunkers that have lost key features, for example, casemates with gaping holes where their shielded artillery was, often look old and forlorn. Sometimes, however, depending on size and site, their character changes. Virilio remarks of bunkers on the Atlantik Wall with a 'Todt Front', that minus their guns they can be compared to Aztec or Egyptian temples. The objective of the Todt Front was to protect the embrasure against artillery bombs and oblique shell hits: it has stepped sides and a concrete cap over the embrasure. These features, once functional, become monumental and decorative. The gap where the shield should be now looks like an entrance to a subterranean chamber. The elements of the Todt Front now seem to emphasize its importance as an entrance, rather than its original function, which was to keep projectiles out.

In arguing that bunkers can only with difficulty become 'ruins', I am not claiming that they are uninteresting or merely functional. I am simply saying that they do not become 'ruined', that they do not become attractive because of decay and the consequent softening of their outline as castles have. Bunkers are still there; their aesthetic features are *sui generis*, a function of their form and site, and those are not altered by the fact the building is no longer in use. No longer functional does not mean ruined. The ruin involves a highly particular aesthetic. Bunkers are not heroic and they are not ancient. If they are of architectural interest, then it must be because of their merit as designs.

The Nazis were acutely aware of the political uses of architecture and the role of monuments in securing and legitimating the future of the regime. Albert Speer, Hitler's architect at the time, wrote an essay in 1938 on the 'theory of the value of ruins'. He argued in solidly anti-modernist terms that: 'the structures built with modern techniques [would not be appropriate as the noble ruins of the future]. My theory was designed to solve this dilemma. I wanted to give up using modern materials found in metallic and concrete constructions. By respecting certain laws of statics, buildings could be constructed that after thousands of years, would clearly resemble Roman models.'[33]

This is the clearest possible statement of the aesthetics of Nazism. Speer had designed the Party assembly complex at Nuremberg, a setting for politics as theatre. The Nazi's aesthetic is a form of 'political romanticism' in Carl Schmitt's terms.[34] The present is lived as if it were a spectacle, as if one were looking at oneself acting. Things are not done in and for themselves, but to create an effect. Politics is aestheticized – which does not mean that the results are beautiful; on the contrary, they are almost guaranteed to be *kitsch*. A building is conceived by Speer with its destiny as a ruin incorporated in it from the start, so that it will evoke a response in spectators a thousand years hence. Desiring the monumental, Speer has his fingers crossed that posterity will admire Nazi architecture because it will have no other choice. A thousand-year Reich is the claim of a regime that did not merit to last one hour, that could not relate to the practical problems of the present and was unable to treat people fairly. Like the inspiration behind Saddam Hussein's monuments in Baghdad, it hopes the sheer scale of its ambitions and ruthlessness will save it.

Alberti saw monuments as part of the *current* life of the city: ancient and modern alike they are part of an ongoing life justified in its own terms and requiring no posterity to valorize and ennoble it.[35] The monuments are *models* and serve to inspire *virtú* in today's citizens. The monuments provide evidence of the greatness of the city by recalling the good and noble deeds of its leading citizens. Speer's relation to the future is perverted, by contrast. It is the aesthetics of a politics that can hope to prevail by pure power alone, that has no real moral or cultural claims, and that is nihilistic to the core. Its obsession with how it will look as a past in the future recalls some of the worst and most necrophiliac concerns of the heritage industry today.

Speer never intended that the bunkers on the Atlantik Wall should serve as the monument to Nazi ambitions. His own grandiose works were mostly never begun or reduced to rubble in Berlin. The 'ignoble' materials of mass concrete and cast steel have survived, and they are a better monument than the regime that created them deserves.

Fortification and Passive Defence since 1945

Fortification as the defence of places ended for all practical purposes with the breaching of the Atlantik Wall in 1944. Thereafter, formal fortifications as a principal means of defence, even on the most extensive scale, were obsolete. Cities had ceased to be defensible by fortifications at least a half-century before. However, fortifications in the sense of mass concrete structures and underground chambers did not disappear after 1945, but either changed their military function or their nature. Increasingly, defence switched from active to passive, from fortification as a means of fighting to the hardening and protection of specific assets. One should not make this division between active and passive too extreme. Thus it can be claimed that forts protected artillery in the same way as hardened silos protect missiles. Yet this is to miss the main point.[36] Fortification classically conceived was not passive: protection, weapons and the layout of the fortified place were all part of a scheme of active defence. Fortifications could be part of an offensive scheme. Thus Vauban's works on France's northern frontier were a jumping-off point and base for campaigns across the frontier; likewise, the German fortifications in Alsace-Lorraine in 1914 were designed to secure the German left while the right advanced into Belgium.

Fortification continued after 1945 in specific roles. The Norwegian and Swedish coastal artillery have continued to use and to develop concealed and hardened gun sites to the present day. They are part of a scheme of preclusive defence designed to keep enemy vessels out of the Norwegian fjords and contained in the combat zone bordered by the Swedish skerries. The continuing value of such fortifications is largely determined by both countries having long coastlines with these peculiar configurations and low population densities. Other countries like Spain have continued to maintain large-scale conventional coast defences long after they were abandoned as obsolete by major maritime powers like the UK and USA.[37]

The two examples of strategic rather than local fortifications in modern times are not encouraging to anyone who believes that formal fortifications will make a come-back. First, Enver Hoxha's regime in Albania fortified everything it could think of in an orgy of mad bunker-building. While never put to the test, the bunkers, which ran into the tens of thousands, were ineptly sited, badly designed and poorly constructed. Israel's use of a fortified line of bunkers on the Suez Canal to prevent an Egyptian crossing into Sinai was a miserable failure in the 1973 war. Intended as a forward observation position and as a tripwire to active mobile defence by armoured forces, it failed in both roles. The bunkers were quickly neutralized and the relieving armoured forces were halted by Egyptian mobile anti-tank missiles, rapidly ferried across the Canal. The line was probably counterproductive in that it lulled the Israelis into a false sense of security.

This is not to say that passive defensive measures are always useless, but they only make sense as part of an extensive and itself well-conceived scheme of active defence. Thus the large-scale water obstacles created by the Iraqis in the first Gulf War against the Iranians blunted attacks by the highly motivated and almost suicidal Iranian Revolutionary Guards. Again, the Greek Army continues to maintain extensive fortifications in Thrace. These were begun in the 1930s and have been added to ever since, in order to prevent a Turkish breakthrough in the event of war.[38] These defences are still seen as vital and are a closely guarded secret. They continue in use because the front here is shallow, the hilly terrain favours the defence and the Greek Army is much smaller than the Turkish. For similar reasons the South Koreans have constructed elaborate, prepared positions where the front line is very close to Seoul, to blunt a surprise North Korean attack.

In the case of civilian defences, the period after 1945 has called even passive fortification measures into question. In 1945 the atomic bomb on the one hand and the V2 rocket on the other threatened to make it impossible to protect civilians, even in deep shelters. Yet the protection of civilians by fortification had long been difficult. Cities had been defenceless against land bombardment since the turn of the century, even as they threw out even more distant and elaborate rings of forts. By the 1930s cities had come to be seen as sitting targets for aerial bombardment. British and German politicians, including Hitler, recognized that the best form of protection for one's own cities was deterrence, and thus the possession of a bomber force that was also capable of destroying the enemy's population centres was vital.[39] Where Germany and the UK differed was in the strategy they came to give to passive defence in the form of shelters and bomb proofing.[40] The UK government before 1939 believed that enough shelters able to protect the bulk of the population against high-explosive bombing would be both too expensive and impractical. Instead they favoured a mixture of dispersal of industry (the 'Shadow Factory' scheme), evacuation of women and children from London, air-raid precautions, and cheap shelters limited to protection against blast and debris from near misses.

In the run-up to war in the later 1930s, the official view was challenged by innovative and radical architects and engineers. The leftist London Borough of Finsbury rejected the official view and sought better protection for its densely settled population. The architecture group Tecton, led by Berthold Lubetkin, and the structural engineer Ove Arup, created designs for shelters that could resist 454 kg bombs.[41] The most advanced of their shelter designs maximized protection through a thick concrete burster slab and minimized cost by building multi-level shelters underneath it with easy access through helical ramps. The outbreak of war put an end to the scheme and nothing was built. The radicals showed that the reasoning against such shelters was fallacious. Assuming a random distribution of bombs, many people were bound to be killed in the statistically inevitable scattered weak shelters, whereas fewer accessible but concentrated shelters with heavy cover were less likely to be hit and would better protect their occupants if they were. In another sense the government was right to favour the cheapest possible measures. Britain had finite fiscal resources and was a democracy; unlike Nazi Germany, it could not spend at will on defence. Shelters also had an opportunity cost; it was necessary to set against expenditure on deep shelters the bombers and fighters foregone.

Given the modest scale of the bombing that resulted in the UK, an elaborate national shelter-building programme would have been counterproductive. The government's apparently callous favouring of cheap solutions in the face of what it believed would be devastating attacks proved to be the right solution, despite the faulty reasoning. Cheap protection like Anderson shelters in gardens and Morrison

shelters inside houses saved lives in Britain's mainly low-density resi-
dential districts. The British government did not just fear deep shelters
on grounds of cost; it also feared such structures because it distrusted
the people. It thought that many essential workers would retreat into
the shelters and refuse to come out, and that shelters would come to
house a feral population beyond official control. During the heavy
night raids on London during the winter of 1940–1, the government
at first sought to prevent people sheltering overnight in the deep stations of the Tube system for just this reason (and for the more reason-
able one that it might need the Tube to evacuate casualties if the streets
were blocked with rubble). Popular pressure and mass disobedience
forced the government to relent and London Transport to convert the
deep underground stations into night-time shelters with provision for
ticketing, food and sanitation. The Tube became a popular shelter
again during the V1 and V2 raids of 1944–5. Tubes were effective
improvised deep shelters, but nothing could have justified the construction of equivalent spaces for purely military purposes. Also the
stations were by no means entirely safe: there were fatalities from
bomb hits at Balham (68), Bank (111), Bounds Green (18) and
Trafalgar Square (7) and from panic at Bethnal Green (173).[42]

Britain thus muddled through; it managed because after the
summer of 1941 it was not heavily bombed. The German experience
was the reverse: Allied raids mounted in intensity from 1942 onwards
and the Nazi regime adopted extensive and elaborate passive defensive measures. They built large above-ground concrete shelters in cities
like Cologne and Hamburg.[43] Such shelters even contained architectural decorative features to fit in with surrounding buildings in historic
centres: the Nazis, far from being ruthlessly utilitarian, showed a
strong and inappropriately timed concern with 'heritage'. These shelters proved worthless against raids on the scale meted out to Hamburg
in 1943. The raids of 27 July created a firestorm that killed 50,000
people in a single night. The thickest concrete was useless against fires
so large that they sucked in all available oxygen and burned at 1,000
degrees centigrade. Concrete shelters became ovens. Afterwards, they
were found to contain the ashes, shrivelled corpses and melted fat of
their occupants. The Tecton shelters would have suffered in just the
same way: they were designed against local blast effects, not the fire-
storms that no one anticipated.

Hamburg, Dresden and Tokyo should have settled the matter.
Passive defence of urban areas was impossible against saturation
bombing. Hiroshima and Nagasaki merely concentrated the devasta-
tion into one bomb. Yet after the war, both the USA and USSR persisted with passive defence in the atomic age. Much of this was

structural. The USSR had dispersed much of its industry east of the Urals before and during the war. After 1945 the USA embraced pro-grammes to disperse industry and to further scatter population. It adopted several measures of de-concentration to survive the sort of A-bomb attack the Soviets were thought to be capable of launching. First, it built a strategic highway network with extensive redun-dancy.[44] Highways would permit evacuation in the crisis running up to an attack and communication after it. The Federal government thus subsidized state and municipal highway-building programmes. This acted as a hidden subsidy to the American automobile industry and also helped to facilitate suburbanization. Second, the government promoted suburban housing and underwrote mortgages.[45] This dis-persed the population from the inner cities and reinforced an already strongly operating trend. Third, the government began to both harden and duplicate its means of command and communication. This involved large-scale and expensive investment in major bunkers. Examples are, for the military, the huge NORAD HQ for air defence inside Cheyenne Mountain, Colorado, finally completed in 1966, and, for the civilian government, the bunker for members of Congress under the Greenbrier Hotel in West Virginia. This concern to secure post-nuclear attack communications eventually led to a de-central-ized networked system of links between computers – ARPANET, the precursor of the Internet. Passive defence considerations helped to shape some of the decisive spatial features of modern America: its dependence on the automobile, its exurbanization and its reliance on virtual communications for a dispersed population.[46]

The USA varied in the emphasis it gave to civilian passive defence in the Cold War period. Initially, just like the Russians, it tended to see the A bomb as just a bigger load of high explosive. In the 1950s it developed extensive civil defence measures against the limited number of A bombs likely to be delivered by the Soviet bombers that survived to penetrate the air defence screen, and that also managed to evade local missile batteries around major cities. The structural measures, like dispersal, would have had some effect; less rational were the par-anoid attempts to get citizens to live in permanent expectation of nuclear war and internalize the DIY survival tactics epitomized by the notorious public information film *Duck and Cover*. The H bomb ren-dered such passive measures all but useless. The Soviet Union tested an H bomb in 1953. By the mid-1960s ballistic missiles were in service on a scale that displaced the bomber as the primary threat. The only possible response was to concentrate on deterrence and to render it credible by ensuring that enough missiles would survive an attack to devastate the enemy cities in return. Civil defence was gradually downgraded in an age of Mutual Assured Destruction. In the USA this involved the dispersal of missiles in remote sites like Montana, then hardening them in silos designed to withstand a near-miss from a one-megaton warhead. Passive defence of weapons by concrete and steel was complemented by duplication of weapon systems and the protection of the means of command and control through mobility rather than hardening. This involved keeping bombers in the air or on standby, putting missiles in nuclear submarines, and creating flying command posts. The hardened sites of the nuclear age were extensive: many became redundant after the US–Soviet weapons reduction programme, START. They were quite unlike classical fortifications and, for all the concrete poured, in function more like the armour plate on tanks and warships. These hardened sites and bunkers are part of the detritus of the Cold War: they mostly remain on site and now attract their own chroniclers and architectural critics. These relics are the inglorious memorials of an age of secrecy and paranoia that is almost as remote as the bunkers of the Atlantik Wall. Once top secret, they are now abandoned and sad.

At the start of the Second World War the British government, at the same time that it was refusing to build hardened shelters for the public, was beginning to build them for itself.[47] These bunkers were hardly Teutonic in scale or design quality. The most obvious was and is the above-ground citadel built on to the side of the Admiralty. The Cabinet War Rooms in Whitehall were hardly secure against a direct hit by a heavy bomb. Churchill hated bunkers and to his credit refused to skulk during raids in the 'Paddock' bunker, at Dollis Hill in north London, designed to accommodate the Cabinet Office staff. After 1945 the government greatly extended this system of bunkers to create a series of secure citadels under London, linked by a network of tunnels. It also created a network of bunkers from which civil servants would govern Britain in the aftermath of a nuclear attack. In the 1950s the UK maintained and extended its network of Civil Defence, Royal Observer Corps (ROC) and radar station bunkers, in an attempt to maintain something like the system that had protected the country from air attack during the last war, but that had hardened to adapt to the A bomb. This system was much less effective than that stood down in 1945; it was also expensive and by the later 1950s was creaking at the seams. The 1957 Defence Review recognized the threats posed by the H bomb and the ballistic missile to a crowded island, and broke up or downgraded many of the components of the existing system. The ROC was abolished as it had ceased to be useful for plotting aircraft and had turned to the task of monitoring fallout. During the Cold War some of these sites, like the Regional Seats of Government bunkers (RSG), were subject to protests by CND and civil disobedience by groups like the Committee of 100. The bunkers were perceived by radicals as the sinister citadels of the secret state. Now what seems truly laughable rather than sinister is the notion of civil servants sitting in bunkers passing one another memos, while trying to carry on the futile business of governing a nuclear wasteland. After 1989 most of this infrastructure was abandoned or sold off, except for certain key hardened military HQs like the bunker in Northwood, Middlesex, and some key bunkers in Whitehall, such as those under the Ministry of Defence and Portcullis House.

Since the attacks on New York and Washington on 11 September 2001, this downgrading of civil protection measures in the UK has been partially reversed. The object, however, is to cope with the aftermath of a terrorist attack, not harden specific sites against it. Protection against terrorism is quite different from that against air attack. Terrorists have the option to attack asymmetrically: they will find vulnerable but significant sites. One could not harden every highrise block in London, for example. Hence uniform passive defence measures based on hardening will be both wasteful and counterproductive. The ease with which Aum Shinrikyo was able to spread sarin gas on the Tokyo subway shows just how vulnerable systems as extensive as the London Underground are. What appropriate prior planning can do is to try to prevent the chaos and ineffective responses seen in the aftermath of the Tokyo attack.[48]

In 2002 the UK government simulated terrorists dive-bombing a Boeing 747 into Bradwell nuclear power station in Suffolk. The results were not encouraging in terms of the preparedness and capacity of the emergency services to meet such an eventuality. The predictable targets like the Houses of Parliament may distract attention from the real threats. Thus central London would have missed the fallout plume from Bradwell, given the winds on the day, but large parts of Kent would not.

Architecture does still have a place in the new security-centred response, however.[49] We can learn from areas of ongoing continuing emergency, like Northern Ireland, where security against bombs has been gradually built into buildings such as police stations and government offices. The 1993 and 1994 attacks on the City of London demonstrated the obvious: that many modern office buildings are highly vulnerable to blast and their glass facades are lethal to those in the surrounding streets. The attack on the Twin Towers has shown that companies without adequate back-up services are likely to fail in the aftermath of a major attack. The responses to such threats have been threefold: first, to design active security measures and passive protection to be incorporated into new buildings where possible; second, to duplicate key systems like dealing rooms, data storage and data-processing in secondary locations; and third, to promote invisibility – thus key facilities like inter-bank transfer centres and back-up offices are sited in inconspicuous buildings and out-of-town locations.

The modern city cannot be a fortress and still function.[50] It is no longer possible to ensure security by external measures, like building a wall round the city in the Middle Ages. Likewise, intensive 'virtual' walls, that is, frequent and thorough security checks, are expensive and after a time alienate the shoppers and tourists on which the prosperity of many cities now depends. As a preventative measure electronic surveillance offers little security – almost none against suicide bombers. It requires vigilant and competent personnel in order to be effective, but most CCTV screens are watched by bored, low-wage people. Slackness is inevitable, even in the harshest police state. If external security is difficult to come by in the city, so is protection within the building. The noble families of many Italian Renaissance cities had towers of refuge attached to their houses. Shops, offices and dealing rooms all require large floor-plates that are hard to protect externally. Like Mr Baldwin's bombers, some terrorists will always get through. The problem now is the one who is carrying a dirty bomb or a vial of anthrax.

Notes

Chapter 2   Cities, Globalization and Governance

1 Thus, for example, Singapore has developed the Central Provident Fund, an innovative public–private scheme for pensions provision, and the city of Porto Allegre in Brazil has pioneered a successful scheme of direct citizenship participation in setting budget and targets.

2 See A. Southall, *The City in Time and Space*, Cambridge University Press, Cambridge, 1998, ch. 5.

3 This is, of course, to say something slightly different from Max Weber's construction of the ideal type of the occidental city. I am not so much trying to construct a conceptual model of cities, but rather to show how our city ideals have functioned as models for actors. The point here is that the city concept, both as institution and place, has dominated Western thinking about cities and, therefore, to a substantial degree cities themselves. See Max Weber, *The City*, The Free Press, New York, 1958.

4 For a critical discussion of this notion, see B. Hindess, 'Imaginary presuppositions of democracy', in *Economy and Society*, 20, 2 (1991): 173–95.

5 On the democracy of Athens, see M. I. Finley, *Democracy Ancient and Modern*, Rutgers University Press, Brunswick, NJ, 1973; J. Ober, *Mass and Elite in Democratic Athens*, Princeton University Press, Princeton, NJ, 1989, and M. H. Hansen, *The Athenian Democracy in the Age of Demosthenes*, Cambridge University Press, Cambridge, 1991.

6 The classic statement is in T. H. Marshall's 'Citizenship and Social Class', in *Sociology at the Crossroads*, Heinemann, London, 1963.

7 The classic statement is to be found in Alexis de Tocqueville's *Democracy in America*, and the most rigorous re-statement is R. A. Dahl, *A Preface to Democratic Theory*, University of Chicago Press, Chicago, 1956; see also M. E. Warren, *Democracy and Association*, Princeton University Press, Princeton, NJ, 2001.

8   This point is well made in Manuel de Landa's *A Thousand Years of Non-Linear History*, Swerve, New York, 2000.

9   See P. Veyne, *Bread and Circuses*, Allen Lane, London, 1990.

10 On the Ancient city as a built environment see R. E. Wycherly, *How the Greeks Built Cities*, Macmillan, London, 1962, for a lucid interpretation, and R. Tomlinson, *From Mycenae to Constantinople*, Routledge, London, 1992, for a modern survey.

11 The change in late Antique elites is well portrayed in P. Brown, *The World of Late Antiquity*, Thames and Hudson, London, 1971.

12 On the growth of medieval cities see H. Pirenne, *Medieval Cities*, Princeton University Press, Princeton, NJ, 1952, and P. M. Hohenburg and L. Hollen Lees, *The Making of Urban Europe 1000–1994*, Harvard University Press, Cambridge, MA, 1995. Even though it is old, Pirenne's book remains an unrivalled interpretation.

13 See R. MacKenney, *The City State 1500–1700*, Macmillan, Basingstoke, 1989, ch. 1.

14 See M. Van Creveld, *The Rise and Decline of the State*, Cambridge University Press, Cambridge, 1999.

15 See N. Ferguson, *The Cash Nexus*, Allen Lane, London, 2001, ch. 4.

16 F. Braudel makes this point about the 'city centred' nature of commerce and its vulnerability to capture well in *Civilization and Capitalism 15–18th Century*, vol. III, *The Perspective of the World*, Collins, London, 1984, chs 2 and 3. For an example of this shifting balance between cities, see V. Babour, *Capitalism in Amsterdam in the Seventeenth Century*, University of Michigan Press, Ann Arbour, 1966, on its rise at the expense of Antwerp.

17 See A. Minc, *Le Nouveau Moyen Age*, Gallimard, Paris, 1993.

18 See P. Hirst, 'Between the Local and the Global: Democracy in the 21st Century', in R. Axtmann (ed.) *Balancing Democracy*, Continuum, London, 2001.

19 See W. Cronon, *Nature's Metropolis: Chicago and the Great West*, W. W. Norton, New York, 1991.

20 See K. T. Jackson, *Crabgrass Frontier: The Suburbanization of the United States*, Oxford University Press, New York, 1985.

21 A good discussion of the impact of IT on cities is in W. J. Mitchell, *e-topia*, MIT Press, Cambridge, MA, 1999.

22 See S. Sassen, *Cities in a World Economy*, Pine Forge Press, Thousand Oaks, CA, 1994, and M. Castells, *The Internet Galaxy: Reflections on the Internet, Business and Society*, Oxford University Press, New York, 2001.

23 See M. Storper and S. Christopherson, 'Flexible Specialization and Regional Industrial Agglomerations: The case of the US Motion Picture Industry', in *Annals of the Association of American Geographers*, 77, 1 (1990): 104–17.

24 See A. Marshall, *Industry and Trade*, Macmillan, London, 1919, and C. Sabel, 'The Re-emergence of Regional Economies', in P. Hirst and J. Zeitlin (eds), *Reversing Industrial Decline*, Berg, Oxford, 1989.

25 M. Gladwell, 'Clicks and Mortar', *The New Yorker*, 6 December 1999, and P. Hirst, 'The Knowledge Economy: Fact or Fiction', in *Renewal*, 8, 2 (2000): 82–9.

26 See K. T. Jackson, *Crabgrass Frontier*, op. cit.

27 See J. Garreau, *Edge City: Life on the New Frontier*, Doubleday, New York, 1991, and M. Sorkin (ed.) *Variations on a Theme Park: The New American City and the End of Public Space*, Hill and Wang, New York, 1992.

28 See A. Ross, *The Celebration Chronicles*, Verso, London, 2000.

29 E. W. Soja, 'Inside Exopolis: Scenes from Orange County', in M. Sorkin (ed.), op. cit.

30 R. Putnam, *Bowling Alone*, Simon and Schuster, New York, 2001.

31 See P. Le Galès, *European Cities*, Oxford University Press, Oxford, 2002.

32 See Sorkin (ed.), op. cit.

33 D. Osborne and T. Gaebler, *Reinventing Government*, Penguin, New York, 1993.

34 Still the exemplary study of this process is E. Weber, *Peasants into Frenchmen*, Chatto and Windus, London, 1977.

35 For N. F. S. Grundtvig, see S. E. Borish, *The Land of the Living: The Danish Folk High Schools and Denmark's Non-Violent Path to Modernization*, Blue Dolphin, Nevada City, CA, 1991.

36 See F. Prochaska, *The Voluntary Impulse*, Faber and Faber, London, 1978.

37 I have discussed this issue further in 'Statism, Pluralism and Social Control', in D. Garland and R. Sparks (eds), *Criminology and Social Theory*, Oxford University Press, Oxford, 2000.

38 Second edn, Polity, Cambridge, 1991. For a coherent account of the alternative view that globalization is taking place, see D. Held et al., *Global Transformations*, Polity, Cambridge, 1999.

39 See K. Ohmae, *The End of the Nation State: The Rise of Regional Economies*, HarperCollins, London, 1995, and M. Castells, *The Information Age: Economy, Society and Culture*, vol. 2, *The Power of Identity*, Blackwell, Oxford, 1997.

40 See H. Spruyt, *The Sovereign State and its Competitors*, Princeton University Press, Princeton, NJ, 1994.

41 For the evidence, see Hirst and Thompson, op. cit., ch. 3.

42 Thus, in the *Financial Times 500*, 2002 survey of the largest global companies, which measures them by stock-market valuation, 441 are located in the EU, Japan and the USA, and 475 in the OECD.

43 See A. Rugman, *The End of Globalization*, Random House Business Books, London, 2000, and for an attempt to argue how corporations could become less fragile see M. C. Scott, *Heartland – How to Build Companies as Strong as Countries*, John Wiley, Chichester, 2001. Needless to say, I don't think the latter succeeds: it merely shows the vast difference between companies and states.

44 See G. Thompson, *Between Hierarchies and Markets: The Logic and Limits of Network Forms of Organization*, Oxford University Press, Oxford, 2003.

45 See P. Hirst, *War and Power in the 21st Century*, Polity, Cambridge, 2001, for an extended version of this argument.

46 See Hirst and Thompson, op. cit., ch. 9.

47 See N. Scheper-Hughes, *Death Without Weeping: The Violence of Everyday Life in Brazil*, University of California Press, Berkeley, CA, 1992.

48 B. de Souza Santos, 'Participatory Budgeting in Porto Alegre: Toward a Redistributive Democracy', in *Politics and Society*, 4 (1998).

49 See R. D. Kaplan, *The Coming Anarchy*, Vintage, New York, 2000.

Chapter 3   Politics and Territory

1 See A. Giddens, *A Contemporary Critique of Historical Materialism*, vol. 2, *The Nation-State and Violence*, Polity, Cambridge, 1985.

2 Thus Crick, in *In Defence of Politics*, Continuum, London, 2000, defines politics in terms of a process of discussion and accommodation between interests within an institutionalized framework, whereas Schmitt in *The Concept of the Political*, Rutgers University Press, New Brunswick, NJ, 1976, conceives politics as derived from friend/enemy relations, an irreconcilable conflict that organizes groups into competing forces.

3 This does not mean that a state has to be highly centralized or authoritarian: it may be federal and pluralist, conceding extensive constitutionally guaranteed power to other public bodies and to civil society. Indeed, a strong capacity for external exclusion and a strong culture of public law make such pluralism more likely; weak states find it hard to be sustainably pluralist. See P. Hirst, *The Pluralist Theory of the State*, UCL Press, London, 1997.

4 See J. Bodin, *On Sovereignty* (ed. J. H. Franklin), Cambridge University Press, Cambridge, 1992, and N. Machiavelli, *The Discourses* (ed. B. Crick), Penguin, Harmondsworth, 1983.

5 This was not always the case. Western views of the Ottoman regime were often positive to begin with, and even Bodin was mild in his comments. See L. Valensi, *The Birth of the Despot: Venice and the Sublime Porte*, Cornell University Press, Ithaca, NY, 1993.

6 On Mongol political institutions, see L. Krader, *The Formation of the State*, Prentice Hall, Englewood Cliffs, NJ, 1968. For visits to Karakorum by contemporary travellers, see I. De Rachewiltz, *Papal Envoys to the Great Khans*, Faber and Faber, London, 1971, and Sir Henry Yule, *Cathay and the Way Thither*, Hakluyt Society, London, 1913–16, vols I–III, for the major travellers' texts.

7 In this sense we can accept the reality of Georges Duby's critique of stylized models of feudalism, while accepting that medieval states were

fundamentally different in their institutions and forms of legitimacy from later ones. See G. Duby, *The Three Orders: Feudal Society Imagined*, University of Chicago Press, Chicago, 1980.

8 See Marc Bloch, *Feudal Society*, 2 vols, Routledge and Kegan Paul, 2nd edn, London, 1965.

9 On the frontier in medieval Europe, see Bartlett and MacKay (eds), *Medieval Frontier Societies*, Clarendon Press, Oxford, 1989.

10 On medieval institutions, see F. Heer, *The Holy Roman Empire*, Phoenix Press, London, 2002, and Walter Ullman, *The Growth of Papal Government in the Middle Ages*, Methuen, London, 1955.

11 P. Dollinger, *The German Hansa*, Macmillan, London, 1970.

12 See A. Black, *Guilds and Civil Society*, Methuen, London, 1984.

13 See S. Zubaida, *Law and Power in the Islamic World*, IB Tauris, London, 2003.

14 On the rise of the modern state, see T. Ertman, *The Birth of the Leviathan*, Cambridge University Press, Cambridge, 1997, H. Spruyt, *The Sovereign State and its Competitors*, op. cit., S. Krasner 'Sovereignty: an institutional perspective' *Comparative Political Studies*, 21, 1 (1988): 66–94, and J. G. Ruggies, 'Territoriality and Beyond: problematizing modernity in international relations', *International Organization*, 47, 1 (1993): 134–72.

15 See P. Hirst, *War and Power*, op. cit., chs 1 and 2, for a more extended discussion.

16 See H. Spruyt, *The Sovereign State*, op. cit.

17 For Sweden, see M. Roberts, *Essays in Swedish History*, Weidenfeld and Nicolson, London, 1967.

18 On the sources of weakness of the Hanseatic League, see P. Hirst, *War and Power in the 21st Century*, op. cit., pp. 50–2, and on the limitations of city-states as forms of extended rule, see ch. 2.

19 As a general introduction to the subject, E. H. Carr's *Nationalism and After*, Macmillan, London, 1945, remains unrivalled.

20 Thus the polarization of the debate on the nature of nationalism between those who favour pre-modern ethnic and cultural foundations for nationalism, like Anthony Smith, and those who see it as a political project, like Benedict Anderson in *Imagined Communities*, Verso, London, 1991, and Eric Hobsbawm, *Nations and Nationalism since 1780*, Cambridge University Press, Cambridge, 1992, is somewhat exaggerated.

21 L. Febvre, '*Frontière*: the word and the concept', in P. Burke (ed.), *A New Kind of History: From the Writings of Febvre*, Routledge and Kegan Paul, London, 1973.

22 See O. von Gierke, *Political Theories of the Middle Age* (1900), new edn, Cambridge University Press, Cambridge, 1988.

23 J. Black, *Maps and Politics*, Reaktion Books, London, 1997, ch. 5, 'Frontiers'.

24 Carl Schmitt, *Land and Sea*, Plutarch Press, Washington, DC, 1997, p. 39.

25 See J. E. Thomson, *Mercenaries, Pirates and Sovereigns*, Princeton University Press, Princeton, NJ, 1994.
26 On nineteenth-century 'globalization', see K. H. O'Rourke and J. G. Williamson, *Globalization and History: The Evolution of a Nineteenth Century Atlantic Economy*, MIT, Cambridge, MA, 1999, and H. James, *The End of Globalization*, Harvard University Press, Cambridge, MA, 2001.
27 See Simon Bromley, 'The Logic of Liberal Sovereignty', in D. Marsh and C. Hay (eds), *Globalisation, Welfare Retrenchment and the State*, Macmillan, London, 2000.
28 See the extensive data in P. Hirst and G. Thompson, *Globalization in Question*, 1st edn, Polity, Cambridge, 1996, ch. 3.
29 For a fuller version of this argument, see P. Hirst, 'Another Century of Conflict', in *International Relations*, 16, 3 (2002): 327–42.
30 See P. Hirst and G. Thompson, 'The Future of Globalization', in *Cooperation and Conflict*, 37, 3 (2002): table 2.
31 See J. F. Helliwell, *How Much Do National Borders Matter?* Brookings Institution, Washington, DC, 1998, and J. F. Helliwell, *Globalization: Myths, Facts and Consequences*, C. D. Howe Institute, Toronto, 2000.
32 See Bodin, *On Sovereignty*, op. cit.
33 For a longer version of this argument, see P. Hirst, 'Power', in T. Dunne et al. (eds), *The Eighty Years Crisis: International Relations 1919–1991*, Cambridge University Press, Cambridge, 1998.
34 For an expanded account, see P. Hirst, 'Between the Local and the Global: Democracy in the 21st Century', in R. Axtmann (ed.), *Balancing Democracy*, Continuum, London, 2001.
35 For examples, see R. D. Kaplan, *Warrior Politics*, Random House, NY, 2002, and Deepak Lal, 'In Defence of Empires', The 2002 Henry Wendt Lecture, American Enterprise Institute.

Chapter 4   The Spatial Dimensions of Military Power

1 C. Clausewitz, *On War*, 3 vols, trans. J. J. Graham, Routledge and Kegan Paul, London, and vol 1, p. 23. The new Paret edition is superior but I am familiar with this one.
2 Hobbes, *Leviathan*, Blackwell, Oxford, 1951.
3 See Carl Schmitt, *The Concept of the Political*, op. cit., for the political consequences of the distinction between friend and enemy.
4 Clausewitz (trans. J. J. Graham), *On War*, op. cit., vol. 1, p. 2.
5 Clausewitz saw that this inherent tendency to escalation in war before modern technology greatly increased the destructive power of weapons. Nuclear missiles made something like absolute war possible in the sense of a totally destructive spasm exchange of warheads. At the same time they all but destroyed war: as Clausewitz understood, it was a morally exacting and purposive struggle.

6 See Carl Schmitt, *Land and Sea*, op. cit.

7 See Schmitt *Land and Sea*, op. cit. and J. H. Perry, *The Discovery of the Sea*, Weidenfeld and Nicolson, London, 1975.

8 This is not to claim that there were not great explorers and seafaring peoples before this. The examples of the Lapita and the Vikings spring to mind. But the Europeans saw space differently. Likewise, other societies have possessed sophisticated techniques of navigation, as David Lewis has shown for the South Sea Islanders in *We, the Navigators*, University of Hawaii Press, Honolulu, 1994. Yet these techniques were tied to particular experiences and practices. They were not capable of abstraction and generalization; they are analogous to Levi Strauss's notion of a 'science of the concrete' in *The Savage Mind*, Weidenfeld and Nicolson, 1966.

9 See I. Clenndinnen, *Aztecs: An Interpretation*, Cambridge University Press, Cambridge, 1991, and Ross Hassig, *Aztec Warfare*, University of Oklahoma Press, Norman, 1988.

10 See Lucy Mair, *Primitve Government*, Penguin, Harmondsworth, 1970, and Max Gluckman, *Politics, Law and Ritual in Tribal Society*, Blackwell, Oxford, 1965.

11 See Max Gluckman, 'The Peace in the Feud', in *Custom and Conflict in Africa*, Blackwell, Oxford, 1965.

12 Classification of societies is essential and Service's basic structural differentiations are rigorous; the problem comes when these are seen in evolutionary terms, as if band societies are conceived of as at a lower level (if not universal stage) of general social evolution. In the end M. Sahlins and E. R. Service's general theoretical work *Evolution and Culture*, University of Michigan Press, Ann Arbor, 1960, fails because it tries the impossible balancing act of seeking to keep general evolutionary judgements based on increasing structural complexity and adaptive potential, but also to separate them from the specific causal processes of social development.

13 See Gluckman, *Custom and Conflict*, op. cit., and E. E. Evans-Pritchard, *The Nuer*, Oxford University Press, Oxford, 1940.

14 See Peter Matthiessen, *Under the Mountain Wall*, Collins Harvill, London, 1989.

15 For Maori warfare and the impact of Westerners, see A. W. Crosby, *Ecological Imperialism*, Cambridge University Press, Cambridge, 1986, ch. 10.

16 See J. C. Beaglehole, *The Life of Captain Cook*, Stanford University Press, Stanford, CA, 1974, chs VIII, XVI and XXII; *The Cambridge History of the Pacific Islanders*, ed. D. Denoon et al., Cambridge University Press, Cambridge, 1997, is also useful but is broken up thematically.

17 H. H. Turney-High, *Primitive War*, University of South Carolina Press, Columbia, 1949, 3rd printing, 1991. See also Arthur Ferrill, *The Origins of War*, Thames and Hudson, London, 1985.

18 R. Lowe, *The Origin of the State*, Harcourt, Brace and Company, New York, *c*. 1927.

19 See D. Morris, *The Washing of the Spears*, and V. D. Hanson, *Why the West Has Won*, Faber and Faber, London, 2001, ch. 8.

20 K. Polanyi, *Dahomey and the Slave Trade*, Washington University Press, Seattle, 1966, and M. J. Herskovits, *Dahomey: an Ancient West African Kingdom*, 2 vols, Augustin, New York, 1938.

21 Gibbon abridged D. M. Low, Chatto and Windus, London, 1960, pp. 598–9; see also the discussion in J. Black, *War and the World*, Yale University Press, New Haven, CN, 1998, pp. 3–13.

22 Ibn Khaldûn, *Muqaddimah: An Introduction to History*, translated from the Arabic by Franz Rosenthal, Routledge and Kegan Paul, London, 1958.

23 It may be no accident that Gibbon and Adam Ferguson, whose *Essays on the History of Civil Society* (1767), Edinburgh University Press, Edinburgh, 1966, is organized around these categories; both had direct experience of the clash between a highly developed commercial society and the backward quasi-tribal, quasi-feudal social structures in the Highlands of Scotland. The categories of savagery, barbarism and civilization were systemactially developed as categories of social classification by Lewis Henry Morgan in his *Ancient Society* (1877) Meridian Books, New York, 1967. Far from being the result of imperialist prejudice (Morgan was an active defender of the American Indians) they remain of sociological interest today.

24 On the early cult of the noble savage, see F. Boas and A. O. Lovejoy, *Primitivism and Related Ideas in Antiquity*, Johns Hopkins University Press, Baltimore, MD, 1935.

25 For southern Egypt, see R. B. Jackson, *At Empire's Edge*, Yale University Press, New Haven, CN, 2002, and for North Africa, but for the whole frontier generally, R. Whittaker, *Frontiers of the Roman Empire*, John Hopkins University Press, Baltimore, MD, 1994. See also D. Williams, *The Reach of Rome: A History of the Roman Imperial Frontier*, St. Martin's Press, New York, 1997.

26 The Romans followed the rest of the Ancient World in seeing peripheral regions not merely as underdeveloped but as inherently primitive and deprived by nature; see *The Edges of the World in Ancient Thought*.

27 E. Luttwak, *The Grand Strategy of the Roman Empire*, Johns Hopkins University Press, Baltimore, MD, 1976. For a critique, see A. Ferrill 'The Grand Strategy of the Roman Empire', in P. Jennedy (ed.), *Grand Strategies in War and Peace*, Yale University Press, New Haven, CN, 1991.

28 See Whittaker, *Frontiers*, op. cit., and D. Williams, *The Reach of Rome*, op. cit.

29 H. Elton, *Warfare in Roman Europe AD 350–425*, Clarendon Press, Oxford, 1996, disputes both these assertions, but his attempts to prove from names that barbarian senior officers were relatively few and that the army remained effective seem difficult to sustain because of the inconclusiveness of the evidence.

30 For the later period, see A. H. M. Jones, *The Later Roman Empire*, 2 vols, Blackwell, Oxford, 1964, and for an attempt at a social rather than a military explanation for the fall of the empire, see F. W. Wallbank, *The Awful Revolution*, Liverpool University Press, Liverpool, 1969.

31 A. Waldron, *The Great Wall of China: From History to Myth*, Cambridge University Press, Cambridge, 1990.

32 See *The Cambridge History of China*, vol. 6, *Alien Regimes and Border States, 907–1368*, ed. H. Franke and D. Twitchett, Cambridge University Press, Cambridge, 1994, and T. J. Barfield, *The Perilous Frontier*, Oxford 1989.

33 See M. Elvin, *The Pattern of the Chinese Past*, Eyre Methuen, London, 1973.

34 O. Lattimore, *Inner Asian Frontiers of China*, American Geographical Society Research Series 21 (1940), New York.

35 See M. Elvin, *The Pattern of the Chinese Past*, op. cit., ch. 7.

36 On Mongol warfare, see J. Chambers, *The Devil's Horsemen*, Weidenfeld and Nicolson, London, 1975, D. Morgan, *The Mongols*, Blackwell, Oxford, 1986, and R. Marshall, *Storm from the East*, Penguin, Harmondsworth, 1994. See also J. Keegan, *History of Warfare*, Hutchinson, London, 1993, ch. 3.

37 See A. Waldron, *The Great Wall of China*, op. cit., ch. 6.

38 See D. Morgan, *The Mongols*, op. cit., pp. 103–7.

39 See L. Krader, *Formation of the State*, op. cit., ch. 6, 'The Tartar State; Turks and Mongols', and Krader, *Social Organization of the Mongol–Turkic Pastoral Nomads*, Humanities Press, New York, 1963.

40 Methuen, London, 1965, p. 25.

41 For Mahan's ideas, see J. T. Sumida, *Inventing Grand Strategy and Teaching Command*, Johns Hopkins University Press, Baltimore, MD, 1997, and the essays by M. T. Sprout in the original 1943 E. M. Earle edn, Princeton University Press, Princeton, NJ, and by P. A. Crowl in the 1986 P. Paret edn, Clarendon Press, Oxford, of *Makers of Modern Strategy*.

42 See P. Padfield, *The Tide of Empires*, 2 vols, Routledge and Kegan Paul, London, 1979 and 1982, and J. Glete, *Warfare at Sea 1500–1650*, Routledge, London, 2000.

43 Glete, op. cit., ch. 5.

44 See J. F. Guilmartin, *Gunpowder and Galleys*, Cambridge University Press, Cambridge, 1974.

45 On Chinese ships and naval technology, see Ronan and Needham, *The Shorter Science and Civilization in China*, vol. 3, Cambridge University Press, Cambridge, 1986, and on Turtle Ships, G. Parker, *The Military Revolution*, Cambridge University Press, Cambridge, 1988, pp. 108–10.

46 On the innovations necessary to the age of discovery, see Conway's *History of the Ship, The Sailing Ship 1000–1650*, Brassey's, London, 1994. On the initial Iberian occupation of the Atlantic islands as a preparation for the

process of discovery and conquest, see F. Fernandez-Armesto, *Before Columbus*, Macmillan, London, 1987.

47 For the Vivaldis, see J. R. S. Phillips, *The Medieval Expansion of Europe*, Oxford University Press, Oxford, 1988, pp. 155–6, and on the technology of the galley, see Conway's *History of the Ship, The Age of the Galley*, Brassey's, London, 1995.

48 See L. Levathes, *When China Ruled the Seas*, Simon and Schuster, New York, 1994.

49 For the central role of guns in European dominance, see C. Cipolla, *Guns and Sails in the Early Phase of European Expansion*, Collins, London, 1965.

50 The best account of the revolution in navigation is still E. G. R Taylor, *The Haven-finding Art: A History of Navigation from Odysseus to Captain Cook*, Hollis and Carter for the Institute of Navigation, London, 1971, and the best account of their use in practice is S. E. Morrison, *Admiral of the Ocean Sea, A Life of Christopher Columbus*, Little Brown, Boston, MA, 1970.

51 C. R. Boxer, *The Portuguese Seaborne Empire* 1415–1825, Carcanet, in association with the Calouste Gulbenkian Foundation, Manchester, 1991.

52 G. Parker, *The Military Revolution*, op. cit., p. 112.

53 See J. H. Elliott 'The Spanish Conquest', in L. Bethell (ed.), *Colonial Spanish America*, Cambridge University Press, Cambridge, 1987, and J. H. Parry, *The Spanish Seaborne Empire*, University of California Press, Berkeley, 1990, c. 1966.

54 P. Padfield, *Tide of Empires: Decisive Naval Campaigns in the Rise of the West*, Routledge and Kegan Paul, London, 1979, vol. I, chs 4–6, and vol. 2, chs 1–4.

55 P. Kennedy, *The Rise and Fall of British Naval Mastery*, Macmillan, London, 1983, chs 8 and 9.

56 *Geographical Journal*, xxiii, 4 (1904); see also Mackinder's *Democratic Ideals and Reality*, Constable, London, 1919, and P. Kennedy, 'Mahan versus Mackinder', in his *Strategy and Diplomacy*, Fontana, London, 1983.

57 See R. J. Overy, *The Air War 1939–45*, Macmillan, London, 1980; see also his *Why the Allies Won*, Jonathan Cape, London, 1995.

58 See P. Kennedy, 'The Eagle has Landed', *Financial Times*, 2 February 2002.

59 See B. Semmel, *Liberalism and Naval Strategy*, Allen and Unwin, London, 1986, and A. H. Imlah, *Economic Elements in the Pax Britannica*, Cambridge, MA, 1958.

60 See H. James, *The End of Globalization*, op. cit.

61 See J. G. Ruggie, *Building the World Polity*, Routledge, London, 1998.

62 Guilmartin, *Gunpowder and Galleys*, op. cit., advances this thesis; see also Glete, *Warfare at Sea*, op. cit., ch. 6, and S. Rose, *Medieval Naval Warfare 1000–1500*, Routledge, London, 2002, ch. 6.

63 F. Braudel, *The Mediterranean and the Mediterranean World in the Age of Philip II*, vol. 1, Collins, London, 1972, and Braudel, *Civilization and Capitalism*, vol. III, Collins, London, 1984, ch. 2.

64 Braudel, *Mediterranean*, Collins, London, 1973, vol. II, pt. 2, vii.

65 For Malta, see E. Bradford, *The Great Siege*, Hodder and Stoughton, London, 1961, and for Lepanto, see Padfield, *Tide*, op. cit., vol. 1, ch. 3, and Braudel, *Mediterranean*, op. cit., vol. II, pt. 3, iv.

Chapter 5   The Frontier, Conquest and Settlement

1 See R. Bartlett, *The Making of Europe: Conquest, Colonization and Cultural Change 950–1350*, Penguin, London, 1994.

2 See R. Bartlett and A. MacKay (eds), *Medieval Frontier Societies*, op. cit.

3 See F. J. Turner, *The Frontier in American History*, Dover, New York, 1996, a collection which includes the 1893 essay along with others on related themes.

4 On the Turner debate in the context of medieval frontier expansion, see R. I. Burns, 'Significance . . .', in Bartlett and MacKay (eds), op. cit. On the Turner thesis in relation to Latin America generally from the Conquest into the twentieth century, see A. Hennessy, *The Frontier in Latin American History*, Edward Arnold, London, 1978.

5 See R. Hofstadter, *The Progressive Historians: Turner, Beard, Parrington*, Knopf, New York, 1968, and D. M. Potter, *People of Plenty: Economic Abundance and the American Character*, University of Chicago Press, Chicago, 1963.

6 W. Cronon, *Nature's Metropolis: Chicago and the Great West*, op. cit.

7 H. Inalcik and D. Quatert (eds), *An Economic and Social History of the Ottoman Empire*, vol. 1, *1300–1916*, Cambridge University Press, Cambridge, 1994, p. 14.

8 D. Obolensky, *The Byzantine Commonwealth*, Phoenix Press, London, 2000, p. 237.

9 Inalcik and Quatert, op. cit., p. 15.

10 See C. Duffy, *Siege Warfare: The Fortress in the Age of Vauban and Frederick the Great, 1660–1789*, Routledge and Kegan Paul, London, 1985, ch. 8.

11 G. Rothenburg, *The Austrian Military Frontier in Croatia 1522–1747*, University of Illinois Press, Urbana, IL, 1960.

12 See H. Kennedy, *Muslim Spain and Portugal*, Longman, London, 1996, ch. 1.

13 E. Lourie, 'A Society Organized for War: Medieval Spain', *Past and Present*, 35 (1966): 56.

14 Lourie, op. cit.: 58.

15 Gonzélez Jiménez in Bartlett and MacKay (eds), op. cit.

16 M. Sanchez-Albornoz, quoted by A. MacKay, *Spain in the Middle Ages: From Frontier to Empire 1000–1500*, Macmillan, London, 1977, p. 38.

17 MacKay, op. cit., p. 39.
18 See N. Housley, *The Later Crusades, 1274–1580*, Oxford University Press, Oxford, 1992.
19 For the military orders, see Lourie, 'A Society . . .' op. cit.
20 For the institution of *behetria*, see Lourie, op. cit.
21 See Lourie, op. cit.: 67–8.
22 See Castaner in Bartlett and MacKay (eds), op. cit., for this point and for cross-border institutions generally.
23 See P. Zagorin, *Rebels and Rulers 1560–1660*, vol II, Cambridge University Press, Cambridge, 1982, pp. 33–7, for Catalonia and Portugal; see also J. H. Elliot, *The Revolt of the Catalans: A Study in the Decline of Spain (1598–1640)*, Cambridge University Press, Cambridge, 1963.
24 See H. Kamen, *Spain's Road to Empire*, Allen Lane, London, 2002, pp. 181–2.
25 For accounts of the conquests, see H. Thomas, *The Conquest of Mexico*, Hutchinson, London, 1993, and J. Hemming, *The Conquest of the Incas*, Penguin, Harmondsworth, 1983. For Aztec society, see I. Clendinnen, *Aztecs: An Interpretation*, Cambridge University Press, Cambridge and New York, 1995.
26 On the role of translation generally and Donna Marina in particular, see S. Greenblatt, *Marvelous Possessions, the Wonder of the New World*, Chicago University Press, Chicago, IL, 1991.
27 On the role of writing in the conquest, see T. Todorov, *The Conquest of America*, Harper and Row, New York, 1984.
28 I. Clendinnen, *Ambivalent Conquests: Maya and Spaniard in Yucatan 1517–1570*, Cambridge University Press, Cambridge, 1987.
29 See D. J. Weber, *The Spanish Frontier in North America*, Yale University Press, New Haven, CN, 1992, ch. 1, on Florida and on Spanish policy and institutions in North America generally.
30 See T. Flannery, *The Eternal Frontier*, Vintage, London, 2002, p. 264.
31 See A. W. Crosby, *The Columbian Exchange: Biological and Cultural Consequences of 1492*, Greenwood Press, Westport, CN, 1972.
32 On seaborne conquest in mainland Spain and the Atlantic islands, see F. Fernandez-Armesto, *Before Columbus*, op. cit.
33 See A. W. Crosby, *Ecological Imperialism*, op. cit., ch. 4.
34 See H. Thomas, *The Conquest of Mexico*, op. cit.
35 H. Kamen, *Spain's Road to Empire*, op. cit., p. 123.
36 On the Spanish natural law tradition and the rights of the Indians, see A. Pagden, *The Fall of Natural Man*, Cambridge University Press, Cambridge, 1986.
37 P. Seed, *Ceremonies of Possession*, Cambridge University Press, Cambridge, 1995, ch. 3.
38 For the text of the Requirement, see Seed, op. cit., p. 69.
39 For the evolution of the *encomienda* system and the control of native labour generally, see C. Gibson, *The Aztecs Under Spanish Rule*, Stanford

University Press, Stanford, CA, 1964, and his *Spain in America*, Harper and Row, New York, 1966, for the institutions of the Spanish colonial system more generally.

40 See D. J. Weber, *The Spanish Frontier*, op. cit.

41 Flannery, *The Eternal Frontier*, op. cit., p. 268.

42 This section is based on F. Anderson, *Crucible of War: The Seven Years War and the Fate of the Empire, in British North America 1754–1766*, Faber and Faber, London, 2000, and I. K. Steele, *Warpaths: Invasions of North America*, Oxford University Press, New York, 1994.

43 See J. E Cairnes, *The Slave Power: Its Character, Career and Possible Design; being an attempt to explain the real issues involved in the American contest* (1863), David and Charles, Newton Abbot, 1968. Turner was clear on the central role of the West in the Civil War.

44 For this process generally, see A. W. Crosby, *Ecological Imperialism*, op. cit.

45 On migration, see S. Castles and M. J. Miller, *The Age of Mass Migration*, Macmillan, London, 1993.

46 See, for convergence, K. H. O'Rourke and J. G. Williamson, *Globalization and History*, op. cit.

47 See P. Vidal de la Blache, *Principes de géographie humaine publiés d'après les manuscrits de l'auteur par Emmanuel de Martonne*, A. Colin, Paris, 1922, and L. P. V. Febvre (in collaboration with L. Bataillon), *A Geographical Introduction to History*, K. Paul, Trench, Trubner & Co. Ltd, London, and Alfred A. Knopf, New York, 1925.

48 See O. Rackham, *History of the Countryside*, Dent, London, 1986, for England.

49 See M. Warnke, *The Political Landscape*, Reaktion Books, London, 1994, and S. Schama, *Landscape and Memory*, HarperCollins, London, 1995.

50 Febvre, *A Geographical Introduction*, op. cit., p. 304.

Chapter 6   War, Environment and Technology

1 See W. MacNeill, *Keeping Together in Time; Dance and Drill in Human History*, Harvard University Press, Cambridge, MA, 1995.

2 See P. Hirst, *War and Power*, op. cit., ch. 2, and T. K. Rabb, *The Struggle for Political Stability in Europe*, Oxford University Press, New York, 1975.

3 Braudel, *Civilization and Capitalism*, vol. III, op. cit.

4 See F. Tallett, *War and Society in Early-Modern Europe*, Routledge, London, 1992.

5 Braudel, *Civilization and Capitalism*, vol. I, op. cit.

6 W. McNeill, *The Pursuit of Power*, Blackwell, Oxford, 1983, ch. 5, and ideas of pre-modern road conditions can be gathered from N. Ohler, *The Medieval Traveller*, The Boydell Press, Woodbridge, 1989.

7 J. Black, *Maps and History*, Yale University Press, New Haven, CN, 1997, ch. 1.

8 R. I. Burns, 'The Significance of Frontiers in the Middle Ages', in R. Bartlett and A. Mackay (eds), *Medieval Frontier Societies*, op. cit.

9 E. Le Roy Ladurie, *Times of Feast, Times of Famine*, Doubleday, New York, 1971, and B. Fagan, *The Little Ice Age*, Basic Books, New York, 2000.

10 For examples, see B. M. Downing, *The Military Revolution and Political Change*, Princeton University Press, Princeton, NJ, 1992, M. Mann, *The Sources of Social Power*, Cambridge University Press, Cambridge and New York, 1986–93, and B. D. Porter, *War and the Rise of the State*, The Free Press, New York, 1994.

11 On the technology of the gunpowder revolution, see B. S. Hall, *Weapons and Warfare in the Renaissance*, Johns Hopkins University Press, Baltimore, MD, 1997.

12 See R. Murphey, *Ottoman Warfare 1500–1700*, UCL Press, London, 1999.

13 M. S. Anderson, *War and Society in Europe of the Old Regime 1618–1789*, Fontana, London, 1988.

14 G. Parker, 'Mutiny and discontent in the Spanish Army of Flanders 1572–1607', in *Spain and the Netherlands 1559–1659*, Fontana, London, 1990.

15 See C. Duffy, *Siege Warfare Vol. 1: The Fortress in the Early Modern World 1494–1660*, Routledge and Kegan Paul, London, 1979.

16 F. Tallett, *War and Society*, op. cit., pp. 50–68, and M. Van Creveld, *Supplying War: Logistics from Wallenstein to Patton*, Cambridge University Press, Cambridge, 1977, ch. 1.

17 M. Van Creveld, *Supplying War*, op. cit., p. 34.

18 M. Van Creveld , *Supplying War*, op. cit., ch. 5.

19 See R. Murphey, *Ottoman Warfare*, op. cit., and V. Aksan, 'Ottoman War and Warfare 1453–1812', in J. Black (ed.), *War in the Early Modern World 1450–1815*, UCL Press, London, 1999.

20 Inalcik, vol. 1, op. cit., p. 39.

21 G. Parker, *The Army of Flanders and the Spanish Road*, Cambridge University Press, Cambridge, 1972.

22 M. Roberts, *Essays in Swedish History*, op. cit.

23 G. Parker, *The Military Revolution*, op. cit., pp. 52–3.

24 G. Parker, *The Thirty Years War*, Routledge and Kegan Paul, London, 1987, and P. Limm, *The Thirty Years War*, Longman, London, 1984.

25 K-R Bohme, 'Building a Baltic Empire: Aspects of Swedish Experience', in G. Rystad et al. (eds), *The Baltic in Power Politics Vol.1 1500–1890*, Lund University Press, Sweden, 1994.

26 See M. Van Creveld, *Supplying War*, op. cit., ch. 3, and W. McNeill, *The Pursuit of Power*, op. cit., ch. 7.

27 T. Standage, *The Victorian Internet*, Weidenfeld and Nicolson, London,

1998, and M. Van Creveld, *Command in War*, Harvard University Press, Cambridge, MA, 1985, ch. 4.

28 See W. McNeill *Pursuit*, op. cit., ch. 6, and G. Best, *War and Society in Revolutionary Europe 1770–1870*, St Martin's Press, New York, 1982.

29 See M. Van Creveld, *Command in War*, op. cit., chs 4 and 5.

30 A. Bucholz, *Moltke, Schlieffen and Prussian War Planning*, Berg, Providence, RI, 1993.

31 H. Strachan, *European Armies and the Conduct of War* (1983), reprinted Routledge, London, 2000.

32 P. Griffith, *Forward into Battle*, Anthony Bird, Chichester, 1981, ch. 4.

33 D. Hounshell, *From the American System to Mass Production*, Johns Hopkins University Press, Baltimore, MD, 1984.

34 See T. Standage, *The Victorian Internet*, op. cit.

35 K. Alder, *Engineering the Revolution: Arms and Enlightenment in France 1763–1815*, Princeton University Press, Princeton, NJ, 1997.

36 Cited in C. J. Fuller, *War and Western Civilization*, Duckworth, London, 1932, pp. 95–6.

37 For an overview, see H. Strachan, *European Armies*, op. cit., ch. 3, also H. Strachan, *The First World War*, vol. 1, Oxford University Press, Oxford, 2001, ch. 3, and for logistics, see M. Van Creveld, *Supplying War*, op. cit., ch. 4. It should be noted that there never was a 'Schlieffen Plan' in the sense of a vast outflanking movement to the west of Paris. German planning concentrated on beating the French Army in battles within the frontier zone. A march behind Paris would have been logistically impossible in the time available. See T. Zuber, *Inventing the Schlieffen Plan*, Oxford University Press, Oxford, 2002.

38 See M. Van Creveld, *Command in War*, Harvard University Press, Cambridge, MA, 1985, ch. 5.

39 See J. Keegan, *The Face of Battle*, Cape, London, 1976, ch. 4, 'The Somme'.

40 See S. Bidwell and D. Graham, *Fire Power: British Army Weapons and Theories of War*, George Allen and Unwin, London, 1982.

41 The best general history of the First World War remains B. Liddell Hart, *History of the First World War*, Cassell, London, 1970; although it is old and often contentious it is lively and its basic judgements sound. H. Strachan's new history, the first volume of which has appeared, is set to replace it if at vastly greater length.

42 See A. J. Trythall, *'Boney' Fuller*, Cassell, London, 1977, and B. Bond, *Liddell Hart*, Cassell, London, 1977.

43 See E. Warner, 'Douhet, Mitchell, Seversky: Theories of Air Warfare', in E. M. Earle (ed.) *Makers of Modern Strategy*, 1943, op. cit., and D. MacIsaac, 'Voices from the Central Blue: The Air Power Theorists', in P. Paret (ed.) *Makers of Modern Strategy*, 1986, op. cit.

44 Giulio Douhet, 1921, US translation, Coward-McCann, New York, 1942.

45 See R. J. Overy, *The Air War 1939–45*, op. cit.

46 See M. Van Creveld, *Supplying War*, op. cit., ch. 5.

47 See M. Van Creveld, *Supplying War*, op. cit., ch. 7.

48 Bomber Command lost 47,268 killed or missing; see J. Terraine, *A Time for Courage: The RAF in the European War 1939–45*, Macmillan, New York, 1985, p. 682.

49 On the R & D and production history of the V2, see M. J. Neufeld, *The Rocket and the Reich*, Harvard University Press, Cambridge, MA, 1995.

50 B. Liddell Hart, *History of the Second World War*, Cassell, London, 1970, p. 691.

51 See L. Freedman, 'The First Two Generations of Nuclear Strategists', in P. Paret (ed.), *Makers of Modern Strategy*, op. cit.

52 For Antwerp, see *Vesting Antwerpen: De Brialmontforten*, Pandora, Snoeck, Snoek-Ducaju & Zoon, Gent (Ghent), 1997, and for Copenhagen, *The Fortifications of Copenhagen*, National Forest and Nature Agency, The Ministry of Environment and Energy, Copenhagen, 1998, pp. 145–216.

53 C. J. Ashworth, *War and the City*, Routledge, London, 1991.

54 On the technique of the seizure of power whether by revolutionaries or factions of the elite, see E. Luttwak, *Coup d'Etat: A Practical Handbook*, Harvard University Press, Cambridge, MA, 1979.

55 This was well understood by the Communist 3rd International; see A. Neuberg, *Armed Insurrection*, St Martin's, New York, 1970 and 1971.

56 See F. Jellinek, *The Paris Commune of 1871*, Grosset and Dunlap, New York, 1965.

57 On the Germans' error in besieging the city, see J. Erikson, *The Road to Stalingrad*, Weidenfeld and Nicolson, London, 1983, and for a graphic description of the fighting, see A. Beevor, *Stalingrad*, Viking, London, 1998.

58 P. Delaforce, *Smashing the Atlantic Wall – The Destruction of Hitler's Coastal Fortresses*, Cassell, London, 2001.

59 See A. Beevor, *Berlin*, Viking, London, 2002, for the fighting, and J. Erikson, *The Road to Berlin*, Weidenfeld and Nicolson, London, 1983, for the strategy.

60 This is still the case. For example, V. D. Hanson in *Why the West has Won*, op. cit., sees Vietnam as a failure of political will in what is otherwise a triumphalist account of 'Western' victories from Salamis onwards.

Chapter 7   Information, Space and War

1 The post-1945 British Rotor air defence system tied together technologies of different vintages, including the remains of the Chain Home system, and generated numerous problems. See N. J. McCamley, *Cold War Nuclear Bunkers*, Leo Cooper, Barnsley, 2002, ch. 6.

2 On the technology of radar and its evolution, see R. Buderi, *The Invention that Changed the World*, Abacus, London, 1998.

3 See D. Zimmerman, *Britain's Shield: Radar and the Defeat of the Luftwaffe*, Sutton, Stroud, 2001, ch. 1.

4 Even so the RAF based its planning in the 1920s on attacks by the *Armée de L'Air*.

5 Zimmerman, op. cit., ch. 3.

6 See L. Brown, *A Radar History of WWII*, Institute of Physics, Bristol, 1999, chs 1 and 2.

7 Brown, op. cit., pp. 97–9.

8 See Zimmerman, op. cit., and Brown, op. cit., for the British system.

9 It shows that contrary to much ill-informed historical comment British officialdom was neither inherently anti-industrial nor anti-scientific; for the demolition of such myths, see D. Edgerton, *England and the Aeroplane: An Essay on a Militant and Technological Nation*, Macmillan, Basingstoke, 1991.

10 See Buderi, op. cit., chs 17 and 18, and for a detailed description of the Pinetree and DEW lines, see McCamley, op. cit., ch. 2.

11 On the crucial role of the whole system, integrating hardware and software, and its formation, see Zimmerman, op. cit.

12 On the Battle of Britain, see D. Wood and D. Dempster, *The Narrow Margin*, Hutchinson, London, 1961. It is still the best account.

13 See R. V. Jones, *Most Secret War*, Hamish Hamilton, London, 1978, and Brown, op. cit., ch. 6.

14 On Jutland, see A. Marder, *From the Dreadnought to Scapa Flow*, vol. 3, Oxford University Press, London, 1966.

15 On carrier design in this context, see N. Friedman, *US Aircraft Carriers*, US Naval Institute Press, Annapolis, MD, 1983.

16 See Brown, op. cit., ch. 3.

17 See R. Lewin, *Ultra Goes to War*, Grafton, London, 1988, ch. 8.

18 See R. Lewin, *The American Magic*, Penguin, Harmondsworth, 1983, and D. Kahn, *The Codebreakers: The Story of Secret Writing*, Weidenfeld and Nicolson, London, 1965.

19 On the failure at Pearl Harbor, see R. Wohlstetter, *Pearl Harbor Warning and Decision*, Stanford University Press, Stanford, 1962, and Kahn, op. cit.

20 See Brown, op. cit., ch. 5.

21 For Midway from the US perspective, see S. E. Morrison, *History of US Naval Operations in WWII*, vol. 4, Little Brown, Boston, MA, 1949, and from the Japanese, see P. Dull, *A Battle History of the Imperial Japanese Navy*, US Naval Institute Press, Annapolis, MD, 1978, chs 8–11.

22 The US Navy adopted a concentric ring formation with capital ships at the centre, radar around the periphery, in order both to coordinate radar search patterns and to maximize the effectiveness of controlled AA fire.

23 See Brown, op. cit., ch. 5.5, and Dull, op. cit., ch. 13.

24 This point emerges clearly from the three major radar histories consulted

here, Brown, Buderi and Zimmerman; see also G. Hartcup, *The Challenge of War*, David and Charles, Newton Abbot, 1970.

25 See A. Toffler, *Future Shock*, The Bodley Head, London, 1970, *Third Wave*, Collins, London, 1980, and with Heidi Toffler, *War and Anti-War*, Little Brown, Boston, MA, 1993.

26 J. Baudrillard, *The Gulf War Never Took Place*, Indiana University Press, Bloomington, IN, 1995.

27 See D. Coyle, *The Weightless World*, Capstone, London, 1997, and C. Leadbetter, *Living on Thin Air: The New Economy*, Penguin, London, 2000.

28 G. and M. Friedman, *The Future of War*, St Martin's Press, New York, 1996.

29 J. Arquilla and J. Ronfeld (eds), *In Athena's Camp: Preparing for Conflict in the Information Age*, RAND, Santa Monica, CA, 1997.

30 The public and the media have been interacting since modern mass circulation dailies were created in the nineteenth century; for example, William Russell's reports in *The Times* of the chaos in the Crimea: see *Russell's Dispatches from the Crimea*, André Deutsch, London, 1966. In 1991 TV news galvanized public opinion on behalf of the Kurds; people saw suffering and responded to it.

31 A useful discussion of the civilian dimensions of the notion of information dominance is in C. May, *The Information Society: A Sceptical View*, Polity, Cambridge, 2002.

32 For the role of intellectuals and political theorists, see M. Drake, *The Problematics of Military Power: Government, Discipline and the Subject of Violence*, with a foreword by Paul Hirst, Frank Cass, London and Portland, Oreg., 2002.

33 M. de Landa, *War in the Age of Intelligent Machines*, Swerve Editions, Zone Books, New York, 1991.

34 *Desert Screen*, Continuum, London, 2000, p. 109.

35 For a popular version, see M. Ignatieff, *Virtual War*, Chatto and Windus, London, 2000.

36 See W. Murray and M. Knox, ch. 1, in Murray and Knox (eds), *The Dynamics of Military Revolution 1300–2050*, Cambridge University Press, Cambridge, 2001.

37 See for this evolution, N. Friedman, *Seapower and Space*, Chatham Publishing, London, 2000.

38 In operation 'Enduring Freedom' in 2001–2 in Afghanistan Pakistani cooperation was essential. Had Pakistan continued to support its protégés the Taliban, the US action would have been extremely difficult. Even then it relied on long flights by US carrier aircraft refuelled by RAF tankers and even longer flights by US bombers refuelled by USAF tankers. Pakistan allowed the USA in for old-fashioned reasons of great-power leverage and bribery. Even then the air war was essentially in support of local warlord allies. See M. O'Hanlon, 'A Flawed Masterpiece', in *Foreign Affairs*, May/June 2002: 47–63.

39 For a good overview of the RMA, see E. A. Cohen, 'A Revolution in Warfare', *Foreign Affairs*, March/April 1996: 37–54.

40 J. S. Nye and W. A. Owens, 'America's Information Edge', *Foreign Affairs*, March/April 1996: 20–36.

41 See Arquilla and Ronfeld (eds), op. cit.

42 See R. P. Hallion, 'Precision Guided Munitions and the New Era of Warfare', APSC Paper 53, RAF Base, Fairburn Act, Australia, 1995.

43 E. N. Luttwak, 'A Post-Heroic Military Policy', *Foreign Affairs*, July/ August 1996: 33–44.

44 *The National Security Strategy of the United States of America*, September 2002, The White House, NSC.

45 See J. Bailey, 'The First World War and the Birth of Modern Battle', in Murray and Knox (eds), op. cit., and also S. Bidwell and D. Graham, *Firepower: British Army Weapons and Theories of War 1904–1945*, Allen & Unwin, London, 1982.

46 See K. Macksey, *Armoured Crusader*, Hutchinson, London, 1967.

47 A good critical account of the RMA thesis which places it in the context of history and strategy is C. S. Gray, *Strategy for Chaos*, Frank Cass, London, 2002.

48 Two good sceptical accounts are L. Freedman, *The Revolution in Strategic Affairs*, Adelphi Paper 318 IISS, Oxford University Press, Oxford, 1998, and M. O'Hanlon, *Technological Change and the Future of War*, Brookings Institution, Washington, DC, 2000.

49 See J. W. Kipp and L. W. Grau, 'The Fog and Friction of Technology', *Command and General Staff College Military Review*, Sept/Oct 2001: 1–14.

50 On the parallel with Vietnam, see W. Murray and M. Knox, ch. 10 in Murray and Knox (eds), op. cit.

51 M. Van Creveld, *Command in War*, op. cit., ch. 4.

52 Mao's military theories did not cease to be relevant the day the Chinese stopped taking Communism seriously. The PLA were extremely successful practitioners of 'asymmetrical war' before the term had been invented. For a sympathetic account of theory and practice by a retired US Marines officer, see S. B. Griffith, *The Chinese Peoples' Liberation Army*, Weidenfeld and Nicholson, London, 1968.

53 C. E. Hawkins, 'The Peoples' Liberation Army Looks to the Future', *Joint Forces Quarterly*, summer 2000: 12–16.

54 See P. Hirst, 'Another Century of Conflict', *International Relations*, 16, 3: 327–42.

55 P. S. Anton, R. Silberglitt and J. Schneider, *The Global Technology Revolution: Bio/Nano/Materials Trends and Their Synergies with Information Technology by 2015*, RAND, Santa Monica, CA, 2001.

56 See M. Libicki, 'The Small and the Many', in Arquilla and Ronfeld (eds), op. cit., and for a longer version, see *The Mesh and the Net*, McNair Paper 28, Institute for National Strategic Studies, National Defense University, 1994.

57 Put a Deleuzian spin on this if you like, but you don't need to.
58 See N. Friedman, *Seapower and Space*, op. cit.
59 See G. and M. Friedman, *The Future of War*, op. cit.

Chapter 8   Foucault and Architecture

1 See for example M. Cacciari, F. Rella, M. Tafuri and G. Teyssot, in *Il Dispositivo Foucault*, Cluva Liberia, Venice, 1977; see also a revised translated version of Teyssot's article and the comments by the translator, David Stewart, in *Architecture & Urbanism*, 121 (October 1980): 79–100.
2 The exception is *Madness and Civilization*, Tavistock, London, 1970. This is generally, however, seen in libertarian terms, rather than as prefiguring as it does the concepts of power advanced later.
3 Michel Foucault, *The Order of Things*, Tavistock, London, 1970, and *The Archaeology of Knowledge*, Tavistock, London, 1972.
4 *Discipline and Punish*, Allen Lane, London, 1978, and *History of Sexuality*, vol. 1, Allen Lane, London, 1979.
5 The classic statement of the notion of 'unit ideas' is A. O. Lovejoy, *The Great Chain of Being*, Harvard University Press, Cambridge, MA, *c.* 1964.
6 *Œuvres économiques et philosophiques de F. Quesnay, fondateur du système physiocratique; accompagnées des éloges et d'autres travaux biographiques sur Quesnay par différents auteurs*, with introduction and notes by Auguste Oncken, Frankfurt-on-Main, J. Baer, 1888.
7 *Input-Output Economics*, 2nd edn, Oxford University Press, Oxford, 1986.
8 M. Foucault, *The Birth of the Clinic*, Tavistock, London, 1973.
9 Academy Editions, London, 1973; for modern discussions of Wittkower's book, see H. A. Million, 'Rudolf Wittkower, Architectural Principles in the Age of Humanism and its Influence on the Development and Interpretation of Modern Architecure', *Journal of the Society of Architectural Historians*, 31, 2 (1972): 83–91, and A. A. Payne, 'Rudolf Wittkower and Architectural Principles in the Age of Modernism', *JSAH*, 53, 3 (1994): 322–42.
10 See Ian Hacking, *Why does Language Matter to Philosophy?*, Cambridge University Press, Cambridge, 1975, for an introduction to the philosophy of language from a Foucauldian perspective. See also the excellent discussion in M. Cousins and A. Hussain, *Michel Foucault*, Macmillan, Basingstoke, 1984.
11 Andrea Palladio, *Quattro libri*, Preface Book Four – cited by Wittkower, op. cit., p. 23. A. Palladio, *The Four Books of Architecture*, Dover, New York, 1975.
12 R. Wittkower, op. cit., p. 27.
13 M. Foucault, *Archaeology of Knowledge*, Routledge, London and New York, 2002, p. 38.

14 Erwin Panofsky comments in his essay 'The History of the Theory of Human Proportions as a Reflection of the History of Styles', that: 'The Italian Renaissance, however, looked upon the theory of proportions with unbounded reverence; but it considered it, unlike the Middle Ages, no longer as a technical expedient but as the realisation of a metaphysical postulate . . . the Middle Ages, it is true, were thoroughly familiar with a metaphysical interpretation of the structure of the human body . . . However, insofar as the medieval theory of proportions followed the line of humanistic cosmology, it had no relation to art; and insofar as it stood in relation to art, it had degenerated into a code of practical rules which had lost all connection with humanistic cosmology.' *Meaning in the Visual Arts*, Penguin, Harmondsworth, 1970, p. 118. On Neoplatonism and its conception of similitude in relation to Renaissance art, see also Ernst Gombrich, *Symbolic Images*, Phaidon, Oxford, 1979.

15 Erwin Panofsky, *Renaissance and Renaissances in Western Art*, Paladin, London, 1970.

16 Edgar Wind, *Pagan Mysteries in the Renaissance*, Oxford University Press, Oxford, 1980.

17 Alberti, cited in Wittkower, op. cit., p. 27.

18 J. Hale, *Renaissance Fortification: Art or Engineering?*, Thames and Hudson, London, 1977.

19 Hale, op. cit., p. 46.

20 Cesare Beccaria, *On Crimes and Punishment*, Cambridge University Press, Cambridge, 1995.

21 See also M. Foucault, 'La Politique de la santé au XVIIIeme siecle', in *Machines a guerrir*, Institut de l'Environment, 1976.

22 M. Foucault, *Power/Knowledge*, Colin Gordon (ed.), Pantheon, New York, 1980.

23 See Foucault, in *Machines a guerrir*, op. cit.

24 Giovanni Battista Piranesi, *Le Carceri*, Dover, New York, 1973.

25 M. Tafuri, *Architecture and Utopia*, MIT Press, Cambridge, MA, 1979; Tafuri has commented elsewhere both on Foucault in Cacciari et al., *Il Dispositivo Foucault*, op. cit., and on Piranesi, 'Giovanni Battista Piranesi. L'utopie negative dans l'architecture', *L'Architecture d'aujourd hui*, 184 (March–April 1978), and *La Sfera e il Labarinto*, Einaudi, Turin 1980. I have avoided discussing the secondary literature of exposition and critique of Foucault both for reasons of length and because I prefer to draw positive implications for work on architecture directly from his own texts. I mention this particular interpretation of Piranesi by Tafuri here because it contrasts so directly with my own. Tafuri's comments in *La Sfera e il Labarinto* extend and qualify his account of Piranesi in *Architecture and Utopia*, but do not in my opinion radically change it.

26 Tafuri, *Architecture and Utopia*, op. cit., p. 18.

27 Tafuri, ibid., p. 19.

28 Interestingly enough there is considerable debate on the influence of the *Carceri* on Dance's design. Sir John Summerson, in *Georgian London*, Penguin, Harmondsworth, 1978, notes such an influence. He also comments that Dance's plan was soon rendered obsolete by prison reform but does not dwell on why. He says: 'This composition is doubly remarkable. First, because of its Piranesian sense of the drama of restriction, and the deft accentuation of mass by recession at certain points. And second because of its vivid articulation . . . Here was no mere "centre and wings" Academy picture, but a forceful expression of purpose, cruelly eloquent in all its parts.' Summerson, ibid., p. 148. Dorothy Stroud, in *George Dance, Architect 1741–1825*, Faber, London, 1971, comments on this frequent comparison, but argues that the Newgate design owes little to Piranesi. Accepting Dance's familiarity with Piranesi's work, she points to a Palladian influence (p. 98). John Wilton-Ely, *The Mind and Art of Giovanni Piranesi*, Thames and Hudson, London, 1978, on balance accepts the primacy of a Piranesian influence; he is especially interesting on theatre sets for imaginary prisons in early eighteenth-century Italy and on post-Piranesian projects for monumental prisons; see ch. V. It is also only fair to mention here that monumental-expressive stylistic features continued to appear in prison designs and buildings throughout the nineteenth century – in gate houses, crenellated walls, castle turrets, etc. However, in general, the design of cell blocks and their relation one to another did pay regard to the demands of inspection and circulation in a way earlier prisons did not.

29 There is now an extensive literature on the new prisons, on mental hospitals, etc., and their development from the late eighteenth century onwards. Perhaps the best book on the American systems mentioned above and on the chronology of prison construction is J. D. Rothman, *The Discovery of the Asylum*, Little Brown, Boston, MA, 1971; on American and Italian prisons, see D. Melossi and M. Pavarini, *The Prison and the Factory*, Macmillan, London, 1981; on English prisons, M. Ignatieff, *A Just Measure of Pain*, Macmillan, London, 1978, and R. Evans, *The Fabrication of Virtue: English Prison Architecture 1750–1840*, Cambridge University Press, Cambridge, 1982 (an outstanding work); and on asylums K. Doerner, *Madmen and the Bourgoisie*, Blackwell, Oxford, 1981, M. Donnelly, *Managing the Mind*, Tavistock, London, 1983, and A. Scull, *Museums of Madness*, Allen Lane, London, 1979.

30 See V. Skultans, *English Madness: Ideas on Insanity 1580–1890*, Routledge, London, 1979.

31 Hutchinson, London, 1980. The best modern accounts of governance, both of individual subjects and populations, from a Foucauldian perspective are Nikolas Rose, *Powers of Freedom*, Cambridge University Press, Cambridge, 1999, and M. Dean, *Governmentality: Power and Rule in Modern Society*, Sage, London, 1999.

Chapter 9   The Defence of Places: Fortification as Architecture

1 Now, of course, the heritage industry is so omnivorous it will restore *anything*, including 'Palmerston's Folly' forts outside Portsmouth, for example.

2 J. R. Hale, *Renaissance Fortification: Art or Engineering?*, Thames and Hudson, London, 1977.

3 Michel Foucault, *Discipline and Punish*, Allen Lane, London, 1977.

4 Rudolf Wittkower, *Architectural Principles in the Age of Humanism*, Academy Editions, London, 1973.

5 For Michelangelo's designs, see Quentin Hughes, *Military Architecture*, Hugh Evelyn, London, 1974, pp. 84–7. For Dürer's designs, see Christopher Duffy, *Siege Warfare: The Fortress in the Early Modern World 1494–1660*, Routledge and Kegan Paul, London, 1979, pp. 4–5 and 7.

6 Georg Braun and Franz Hogenburg, *Civitates Orbis Terrarum 1572–1618*, Thames and Hudson, London, 1955.

7 For an account of this concept, see Claude Lévi-Strauss, *Introduction to the Work of Marcel Mauss*, Routledge and Kegan Paul, London, 1987, pp. 25–31.

8 Three studies that integrate military and architectural history or the military and social history relevant to the architectural aspects of fortifications are: B. C. Smail, *Crusading Warfare 1097–1193*, Cambridge University Press, Cambridge, 1956; Geoffrey Parker, *The Army of Flanders and the Spanish Road 1567–1659*, Cambridge University Press, Cambridge, 1972; Simon Pepper and Nicholas Adams, *Firearms and Fortifications: Military Architecture and Siege Warfare in Sixteenth Century Siena*, Chicago University Press, Chicago, IL, 1986.

9 The great exception was the Byzantine Empire and the fortifications of the city of Constantinople. See B. C. P. Tsangadas, *The Fortifications and Defence of Constantinople*, Boulder East European Monographs, 1980, distributed by Columbia University Press, New York.

10 On medieval European expansion and the role of castles in securing it, see Robert Bartlett, *The Making of Europe: Conquest, Colonization and Cultural Change 950–1350*, op. cit., especially ch. 3.

11 On the function of crusader castles, see Smail, op. cit., and on English castles, D. J. Cathcart King, *The Castle in England and Wales*, Routledge, London, 1991. For a modern description of the major crusader castles, see H. Kennedy, *Crusader Castles*, Cambridge University Press, Cambridge, 1994.

12 See Smail, op. cit., pp. 215–44.

13 On the role of 'technology transfer' to the Turks, see J. R. Melville-Jones, *The Siege of Constantinople: Seven Contemporary Accounts*, Adolf M. Hakkert, Amsterdam, 1972, and Nicolo Barbaro, *Diary of the Siege of Constantinople*, Exposition Press, NY, 1969.

14 See Q. Hughes, op. cit., p. 77.

15 Pepper and Adams, op. cit., ch.1, pp. 3–31; see also J. R. Hale, 'The Early Development of the Bastion: An Italian Chronology c.1450–c.1534', in J. R. Hale et al. (eds), *Europe and the Later Middle Ages*, Faber and Faber, London, 1965.

16 See Q. Hughes, op. cit., pp. 70–3.

17 See Q. Hughes, op. cit., pp. 72–3.

18 Duffy, op. cit., p. 20; Hughes, op. cit., p. 87.

19 E. E. Viollet-le-Duc, *Military Architecture*, Greenhill Books, London, 1990, pp. 205–6, 212–17, 226–34.

20 Pepper and Adams, op. cit., especially ch. 2 and ch. 5.

21 The total artillery stock of all Florentine fortresses and galleys in 1552 was 625, of which fully half were light weapons of approximately 1½ kg or less weight of shot: these included 265 *moschetto*, heavy muskets for anti-personnel use. See Pepper and Adams, op. cit., pp. 12–14.

22 On the growth of the iron industry and the shortage of bronze guns, see Carlo Cipolla, *Guns and Sails in the Early Phase of European Expansion 1400–1700*, Collins, London, 1965.

23 See Pepper and Adams, op. cit., p. 24, for Porta Ardeatina, and pp. 38–49 for Porta San Viene.

24 Nelson Goodman and Catherine Z. Elgin, *Reconceptions in Philosophy and other Arts and Sciences*, Routledge, London, 1988, p. 32.

25 In this way Goodman shifts aesthetic judgement back towards the object, as against Kant's emphasis of the experience of the viewing subject in the *Critique of Judgement*.

26 See C. J. Ashworth, *War and the City*, Routledge, London, 1991, pp. 54 and 113.

27 A point forcefully made by John Keegan in his pathbreaking *The Face of Battle*, Cape, London, 1976.

28 Leon Battista Alberti, *On the Art of Building in Ten Books*, trans. J. Rykwert et al., MIT Press, Cambridge, MA, 1988, p. 245.

29 Alberti, op. cit., p. 261.

30 Patricia Seed has explained the political functions of these events in her *Ceremonies of Possession*, Cambridge University Press, Cambridge, 1995, ch. 2. See also Frances A. Yates, *Astraea: The Imperial Theme in the Sixteenth Century*, Routledge and Kegan Paul, London, 1975, part III, 'The Entry of Charles IX and his Queen into Paris 1571', and Roy Strong, *Art and Power: Renaissance Festivals 1450–1680*, Boydell, Woodbridge, 1984.

31 Horst De La Croix, *Military Considerations in City Planning*, George Braziller, New York, 1972.

32 See Martha D. Pollack, *Military Architecture, Cartography and the Representation of the Early Modern City*, The Newberry Library, Chicago, IL, 1991, which is a compendium of the title pages and illustrations from treatises on fortifications. *Les Invalides* in Paris contains a remarkable collection of models of French fortifications.

33 This point has been developed with particular reference to the centrally planned church in chapter 8.

34 See Quentin Hughes, op. cit., pp. 211–12.

35 See Sir George Sydenham-Clarke, *Fortification: Its Past Achievements, Recent Developments and Future Progress*, Beaufort, Liphook, Hants. Reprint of the 2nd edn of 1907. Clarke had seen in the 1890s that modern weapons had put an end to regular geometric fortification – however modern its methods of construction or materials.

36 For Brialmont's designs, see Keith Mallory and Arvid Ottar, *Architecture of Aggression – A History of Military Architecture in North West Europe 1900–1945*, Architectural Press, London, 1973, pp. 21–7; see also *Vesting Antwerpen*, op. cit.

37 On Verdun's forts and the battle of 1916, see Mallory and Ottar, op. cit., pp. 27–33.

Chapter 10   The Defence of Places: From Sieges to Silos

1 Thomas A. Markus, *Buildings and Power: Freedom and Control in the Origin of Modern Building Types*, Routledge, London, 1993. The same is true of Nicholas Pevsner's earlier *A History of Building Types*, Thames and Hudson, London, 1979.

2 John Keegan's *The Face of Battle*, Jonathan Cape, London, 1976, shows how false this assumption is and how difficult it is to take eyewitness accounts of battles or those of chroniclers at face value.

3 G. Parker, *The Army of Flanders and the Spanish Road 1567–1659*, Cambridge University Press, Cambridge, 1972, p. 19. This is one of the best studies of early-modern warfare. By concentrating on logistics and organization it gives due emphasis to the importance of sieges in the warfare of the sixteenth and seventeenth centuries. See also Martin Van Creveld, *Supplying War*, op. cit., chs 1 and 2.

4 See Quentin Hughes, *Military Architecture*, Hugh Evelyn, London, 1974, p. 117.

5 Parker, 1972, op. cit., plate 4 shows the outline of the siege-works of Amiens in a contemporary print of 1597 and their trace of patterns in crops in fields in 1964.

6 In 1601 the Dutch besieged s'-Hertogenbosch with 22 cannon and failed to take it, whereas in 1629 they used 116 guns and were success-ful. Similarly at Gronelo in 1595, the Dutch had only 16 guns and 14 in 1597, but, in 1627, 80 cannon were brought to bear. Undoubtedly, they were the result of Dutch enterprise in Sweden and the import of iron guns from the new factories there. See G. Parker, 1972, op. cit., p. 18.

7 See 'Mutiny and Discontent in the Spanish Army of Flanders 1572–1607', in G. Parker, *Spain and the Netherlands 1559–1659*, Fontana, London, 1979.

8 Sebastien Le Prestre de Vauban, *A Manual of Siegecraft and Fortification*, trans. G. A. Rothwrock, University of Michigan Press, Ann Arbor, 1968.

9 See F. H. Hinsley, *Power and the Pursuit of Peace*, Cambridge University Press, Cambridge, 1963.

10 Monluc, quoted in C. Duffy, *Siege Warfare – The Fortress in the Early Modern World 1494–1660*, Routledge and Kegan Paul, London, 1979, p. 250.

11 Simon Pepper and Nicholas Adams, *Firearms and Fortifications: Military Architecture and Siege Warfare in Sixteenth Century Siena*, Chicago University Press, Chicago, IL, 1986, p. 138.

12 Duffy, op. cit., p. 252.

13 George Sydenham-Clarke, *Fortification: Its Past Achievements, Recent Developments and Future Progress*, Beaufort, Liphook, Hants., reprint of 2nd edn of 1907.

14 *La Guerre Future*, cited in P. Paret (ed.) *Makers of Modern Strategy*, Clarendon Press, Oxford, 1986, p. 512, and I. F. Clarke, *Voices Prophesying War 1763–1984*, Panther, London, 1970.

15 See the eyewitness accounts in Martin Middlebrook's *The First Day on the Somme*, Penguin, Harmondsworth, 1984, and the reconstruction by John Keegan in *The Face of Battle*, op. cit.

16 Anthony Kemp, *The Maginot Line: Myth and Reality*, Warne, London, 1981, p. 12. All earlier books on the Maginot Line are factually unreliable to a greater or lesser degree; however, V. Rowe, *The Great Wall of France*, Putnam, London, 1959, is still of some value.

17 They were modernized and recreated in the later nineteenth century as a national redoubt. See Douwe Koen, *De Hollandse Waterlinie*, Buijten & Schipperheijn, Amsterdam, 1996.

18 Kemp, op. cit., p. 37.

19 For Metz, see A. Kemp, *The Unknown Battle: Metz 1944*, Stein and Day, New York, 1981.

20 For the Czech fortifications and twentieth–century European fortifications generally, see J. E. Kaufmann and R. M. Jurga, *Fortress Europe: European Fortifications in WWII*, Greenhill Books, London, 1999.

21 On the Westwall, see Keith Mallory and Arvid Ottar, *The Architecture of Aggression*, op. cit., ch. 6.

22 The Germans also camouflaged their buildings on the Atlantik Wall, some also got up in droll disguises. See A. Saunders, *Hitler's Atlantik Wall*, Sutton, Stroud, Glos, 2001.

23 See Colin Partridge, *Hitler's Atlantic Wall*, D. I. Publications, Guernsey, 1976.

24 Paul Virilio, *Bunker Archaeology*, Princeton Architectural Press, New York, 1994.

25 Paul Virilio, 'Bunker archéologie', *Architecture Principe*, 7 (March 1967).

26 Mallory and Ottar, op. cit. This book is historically very thorough and its

architectural judgements are of a very high standard. It covers the whole field of military construction, including temporary housing, Mulberry harbours, air-raid shelters, etc.

27 Erich Mendelsohn, *Complete Works of the Architect*, Triangle Architectural Publishing, London, 1992, plates, pp. 45, 78 and 93. In exile Mendelsohn was ironically given the task of building copies of German housing so that the USA could assess how best to destroy it by bombing.

28 See Silke Weng (ed.), *Erinnerungsorte aus Beton: Bunker in Stadten und Landsschaften*, Ch. Links Verlag, Berlin, 2001.

29 The most notorious were the Mittelwerke tunnels for producing V2s with slave labour. See M. J. Neufeld, *The Rocket and the Reich*, op. cit.

30 Mallory and Ottar, op. cit., ch. 11 and ch. 12, for British and German shelter provision respectively.

31 Mallory and Ottar, op. cit., ch. 7 and ch. 10, for the sea forts and the Mulberry harbours.

32 Virilio, 1994, op. cit., p. 46.

33 Cited in Virilio, 1994, op. cit., p. 56.

34 Carl Schmitt, *Political Romanticism*, MIT Press, Cambridge, MA, 1986. Schmitt is the source for Walter Benjamin's view on the aesthetics of fascism in 'The Work of Art in the Age of Mechanical Reproduction', in *Illuminations*, Fontana, London, 1973. Samir-al-Khalil's *The Monument*, André Deutsch, London, 1991, examines Saddam Hussein's triumphal arches in Baghdad not only as vile *kitsch* but also as a form of political aestheticization through monuments.

35 Leon Battista Alberti, *On the Art of Building in Ten Books*, trans. J. Rykwert et al., MIT Press, Cambridge, MA, 1988.

36 Thus T. Vanderbilt, in *Survival City – Adventures Among the Ruins of Atomic America*, Princeton Architectural Press, New York, 2002, says: 'If forts were once constructed to house armaments, here there is no distinguishing between the weapon and the system to house the weapon: the architecture is the gun, the missile the bullet,' p. 38.

37 See Kaufmann and Jurga, op. cit., *Fortress Europe*, and for today any recent volume of *Jane's Armour and Artillery*, section on coastal artillery.

38 Kaufmann and Jurga, op. cit., ch. 12.

39 See G. H. Quester, *Deterrence Before Hiroshima: The Airpower Background of Modern Strategy*, Wiley, New York, 1966.

40 For the contrast between Britain and Germany on shelter-building, see Mallory and Ottar, op. cit., chs 11 and 12.

41 On the shelter controversy, see Mallory and Ottar, ch. 11, and J. Allan, *Berthold Lubetkin*, RIBA, London, 1992, ch. 8.

42 J. Gregg, *The Shelter of the Tube*, Capital Transport, Harrow Weald, 2001, and A. Calder, *The People's War*, Pimlico, London, 1992, pp. 179–87.

43 See Mallory and Ottar, ch. 12, and for the effects of the bombing of Hamburg, see S. Lindquist, *A History of Bombing*, Granta, London, 2001, sections 200–10.

44 On the construction of the highway network, see K. Easterling, *Organization Space: Landscapes, Highways and Houses in America*, MIT Press, Cambridge, MA, 1999.

45 See K. T. Jackson, *Crabgrass Frontier*, op. cit.

46 On American nuclear era bunkers, see N. J. McCamley, *Cold War Secret Nuclear Bunkers*, op. cit., chs 1–4, and T. Vanderbilt, op. cit. See his comments on the Internet, pp. 197–9.

47 On UK wartime and Cold War bunkers, see N. J. McCamley, op. cit., chs 6–12; A. Clayton, *Subterranean City: Beneath the Streets of London*, Historical Publications, London, 2000, and P. Laurie, *Beneath the City Streets*, Panther, London, 1979.

48 On Tokyo, see H. Murakami, *Underground*, Harvill, London, 2001.

49 On terrorism and architecture, see M. Pawley, *Terminal Architecture*, Reaktion Books, London, 1999, ch. 9, and see also Vanderbilt, op. cit., ch. 6 and Postscript.

50 In this sense the general argument of E. Eis's *Forts of Folly*, Oswald Wolff, London, 1959, that fortification is futile, while wrong for much of military history, holds true for the attempt to fortify the city against modern terrorism.

Index

Pages containing illustrations are shown in italics.

Lightning Source UK Ltd.
Milton Keynes UK
19 May 2010

154379UK00002B/75/P

9 780745 634562